INFORMATION MANAGEMENT

ABDULLAH
Assistant Professor, (MCA Department)
Institute of Environment and Management
Barabanki

First Edition: 2012

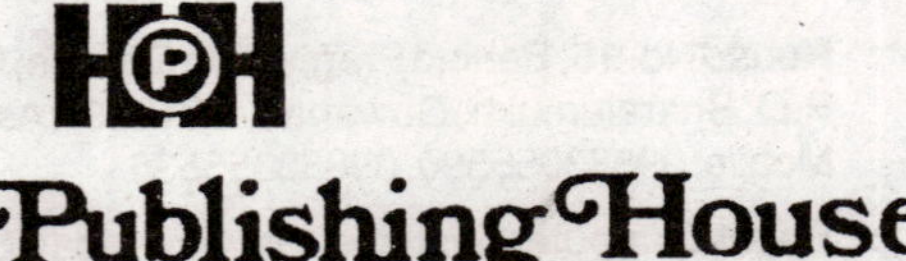

MUMBAI • NEW DELHI • NAGPUR • BENGALURU • HYDERABAD • CHENNAI • PUNE • LUCKNOW • AHMEDABAD • ERNAKULAM • BHUBANESWAR • INDORE • KOLKATA • GUWAHATI

First Edition: 2012

Published by : Mrs. Meena Pandey for **Himalaya Publishing House Pvt. Ltd.,**
"Ramdoot", Dr. Bhalerao Marg, Girgaon, **Mumbai - 400 004.**
Phone: 022-23860170/23863863, Fax: 022-23877178
E-mail: himpub@vsnl.com; Website: www.himpub.com

Branch Offices :

New Delhi : "Pooja Apartments", 4-B, Murari Lal Street, Ansari Road, Darya Ganj, New Delhi - 110 002. Phone: 011-23270392, 23278631; Fax: 011-23256286

Nagpur : Kundanlal Chandak Industrial Estate, Ghat Road, Nagpur - 440 018. Phone: 0712-2738731, 3296733; Telefax: 0712-2721215

Bengaluru : No. 16/1 (Old 12/1), 1st Floor, Next to Hotel Highlands, Madhava Nagar, Race Course Road, Bengaluru - 560 001. Phone: 080-32919385; Telefax: 080-22286611

Hyderabad : No. 3-4-184, Lingampally, Besides Raghavendra Swamy Matham, Kachiguda, Hyderabad - 500 027. Phone: 040-27560041, 27550139; Mobile: 09390905282

Chennai : No. 8/2, Modley 2nd Street, Ground Floor, T. Nagar, Chennai - 600 017. Phone: 044-28144004/28144005; Mobile: 09345345051

Pune : First Floor, "Laksha" Apartment, No. 527, Mehunpura, Shaniwarpeth (Near Prabhat Theatre), Pune - 411 030. Phone: 020-24496323/24496333; Mobile: 09370579333

Lucknow : Jai Baba Bhavan, Church Road, Near Manas Complex and Dr. Awasthi Clinic, Aliganj, Lucknow - 226 024 (U.P.). Phone: 0522-2339329, 4068914; Mobile: 09307501550

Ahmedabad : 114, "SHAIL", 1st Floor, Opp. Madhu Sudan House, C.G. Road, Navrang Pura, Ahmedabad - 380 009. Phone: 079-26560126; Mobile: 09377088847

Ernakulam : 39/104 A, Lakshmi Apartment, Karikkamuri Cross Rd., Ernakulam, Cochin - 622011, Kerala. Phone: 0484-2378012, 2378016; Mobile: 09344199799

Bhubaneswar : 5 Station Square, Bhubaneswar - 751 001 (Odisha). Phone: 0674-2532129, Mobile: 09338746007

Indore : Kesardeep Avenue Extension, 73, Narayan Bagh, Flat No. 302, IIIrd Floor, Near Humpty Dumpty School, Indore - 452 007 (M.P.). Mobile: 09301386468

Kolkata : 108/4, Beliaghata Main Road, Near ID Hospital, Opp. SBI Bank, Kolkata - 700 010, Phone: 033-32449649, Mobile: 09910440956

Guwahati : House No. 15, Behind Pragjyotish College, Near Sharma Printing Press, P.O. Bharalumukh, Guwahati - 781009, (Assam). Mobile: 09883055590, 09883055536

DTP by : Bright Computer Systems, Gayatri Nagar, Sitapur Road, Lucknow Mobile : 9450614766, 9793630385

Printed at : Shri Krishna offset Press Delhi-93

Dedication

I would like to dedicate this book to my father, Mr. Abdul Aziz, who has been so caring, loving and patient with me. Thank you, this is for you.

There are many people who have helped me get to where I am today. I would like to thank my family and especially my mother and wife for always supporting me and believing that I can do anything that I put my mind. Thanks to my grandfather Mr. Abdul Rauf and Uncle Dr. Abdul Haseeb for being proud of me and making me feel like I have wings to fly.

Last but definitely not least, I am dedicating this book to my grandmother Mrs. Trabbunnisha, I love you more and more each day, thanks for loving me, believing me, supporting me and most importantly just being you.

Abdullah

OBJECTIVE

The goal of my book "Information Management" is to provide the reader with a comprehensive introduction to the information system tools and skills required to build a good manager. This book serves the requirements of both students and professional. In fact it is aimed at all those students who desire to have knowledge of information system in depth.

Unique features

- Student friendly. The book is written in clear, concise and lucid manner.
- Independent thinking and research on the subject imparts a practitioner's perspective to it and makes the text thoroughly enjoyable.
- All ideas and concepts are presented with clear examples.
- Historical perspective describes components, system, or events from the past.
- Text is well structured and well supported with suitable diagrams.
- Coverage of new and emerging topics.
- Inter- chapter dependencies are kept to a minimum.
- Chapter objectives, summary at the end of each chapter, and review questions.

Target Audience

Primary usage as a text book for students of BBA, MBA, BCA, B.Tech (CS & IT), MSc (CS & IT) and MCA courses offered by management computer science, Computer engineering and information technology department in colleges and universities.

Also useful as a textual resource in vocational training courses offered by many colleges.

Feedback

For any suggestion and comments about this book, please feel free to send your e-mail at **abdullahkhan.ap@gmail.com**

Hope you enjoy reading this book as much as we have enjoyed writing it.

(Abdullah)

PREFACE

An information system (IS) is any combination of information technology and people's activities using that technology to support operations, management, and decision-making. In a very broad sense, the term information system is frequently used to refer to the interaction between people, algorithmic processes, data and technology. In this sense, the term is used to refer not only to the information and communication technology (ICT) an organization uses, but also to the way in which people interact with this technology in support of business processes.

Some make a clear distinction between information System, and computer System ICT, and business processes. Information System are distinct from information technology in that an information system is typically seen as having an ICT component. Information System are also different from business processes. Information System help to control the performance of business processes.

Alter argues for an information system as a special type of work system. A work system is a system in which humans and/or machines perform work using resources (including ICT) to produce specific products and/or services for customers. An information system is a work system whose activities are devoted to processing (capturing, transmitting, storing, retrieving, manipulating and displaying) information.

Part of the difficulty in defining the term *information system* is due to vagueness in the definition of related terms such as system and information. Beynon-Davies argues for a clearer terminology based in systemic and semiotics. He defines an information system as an example of a system concerned with the manipulation of signs. An information system is a type of socio-technical system. An information system is a mediating construct between actions and technology.

As such, information system inter-relate with data system on the one hand and activity system on the other. An information system is a form of communication system in which data represent and are processed as a form of social memory. An information system can also be considered a semi-formal language which supports human decision making and action.

Information system are the primary focus of study for the information system discipline and for organizational informatics.

A management information system (MIS) is a system that provides information needed to manage organizations effectively. Management information system are regarded to be a subset of the overall internal controls procedures in a business, which cover the application of people, documents, technologies, and procedures used by management accountants to solve business problems such as costing a product, service or a business-wide strategy. Management information system are distinct from regular information system in that they are used to analyze other information system applied in operational activities in the organization. Academically, the term is commonly used to refer to the group of information management methods tied to the automation or support of human decision making, e.g. Decision Support System, Expert system, and Executive information system.

Initially in businesses and other organizations, internal reporting was made manually and only periodically, as a by-product of the accounting system and with some additional statistic(s), and gave limited and delayed information on management performance. Previously, data had to be separated individually by the people as per the requirement and necessity of the organization. Later, data was distinguished from information, and so instead of the collection of mass of data, important and to the point data that is needed by the organization was stored.

Earlier, business computers were mostly used for relatively simple operations such as tracking sales or payroll data, often without much detail. Over time, these applications became more complex and began to store increasing amount of information while also interlinking with previously separate information system. As more and more data was stored and linked, man began to analyze this information into further detail, creating entire management reports from the raw, stored data. The term "MIS" arose to describe these kinds of applications, which were developed to provide managers with information about sales, inventories, and other data that would help in managing the enterprise. Today, the term is used broadly in a number of contexts and includes (but is not limited to): decision support system, resource and people management applications, Enterprise Resource Planning (ERP), Supply Chain Management (SCM), Customer Relationship Management (CRM), project management and database retrieval applications.

An 'MIS' is a planned system of the collection, processing, storage and dissemination of data in the form of information needed to carry out the management functions. In a way, it is a documented report of the activities that were planned and executed. According to **Philip Kotler** "A marketing information system consists of people, equipment, and procedures to gather, sort, analyze, evaluate, and distribute needed, timely, and accurate information to marketing decision makers."

The terms MIS and information system are often confused. Information system include system that are not intended for decision making. The area of study called MIS is sometimes referred to, in a restrictive sense, as information technology management. That area of study should not be confused with computer science. IT service management is a practitioner-focused discipline. MIS has also some differences with ERP which incorporates elements that are not necessarily focused on decision support.

Any successful MIS must support a business's Five Year Plan or its equivalent. It must provide for reports based upon performance analysis in areas critical to that plan, with feedback loops that allow for titivation of every aspect of the business, including recruitment and training regimens. In effect, MIS must not only indicate how things are going, but why they are not going as well as planned where that is the case. These reports would include performance relative to cost centers and projects that drive profit or loss, and do so in such a way that identifies individual accountability, and in virtual real-time.

Anytime a business is looking at implementing a new business system, it is very important to use a system development method such as System Development Life Cycle. The life cycle includes Analysis, Requirements, Design, Development, Testing and Implementation.

Feedback

For any suggestion and comments about this book, please feel free to send your e-mail at **abdullahkhan.ap@gmail.com**

Hope you enjoy reading this book as much as we have enjoyed writing it.

(Abdullah)

ACKNOWLEDGEMENT

The book Information Management has been written for the Management & Technical students of various Universities. It clearly explains the fundamentals of the subject and is designed to give an insight to the student with an appropriate example. The book is written in simple language so that it can be understood by the students and teachers.

- First of all I am thankful to my publisher's Himalaya Publishing House, their editorial team and panel reviewers for their valuable contributions towards content enrichment. Especially to Mr. M.C. Pandey (Branch Manager North), Mr. Pankaj Srivastava (Assistant Branch Manager) and Mr. Bacchan Singh (Senior Sales Representative), for their initial motivation.
- I express my special thanks to Dr. Pradeep Kumar (Chairman) IEM Group of Institutions as he has been a source of inspiration to write this book.
- I am also grateful to my all family members, especially my parents, wife Anwari Kausar, grandfather Mr. Abdul Rauf and Sister Shakeela Khatoon for their heartly cooperation and moral support without this the manuscript would not completed successfully.
- Also, I would like to express my thanks to all faculty members of The Institute of Environment and Management, Kursi Road, Lucknow.
- Finally, I would like to express my thanks specially Mr. Sanjay Kumar Pandey, Assistant Prof. who gives me suggestion and motivate to write this book.
- Above all, I am grateful to Allah (God) for his blessing and grace and I dedicate this humble publication to His Lotus Feet as an offering unto Him.

(Abdullah)

CONTENTS

1 INFORMATION SYSTEM

An **information system** (IS) is any combination of nformation technology and people's activities using that technology to support operations, management, and decision-making. In a very broad sense, the term information system is frequently used to refer to the interaction between people, algorithmic processes, data and technology. In this sense, the term is used to refer not only to the information and communication technology (ICT) an organization uses, but also to the way in which people interact with this technology in support of business processes.

Some make a clear distinction between information system, and computer system ICT, and business processes. Information system are distinct from information technology in that an information system is typically seen as having an ICT component. Information system are also different from business processes. Information system help to control the performance of business processes.

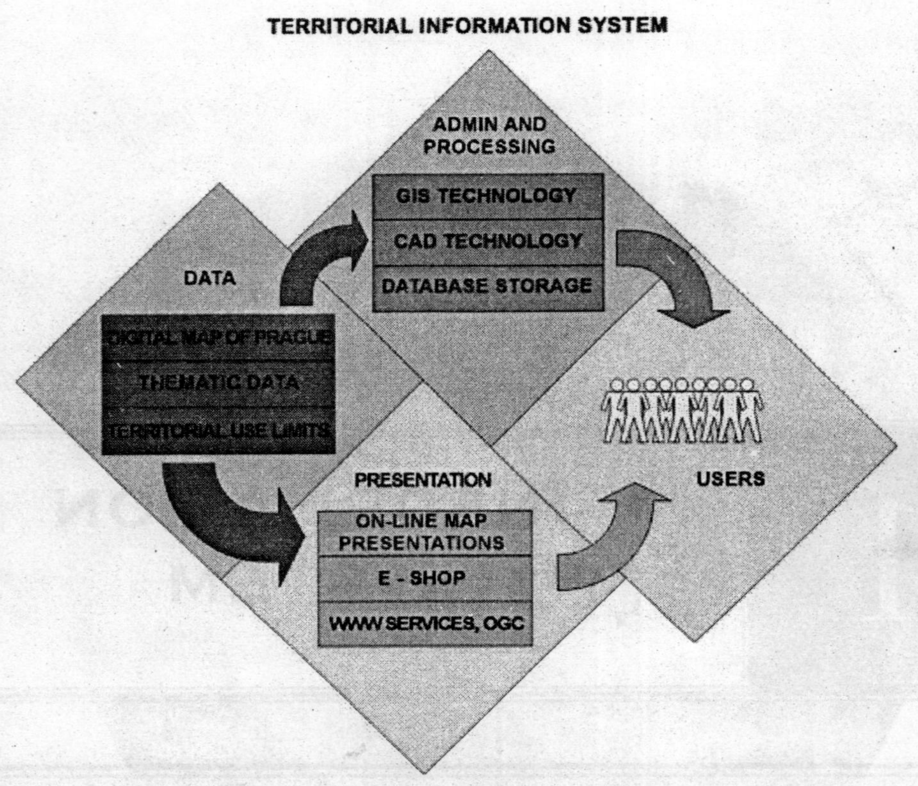

Alter argues for an information system as a special type of work system. A work system is a system in which humans and/or machines perform work using resources (including ICT) to produce specific products and/or services for customers. An information system is a work system whose activities are devoted to processing (capturing, transmitting, storing, retrieving, manipulating and displaying) information.

Part of the difficulty in defining the term information system is due to vagueness in the definition of related terms such as system and information. Beynon-Davies argues for a clearer terminology based in systemic and semiotics. He defines an information system as an example of a system concerned with the manipulation of signs. An information system is a type of socio-technical system. An information system is a mediating construct between actions and technology.

As such, information system inter-relate with data system on the one hand and activity system on the other. An information system is a form of communication system in which data represent and are processed as a form of social memory. An information system can also be considered a semi-formal language which supports human decision making and action.

Information system are the primary focus of study for the information system discipline and for organizational informatics.

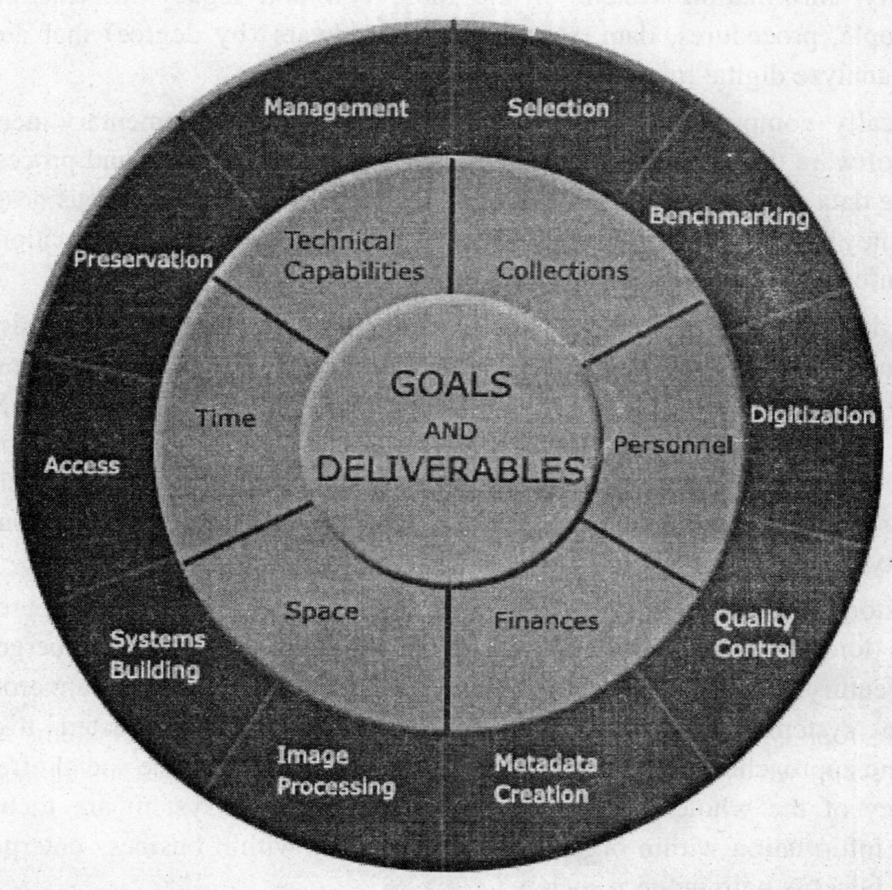

Information System

Information System (IS) is a professional and academic discipline concerned with the strategic, managerial and operational activities involved in the gathering, processing, storing, distributing and use of information, and its associated technologies, in society and organizations. As an area of study, IS bridges the multidisciplinary business field and the interdisciplinary computer science field that is evolving toward a new scientific discipline.

An information system discipline therefore is supported by the theoretical foundations of information and computations such that undergraduate students have unique opportunities to explore the academics of various business models as well as related algorithmic processes within a computer science discipline.

Typically, information system or the more common legacy information system include people, procedures, data, software, and hardware (by degree) that are used to gather and analyze digital information.

Specifically computer-based information system are complementary networks of hardware/software that people and organizations use to collect, filter, and process, create, & distribute data (computing). A majority of IS programs are located in business schools; however, they may have different names such as management information system, computer information system, or business information system.

All IS degrees combine business and computing topics, but the emphasis between technical and organizational issues varies among programs. For example, programs differ substantially in the amount of programming required Computer Information System(s) (CIS) may also be a track within the computer science field studying computers and algorithmic processes, including their principles, their software & hardware designs, their applications, and their impact on society. Overall, an IS discipline emphasizes functionality over design.

The history of **information system** coincides with the history of computer science that began long before the modern discipline of computer science emerged in the twentieth century. Regarding the circulation of information and ideas, numerous legacy information system still exist today that are continuously updated to promote ethnographic approaches, to ensure data integrity, and to improve the social effectiveness & efficiency of the whole process. In general, information system are focused upon processing information within organizations, especially within business enterprises, and sharing the benefits with modern society.

Classification of Information System

Classified information is sensitive information to which access is restricted by law or regulation to particular classes of persons. A formal security clearance is required to handle classified documents or access classified data. The clearance process requires a satisfactory background investigation. There are typically several levels of sensitivity, with differing clearance requirements. This sort of hierarchical system of secrecy is used by virtually every national government. The act of assigning the level of sensitivity to data is called data classification.

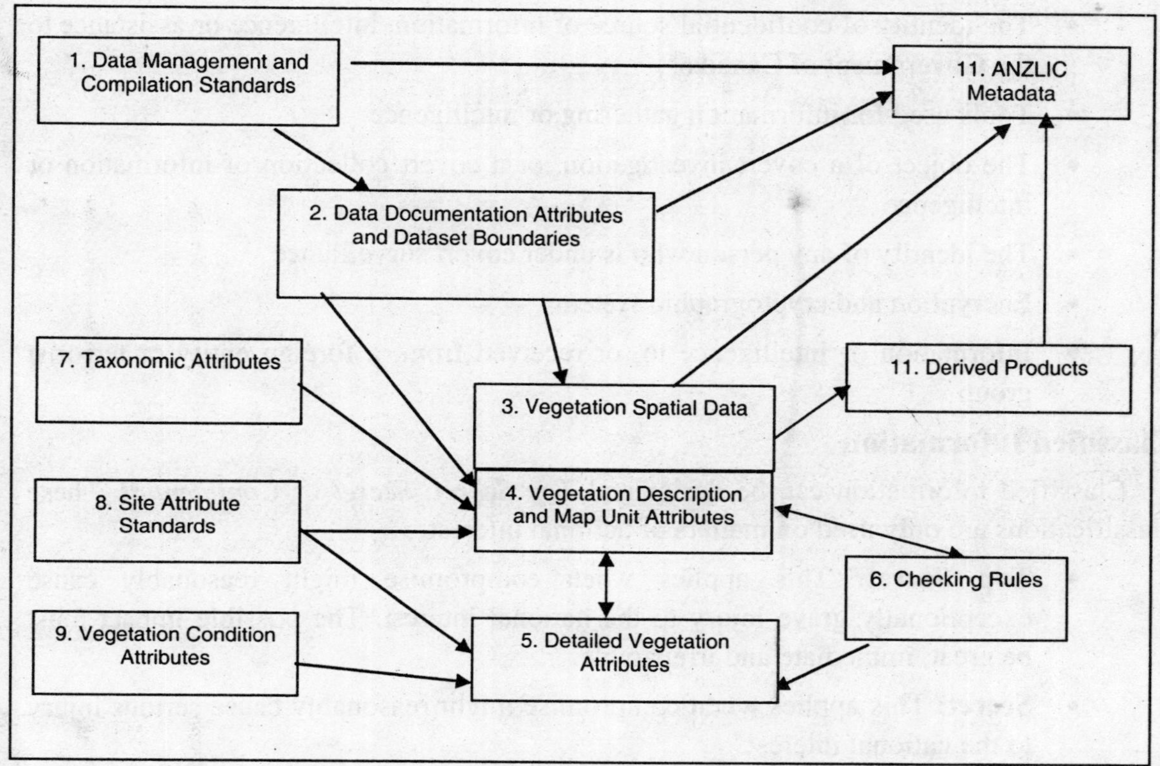

Some corporations and non-government organizations also assign sensitive information to multiple levels of protection, either from a desire to protect trade secrets, or because of laws and regulations governing various matters such as personal privacy, sealed legal proceedings and the timing of financial information releases.

Government Classification

The purpose of classification is ostensibly to protect information from being used to damage or endanger national security. Classification formalizes what constitutes a "state secret" and accords different levels of protection based on the expected damage the information might cause in the wrong hands.

Special Operational Information

It is defined under the **Security of Information Act**, and unauthorized release of such information constitutes a higher breach of trust, with penalty of life imprisonment. SO Is including:

- Military operations in respect of a potential, imminent or present armed conflict.

- The identity of confidential source of information, intelligence or assistance to the Government of Canada
- Tools used for information gathering or intelligence
- The object of a covert investigation, or a covert collection of information or intelligence
- The identity of any person who is under covert surveillance
- Encryption and cryptographic system
- Information or intelligence to, or received from, a foreign entity or terrorist group

Classified Information

Classified information can be designated *Top Secret*, *Secret* or *Confidential*. These classifications are only used on matters of national interest.

- **Top Secret:** This applies when compromise might reasonably cause exceptionally grave injury to the national interest. The possible impact must be great, immediate and irreparable.
- **Secret:** This applies when compromise might reasonably cause serious injury to the national interest.
- **Confidential:** When disclosure might reasonably cause injury to the national interest.

Value of Information

Value of information (VOI or VoI) is the amount a decision maker would be willing to pay for information prior to making a decision.

Similar terms

VoI is sometimes distinguished into **value of perfect information**, also called **value of clairvoyance (VoC)**, and **value of imperfect information**. They are closely related to the widely known expected value of perfect information and expected value of sample information.

Definitions

A simple example best illustrates the concept. Consider a decision situation with one decision, for example deciding on a 'Vacation Activity'; and one uncertainty, for example what wills the **'Weather Condition'** be? But we will only know the **'Weather Condition'** after we have decided and begun the **'Vacation Activity'**.

- The Value of perfect information on *Weather Condition* captures the value of being able to know *Weather Condition* even before making the *Vacation Activity* decision. It is quantified as the highest price the decision-maker is willing to pay for being able to know *Weather Condition* before making the *Vacation Activity* decision.
- The Value of imperfect information on *Weather Condition*, however, captures the value of being able to know the outcome of another related uncertainty, e.g., *Weather Forecast*, instead of *Weather Condition* itself before making *Vacation Activity* decision. It is quantified as the highest price the decision-maker is willing to pay for being able to know *Weather Forecast* before making *Vacation Activity* decision. Note that it is essentially the value of perfect information on *Weather Forecast*.

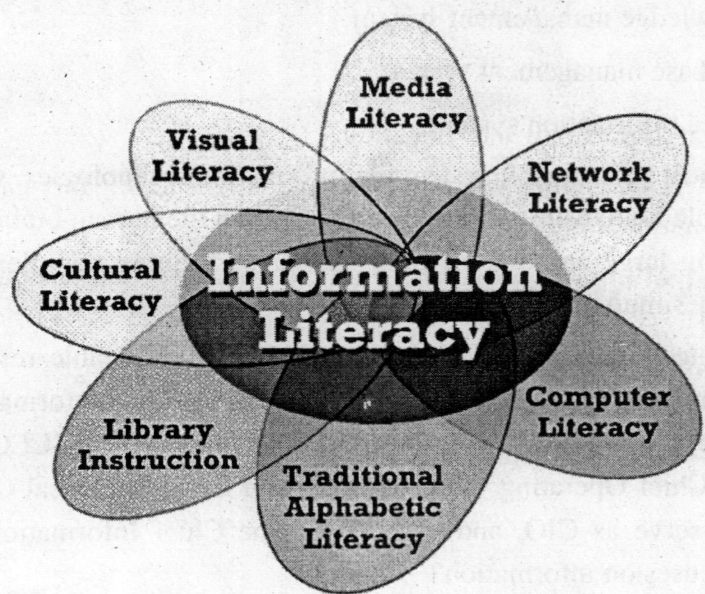

Characteristics

There are two extremely important characteristics of VoI that always hold for any decision situation;

- Value of information can never be less than zero since the decision-maker can always ignore the additional information and makes decision as if such information is not available.

- No other information gathering/sharing activities can be more valuable than that quantified by value of clairvoyance.

Information system are implemented within an organization for the purpose of improving the effectiveness and efficiency of that organization. Capabilities of the information system and characteristics of the organization, its work system, its people, and its development and implementation methodologies together determine the extent to which that purpose is achieved.

There are various types of information system, for example:

- Transaction processing system
- Office system
- Decision support system
- Knowledge management system
- Database management system
- Office information system.

Critical to most information system are information technologies, which are typically designed to enable humans to perform tasks for which the human brain is not well suited, such as: handling large amounts of information, performing complex calculations, and controlling many simultaneous processes.

Information technologies are a very important and malleable resource available to executives. Many companies have created a position of Chief Information Officer (CIO) that sits on the executive board with the Chief Executive Officer (CEO), Chief Financial Officer (CFO), Chief Operating Officer (COO) and Chief Technical Officer (CTO). The CTO may also serve as CIO, and vice versa. The Chief Information Security Officer (CISO), who focuses on information?

Types of Information System

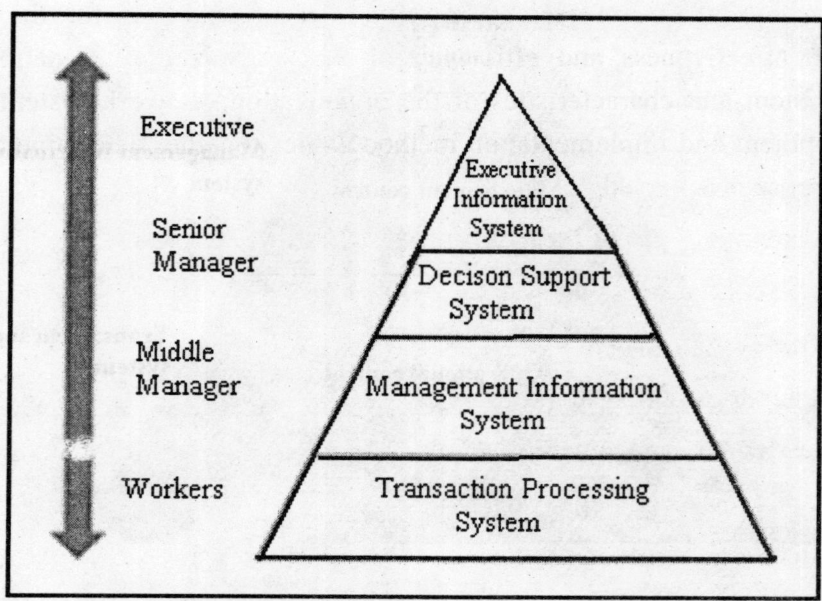

Types of Information System

A four level pyramid model of different types of Information System based on the different levels of hierarchy in an organization.

The 'classic' view of Information system found in the textbooks of the 1980s was of a pyramid of system that reflected the hierarchy of the organization, usually Transaction processing system at the bottom of the pyramid, followed by Management information system, Decision support system and ending with Executive information system at the top. Although the pyramid model remains useful, since it was first formulated a number of new technologies have been developed and new categories of information system have emerged, some of which no longer fit easily into the original pyramid model.

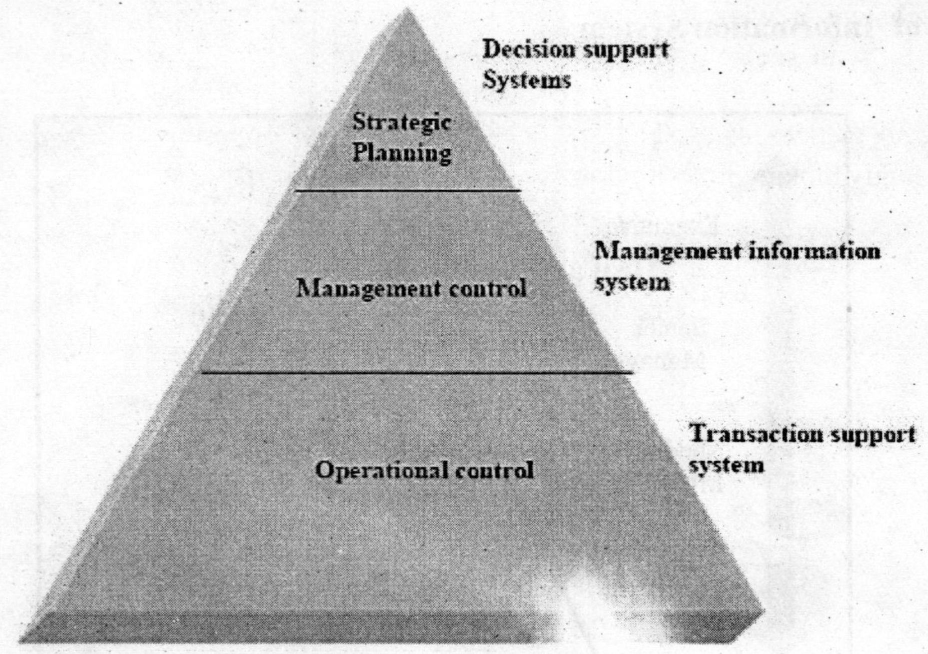

Some examples of such system are:

- Data warehouses
- Enterprise resource planning
- Enterprise system
- Expert system
- Geographic information system
- Global information system
- Office Automation

Information system career pathways

Information System have a number of different areas of work:

- Information system strategy
- Information system management
- Information system development
- Information system security
- Information system iteration

There are a wide variety of career paths in the information system discipline. "Workers with specialized technical knowledge and strong communications skills will have the best prospects. Workers with management skills and an understanding of business practices and principles will have excellent opportunities, as companies are increasingly looking to technology to drive their revenue.

Heat and Health: Information for Prevention, Equity and Sustainability

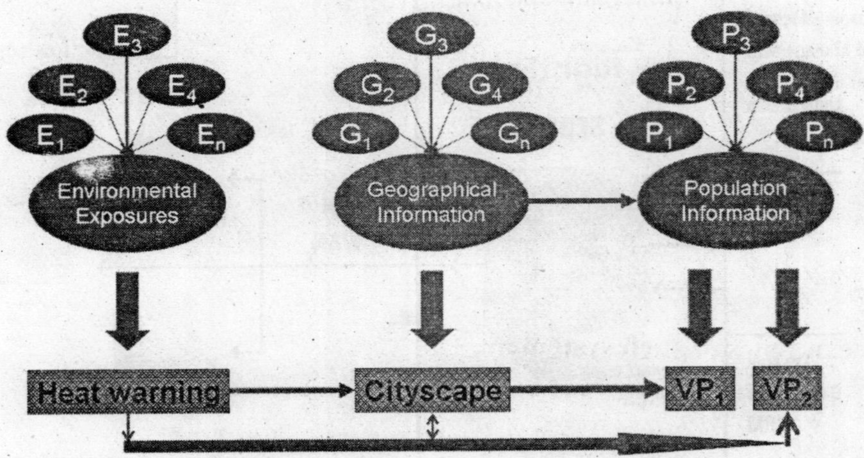

Introduction to Information System in Business framework

Aims and Objectives

The aim of this topic is to introduce information system engineering in organizations. The following topics will be discussed:-

- The reasons why Information Technology and Information System are crucial to modern organizations and thus subject to professional management.
- The factors influencing information system engineering.

The Importance of Information Technology and Information System

All medium to large organizations depend on Information technology for their continued survival. Consider organizations like British Gas, British Telecom, the Power and Water companies having to manually calculate, millions of customer bills every month or quarter! Clearly the clerical effort involved would make it difficult if not impossible for the organization to make a profit.

Similar arguments apply to many other organizations such as the high street banks, central and local government. A recent articie in the Daily Telegraph IT supplement suggested that many large organizations could last no longer than 24 hours without IT support! There should be little wonder that attitudes to the development of information system have changed over the years from an ad hoc almost cavalier approach to a professionally managed, disciplined, planned, and engineering approach.

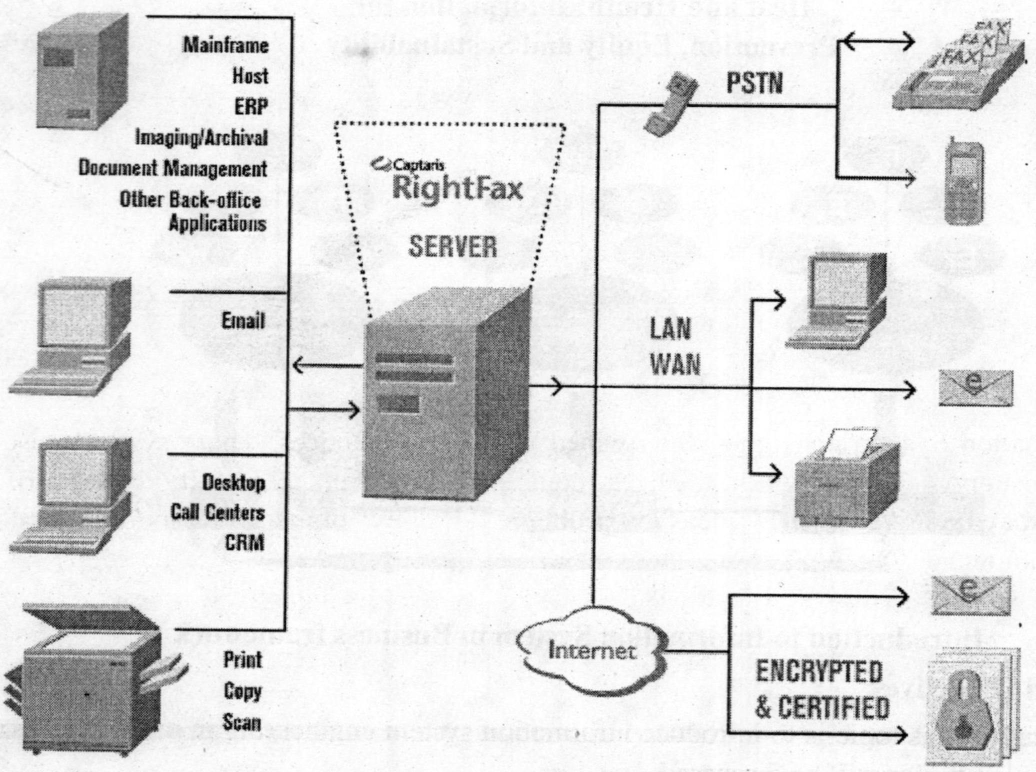

What is an Information System?

An Information System is a combination of work practices, information, people and information technologies organized to accomplish goals in an organization. Management Information System are those that support all management levels in the conduct of their functions, such as operations, administration, or planning and programming. Work practices are the methods used by people and technology to perform work. The information in an information system can include formatted data, text, pictures and sounds. Except when they totally automate a task, information system include people who enter process or use data.

The users of information system are managers of all levels who would require that data be processed, collated and analyzed before it can be useful for making decisions. Types of decisions made are those that range from everyday transactions, longer ranging tactical or monthly reports to longer ranging strategic types that are useful in making projections typically in years.

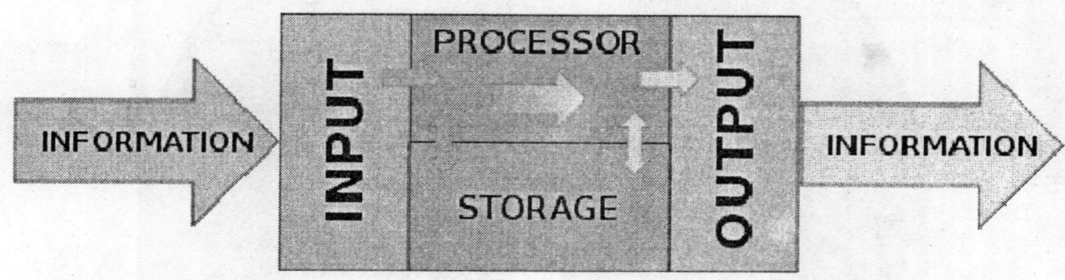

(Information processing)

What are the sources of change in information system?

Information System are tightly intertwined with work practices. These system must change to support the new work practices required to compete successfully. New work practices may be driven by new ideas, by problems, and buy competitive, environmental and technological forces. In turn, these work practices often require adaptations by people, different information and new ways to use information technology.

What is the major business trends related to information system?

Major business trends include greater pervasiveness of computers, continuing convergence of computing and communication, greater automation of work, more value residing in information, new forms of organization and management, faster pace of business, accelerating global competition, and gradual acceptance of global standards. The reliance of business organizations on computer networks, expert system and software manifests the global acceptance of electronic data processing as a universal extension of the human mind and intellect.

What are the roles of information system in organizations?

Information system are organizational subsystem that perform work related to processing information. Information system can play the following roles: (1) participating in the execution of tasks (2) linking planning, execution and control within a subsystem (3) coordinating and integrating subsystem. All types of management system and functions depend on an efficient information system to provide the manager with timely, relevant and accurate information for wise decision making.

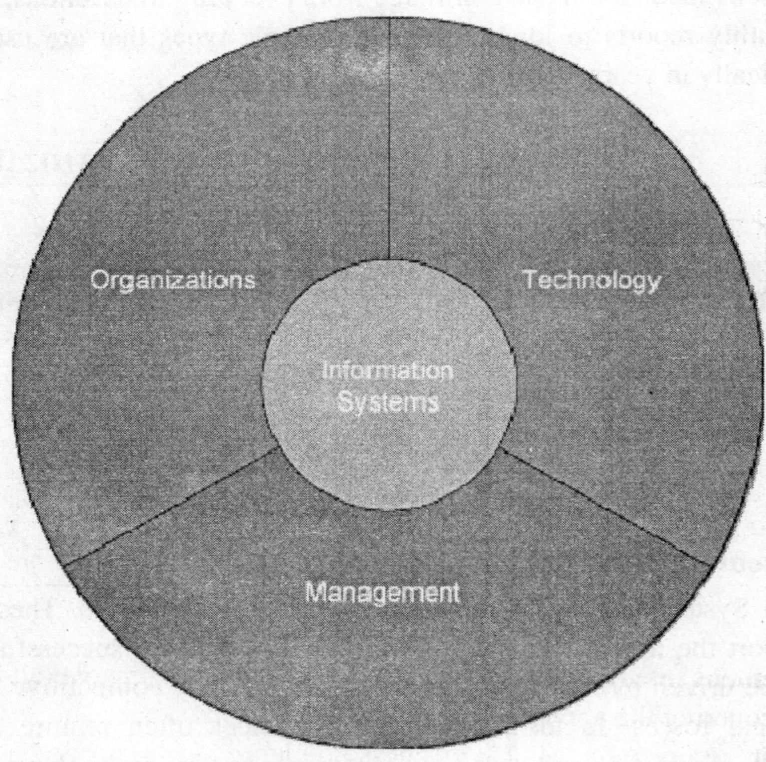

What is the difference between data, information and knowledge?

Data are facts, images or sounds that may or may not be pertinent to a particular task.

Information is data whose form and content are appropriate for a particular use.

Knowledge is a combination of instincts, ideas, rules and procedures that guide actions and decisions. Knowledge is used to transform data into information that is useful in a situation.

In addition, knowledge helps users interpret and act on information. The role of the information manager is to identify what decisions are to be made and to go about providing the information through an information system. Data is processed into information and together with ideas, instincts, rules and procedures; the manager makes the appropriate decision.

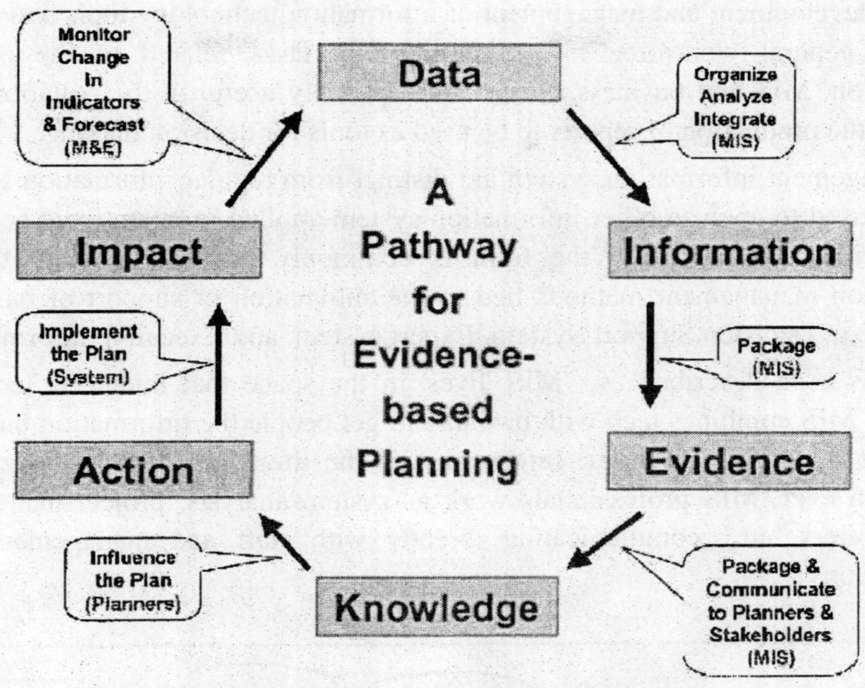

Management Information System

A **management information system** (MIS) is a subset of the overall internal controls of a business covering the application of people, documents, technologies, and procedures by management accountants to solve business problems such as costing a product, service or a business-wide strategy.

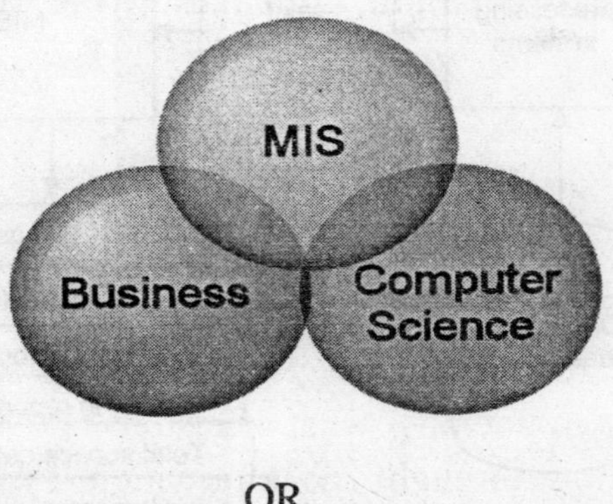

OR

Definition: Management Information System (MIS) is the term given to the discipline focused on the integration of computer system with the aims and objectives on an organization.

The development and management of information technology tools assists executives and the general workforce in performing any tasks related to the processing of information. MIS and business system are especially useful in the collation of business data and the production of reports to be used as tools for decision making.

Management information system are distinct from regular information system in that they are used to analyze other information system applied in operational activities in the organization. Academically, the term is commonly used to refer to the group of information management methods tied to the automation or support of human decision making, e.g. Decision Support System, Expert system, and Executive information system.

It has been described as, "MIS 'lives' in the space that intersects technology and business. MIS combines tech with business to get people the information they need to do their jobs better/faster/smarter. Information is the lifeblood of all organizations - now more than ever. MIS professionals work as system analysts, project managers, system administrators, etc., communicating directly with staff and management across the organization."

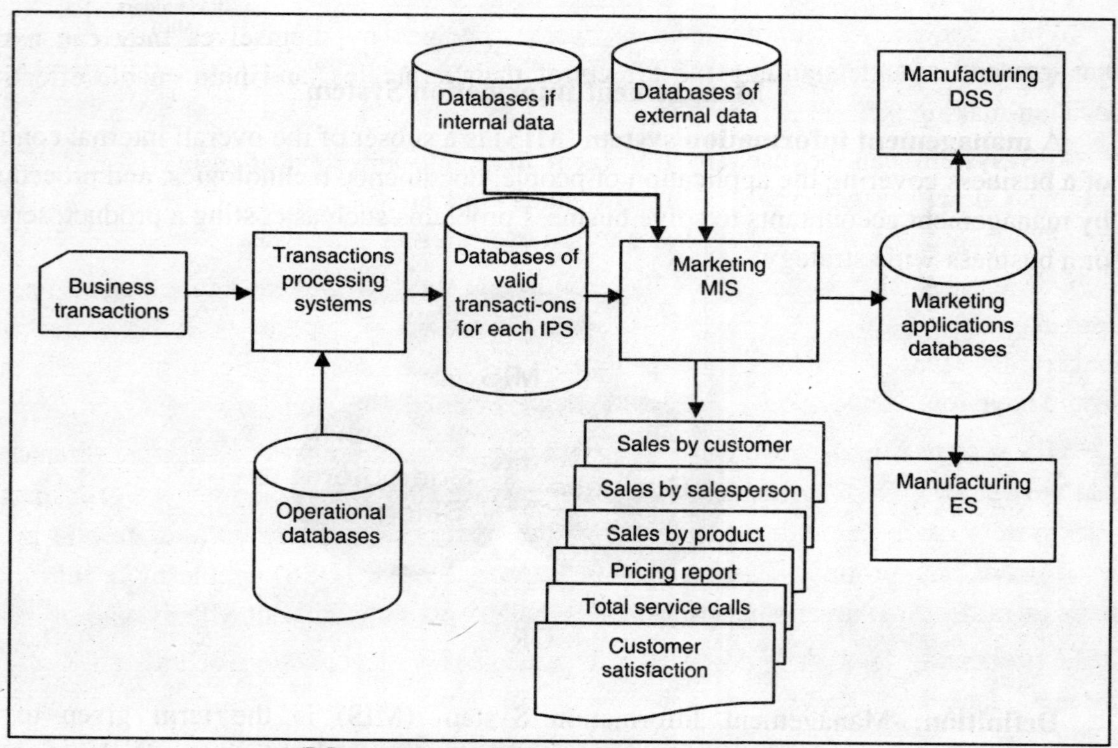

(Management Information System)

Desirable features of an MIS

- **Be flexible -** allowing for different ways of analyzing data and evaluating information.
- **Be able to** support a range of skills and knowledge.
- **Provide interpersonal** communication with other people in the organization.
- **Not require extensive** periods of concentration as manager's switch between different tasks.
- **Make it easy to interrupt** the work and return to it at a later time Protect a manager, from information overload.

Applications of MIS

With computers being as ubiquitous as they are today, there's hardly any large business that does not rely extensively on their IT system.

However, there are several specific fields in which MIS has become invaluable.

Strategy Support

While computers cannot create business strategies by themselves they can assist management in understanding the effects of their strategies, and help enable effective decision-making.

MIS system can be used to transform data into information useful for decision making. Computers can provide financial statements and performance reports to assist in the planning, monitoring and implementation of strategy.

MIS system provide a valuable function in that they can collate into coherent reports unmanageable volumes of data that would otherwise be broadly useless to decision makers. By studying these reports decision-makers can identify patterns and trends that would have remained unseen if the raw data were consulted manually.

MIS system can also use these raw data to run simulations – hypothetical scenarios that answer a range of 'what if' questions regarding alterations in strategy. For instance, MIS system can provide predictions about the effect on sales that an alteration in price would have on a product. These Decision Support System (DSS) enable more informed decision making within an enterprise than would be possible without MIS system.

Data processing not only do MIS system allow for the collation of vast amounts of business data, but they also provide a valuable time saving benefit to the workforce. Where in the past business information had to be manually processed for filing and analysis it can now be entered quickly and easily onto a computer by a data processor, allowing for faster decision making and quicker reflexes for the enterprise as a whole.

Management by Objectives

While MIS system are extremely useful in generating statistical reports and data analysis they can also be of use as a Management by Objectives (MBO) tool.

MBO is a management process by which managers and subordinates agree upon a series of objectives for the subordinate to attempt to achieve within a set time frame. Objectives are set using the SMART ratio: that is, objectives should be Specific, Measurable, Agreed, Realistic and Time-Specific.

The aim of these objectives is to provide a set of key performance indicators by which an enterprise can judge the performance of an employee or project. The success of any MBO objective depends upon the continuous tracking of progress.

In tracking this performance, it can be extremely useful to make use of an MIS system. Since all SMART objectives are by definition measurable they can be tracked through the generation of management reports to be analyzed by decision-makers.

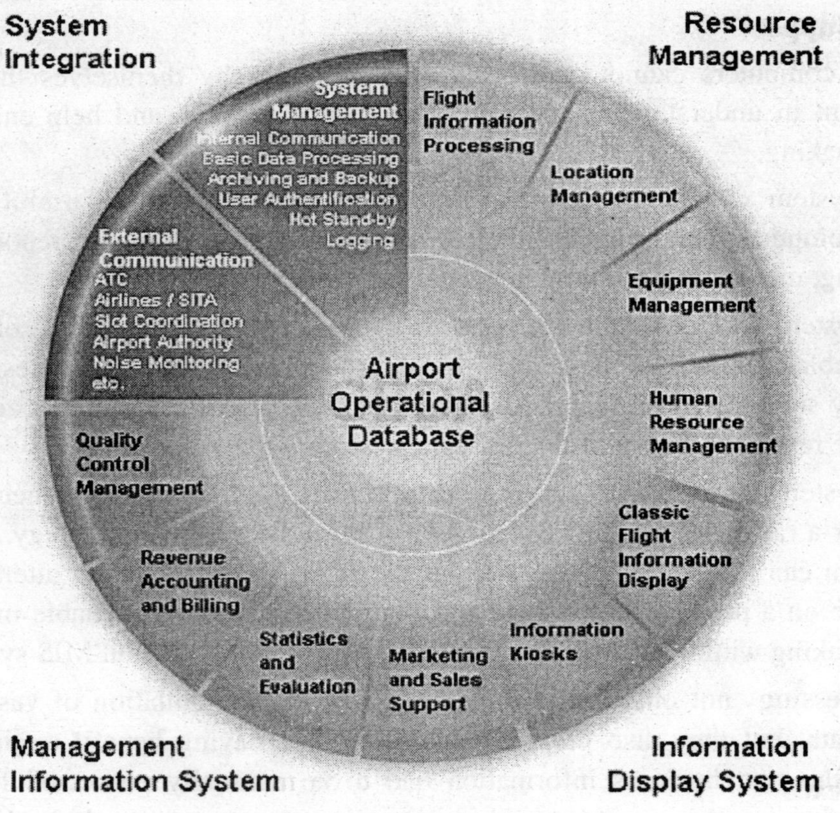

Benefits of MIS

The field of MIS can deliver a great many benefits to enterprises in every industry. Expert organizations such as the Institute of MIS along with peer reviewed journals such as MIS Quarterly continue to find and report new ways to use MIS to achieve business objectives.

Core Competencies

Every market leading enterprise will have at least one core competency – that is, a function they perform better than their competition. By building an exceptional management information system into the enterprise, it is possible to push out ahead of the competition. MIS system provide the tools necessary to gain a better understanding of the market as well as a better understanding of the enterprise itself.

Enhance Supply Chain Management

Improved reporting of business processes leads inevitably to a more streamlined production process. With better information on the production process comes the ability to improve the management of the supply chain, including everything from the sourcing of materials to the manufacturing and distribution of the finished product.

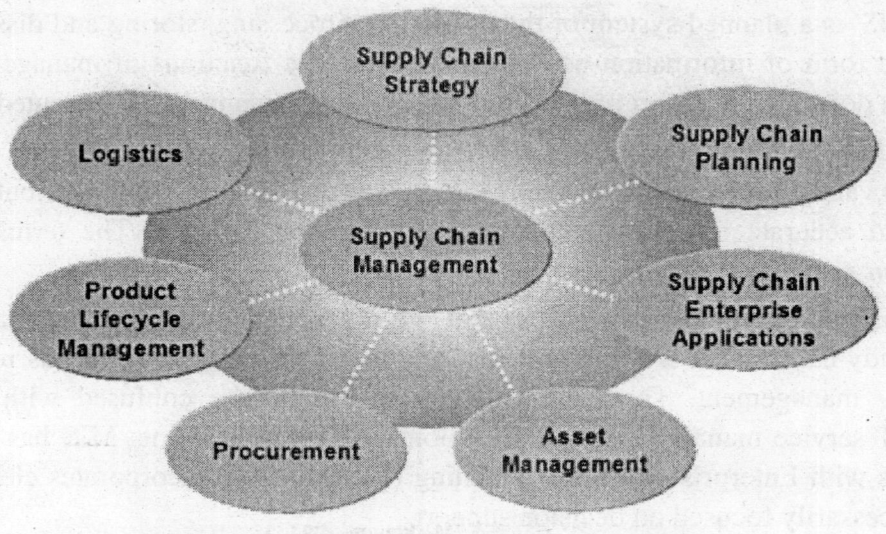

(SCM Functioning)

Quick Reflexes

As a corollary to improved supply chain management comes an improved ability to react to changes in the market. Better MIS system enable an enterprise to react more quickly to their environment, enabling them to push out ahead of the competition and produce a better service and a larger piece of the pie.

Further information about MIS can be found at the Bentley College Journal of MIS and the US Treasury's MIS handbook, and an example of an organizational MIS division can be found at the Department of Social Services for the state of Connecticut.

Overview

At the start, in businesses and other organizations, internal reporting was made manually and only periodically, as a by-product of the accounting system and with some additional statistics, and gave limited and delayed information on management performance.

In their infancy, business computers were used for the practical business of computing the payroll and keeping track of accounts payable and accounts receivable. As applications were developed that provided managers with information about sales, inventories, and other data that would help in managing the enterprise, the term "MIS" arose to describe these kinds of applications. Today, the term is used broadly in a number of contexts and includes (but is not limited to): decision support system, resource and people management applications, project management and database retrieval application.

An 'MIS' is a planned system of the collecting, processing, storing and disseminating data in the form of information needed to carry out the functions of management. In a way, it is a documented report of the activities those were planned and executed.

According to Philip Kotler, "A marketing information system consists of people, equipment, and procedures to gather, sort, analyze, evaluate, and distribute needed, timely, and accurate information to marketing decision makers." The terms *MIS* and *information system* are often confused.

Information system include system that are not intended for decision making. The area of study called MIS is sometimes referred to, in a restrictive sense, as information technology management. That area of study should not be confused with computer science. IT service management is a practitioner-focused discipline. MIS has also some differences with Enterprise Resource Planning (ERP) as ERP incorporates elements that are not necessarily focused on decision support.

Professor Allen S. Lee states that "...research in the information system field examines more than the technological system, or just the social system, or even the two side by side; in addition, it investigates the phenomena that emerge when the two interact."

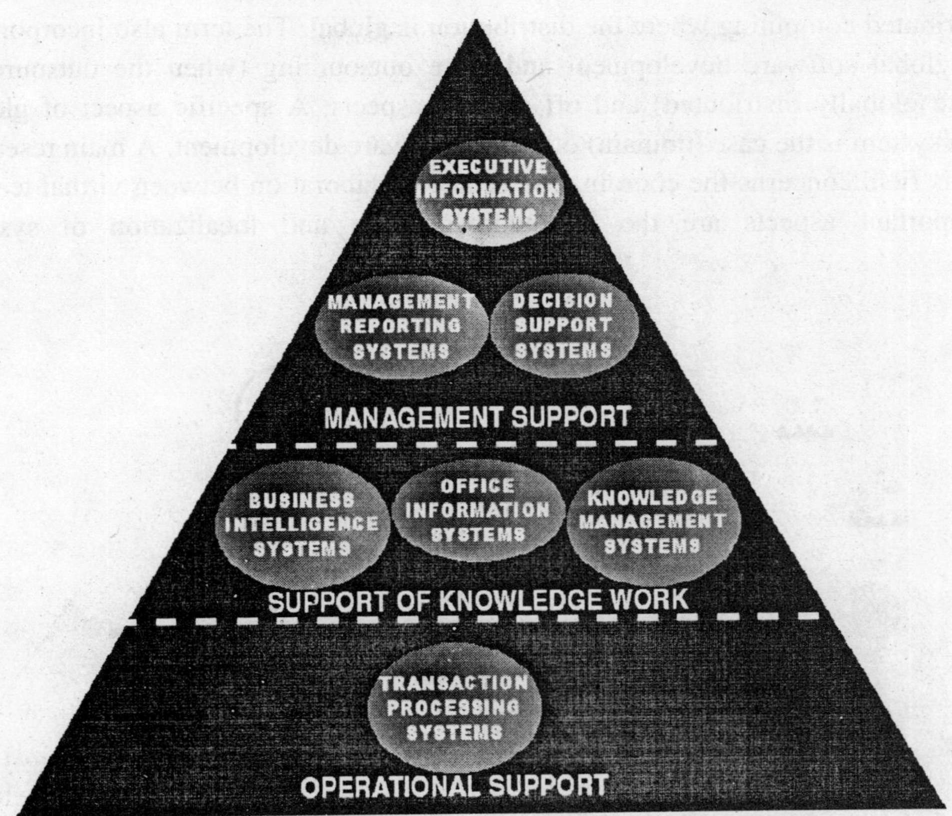

Global Information System

Definition

There is a variety of definitions and understandings of a Global Information System (GIS, GLIS), such as

- **A global information system (GLIS)** is an information system which is developed and / or used in a global context.
- A **global information system** (GLIS) is any information system which attempts to deliver the totality of measurable data worldwide within a defined context. (USF)

The term Global Information System has the same acronym is the same, the meaning is different from the term Geographic Information System.

Common to this class of information system is that the context is a global setting, either for its use or development process. This means that it highly relates to distributed system/distributed computing where the distribution is global. The term also incorporates aspects of global software development and there outsourcing (when the outsourcing locations are globally distributed) and off shoring aspects. A specific aspect of global information system is the case (domain) of global software development. A main research aspect in this field concerns the coordination of and collaboration between virtual teams. Further important aspects are the internationalization and localization of system components.

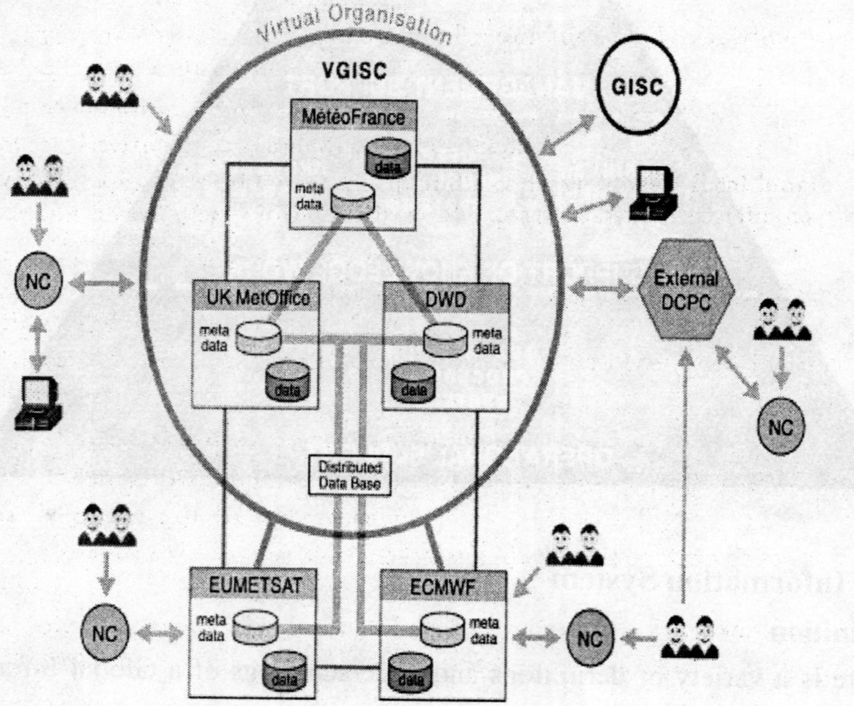

Tasks in Global Information System Design

Critical tasks in the design of Global Information System are

- **Process and System Design:** How are the processes between distributed actors organized how are the system distributed / integrated.
- **Technical architecture:** What is the technical infrastructure enabling actor to collaborate?
- **Support mechanisms:** How are actors in the process of communication, collaboration, cooperation supported?

A variety of examples can be found - basically, every multi-lingual website can be seen as a global information system. However, mostly a GLIS is referred as a specific system developed or used in the global context.

Examples

Specific examples are

- System developed for multinational users, e.g., SAP as a global ERP system
- Global Information System for Education: The Global Learning Objects Brokered Exchange

Support system for global cooperation: System, e.g. Plantar

Factors Influencing the System Development Effort

A variety of factors influence Information System Engineering, ranging from high level strategic to detailed technical issues. The following factors are considered, however the list is by no means exhaustive and you may well care to add your own:-

- Strategic Information System Planning
- Corporate Data Management,
- Business Process Re-Engineering,
- The Technical Environment,
- Models & Methodologies,
- Socio-Behavioral Development,
- Supporting Tools,
- Quality Assurance,
- Project Management,
- Human Resources,
- End-User System Development.

(2) Strategic Information System Planning

Organizations typically develop rolling business plans, they are constructed by taking into account the current business, the external influences on the business (e.g. the economy, government policy and technological advances), and the aims and objectives of the most senior levels of management. The strategic business plan describes how the organization will strive to move from the current business to the target business.

Information System support is necessary to achieve the strategic business plan, so the business plan feeds into a Strategic Information System Plan (SISP), which describes how the current IT system are intended to evolve into the target IT system. A 'big bang' approach is infeasible; therefore a project based approach is used. The output of the SISP is a series of development projects which will either involve modifying existing system or developing new system (which are likely to have to interface or integrate with existing system).

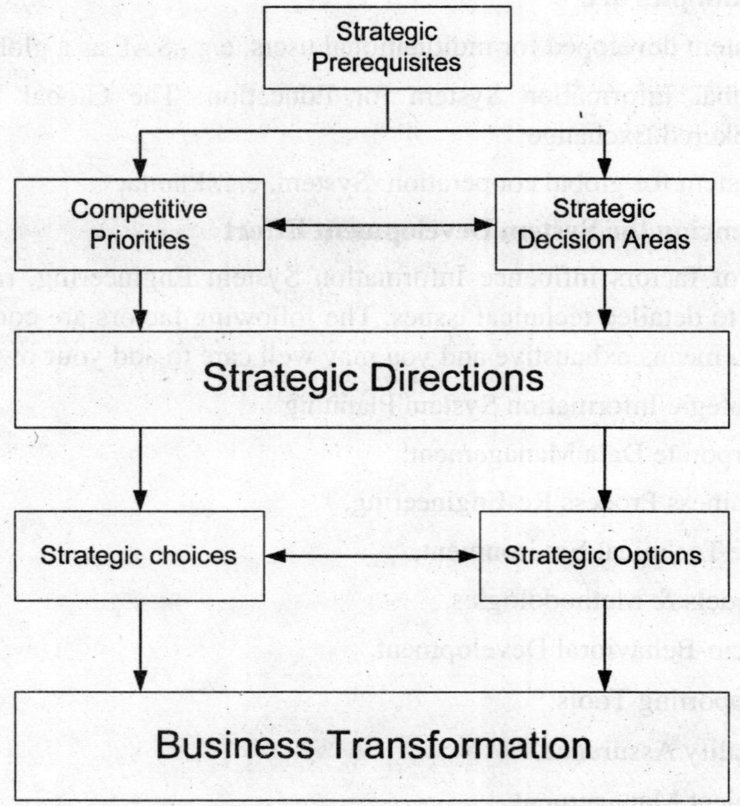

In the past information system were developed simply to improve the efficiency of specific business functions. More recently information system have been viewed as tools for obtaining competitive advantage. Avison and Fitzgerald (1995) have discussed the following ways in which information system can help to achieve competitive advantage:-

"Redefine the boundaries of particular industries,

Develop new products or services,

Change the relationships between suppliers and customers,

Establish barriers to deter new entrants to *marketplaces*."

Porter (1980) identifies five competitive forces that any organization needs to consider:

1. Threat of new entrants.
2. Bargaining power of customers.
3. Threat of substitute products or services.
4. Bargaining power of suppliers.
5. Rivalry among existing firms.

Corporate Data Management

Organizations like British Gas, British Telecom and the NHS have come to realize that on a replacement cost basis their computerized databases are amongst their most valuable assets (consider how much it would cost for British Gas to recapture its customer database) and that as such they need to be professionally managed.

These companies have realized how important data accuracy and consistency is and have developed company system and data architectures. These are very high level models which describe the main processes the organization carries out and the main entities and relationships required to support these business processes. The development of application system is constrained by the need to be consistent with the overarching, high level, companywide view of its data.

Business Process Re-Engineering / Process Innovation

The idea of process innovation (Davenport and Short, 1990, Davenport, 1993) is closely linked with the techniques of Business Process Re-engineering. The argument is that computerizing existing system is only likely to yield marginal gains. In many cases, the only means of achieving radical improvements is to radically re-engineer the business process itself and use IT to enable to re-engineered process. Process Innovation illustrates the main argument of the paper, i.e. that an effective methodology for ISE should adopt a rigorous, structured approach to data design and a dynamic approach to process design.

The Technical Environment

A company which has made a substantial investment in ICL hardware and the INGRES Relational Database Management System (RDBMS) does not decide to convert to IBM and DB2 lightly, so realistically the development is constrained by the existing technical environment.

Object Orientation

In this approach, information system can be viewed as networks of objects, communicating with each other via messages. An object consists of data attributes and a set of methods which enable objects to be created, updated queried and deleted. One of the objectives of object orientation is software re-use. The idea is that all the processing complexities are encapsulated within the object. In this scenario, information system can be engineered from existing objects.

Supporting Tools

Standard tools are likely to be used, e.g. Case tools, data dictionaries, analyst workbenches and 4th Generation Environments (4GE). These are often linked with methodologies, e.g. the PC/Select Case product has add-on toolkits for SSADM and Yourdon. Again organizations using these tools are choosing to constrain their system development process.

Overview

Foundation Concepts: Foundations of Information in Business presents an overview of the five basic areas of information system knowledge needed by business professionals, including the conceptual system components and **major** types of information system.

Why Information System are Important – An understanding of the effective and responsible use and management of information system and technologies is important for managers, business professionals, and other knowledge workers in today's internet worked enterprises. Information system play a vital role in the e-business and e-commerce operations, enterprise collaboration and management, and strategic success of businesses that must operate in an internet worked global environment. Thus, the field of information system has become a major functional area of business administration.

An IS Framework for Business Professionals – The IS knowledge that a business manager or professional needs to know is illustrated in Figure 1.2 and covered in this chapter and text. This included

(1) **Foundation concepts:** fundamental behavior, technical, business, and managerial concepts like system components and functions, or competitive strategies;

(2) **Information technologies**: concepts, developments, or management issues regarding hardware, software, data management, networks, and other technologies;

(3) **Business applications:** major uses of IT for business processes, operations, decision making, and strategic/competitive advantage;

(4) **Development processes**: how end users and IS specialists develop and implement business/IT solutions to problems and opportunities arising in business; and

(5) **Management challenges:** how to effectively and ethically manage the IS function and IT resources to achieve top performance and business value in support of the business strategies of the enterprise.

System Concepts – A system is a group of interrelated components working toward the attainment of a common goal by accepting inputs and producing outputs in an organized transformation process. Feedback is data about the performance of a system.

Control is the component that monitors and evaluates feedback and makes any necessary adjustments to the input and processing components to ensure that proper output is produced.

An Information System Model – An information system uses the resources of people, hardware, software, data, and networks to perform input, processing, output, storage, and control activities that convert data resources into information products. Data are first collected and converted to a form that is suitable for processing (input). Then the data are manipulated and converted into information (processing), stored for future use (storage), or communicated to their ultimate user (output) according to correct processing procedures (control).

IS Resources and Products

- Hardware resources include machines and media used in information processing.
- Software resources include computerized instructions (programs) and instruction for people (procedures).
- People resources include information system specialists and users.
- Data resources include alphanumeric, text, image, video, audio, and other forms of data.
- Network resources include communications media and network support. Information products produced by an information system can take a variety of forms, including paper reports, visual displays, multimedia documents, electronic messages, graphics images, and audio responses.

Information System Resources

The basic IS model shows that an information system consists of five major resources:

- People resources
- Hardware resources
- Software resources
- Data resources
- Network resources

People Resources

People are required for the operation of all information system. These people resources include end users and IS specialists.

End Users

(Also called users or clients) are people who use an information system or the information it produces. Most of us are information system end users. And most end users in business are knowledge

Workers, that is, people who spend most of their time communicating and collaborating in teams of workgroups and creating, using, and distributing information.

IS Specialists are people who develop and operate information system. They include system analysts, Software developers, system operators, and other managerial, technical, and clerical IS personnel.

System analysts – design information system based on the information requirements of end users.

Software developers – create computer programs based on the specifications of system analysts.

System operators – monitor and operate large computer system and networks.

Hardware Resources

Hardware resources include all physical devices and materials used in information processing.

Machines- physical devices (computers, peripherals, telecommunications networks, etc.)

Media

All tangible objects on which data are recorded (paper, magnetic disks etc.) Examples of hardware in computer-based information system are:

Computer System – which consist of central processing units containing microprocessors, and a variety of interconnected peripheral devices.

Computer peripherals – which are devices such as a keyboard or electronic mouse for input of data and commands, a video screen or printer for output of information, and magnetic or optical disks for storage of data resources.

Software Resources

Software resources include all sets of information processing instructions.

Program - a set of instructions that causes a computer to perform a particular task.

Procedures - set of instructions used by people to complete a task.

Examples of software resources are:

System software – such as an operating system program, that controls and supports the operations of a Computer system.

Application software– are programs that direct processing for a particular use of computers by end users.

Procedures– are operating instructions for the people who will use an information system.

Data Resources

Data constitutes a valuable organizational resource. Thus, **data resources** must be managed effectively to benefit all end users in an organization. The data resources of information system are typically organized into:

Databases - a collection of logically related records or files. A database consolidates many records previously stored in separate files so that a common pool of data records serves many applications.

Knowledge Bases - which hold knowledge in a variety of forms such as facts and rules of inference about various subjects.

Network Resources

Telecommunications networks like the Internet, intranets, and extranets have become essential to the successful electronic business and commerce operations of all types of organizations and their computer-based information system. Telecommunications networks consist of computers, communications processors, and other devices interconnected by communications media and controlled by communications software. The concept of **network** resources emphasizes that communications networks are a fundamental resource component of all information system. Network resources include:

Communications media (twisted-pair wire, coaxial cable, fiber-optic cable, and microwave, cellular, and **satellite** wireless system.

Network support (people, hardware, software, and data resources that directly support the operation and use of a communications network).

Information System Activities

Information processing (or data processing) activities that occur in information system include the following:

- Input of data resources
- Processing of data into information
- Output of information products
- Storage of data resources
- Control of system performance

Data versus Information

Data:- Are raw facts or observations, typically about physical phenomena or business transactions. More specifically, data are objective measurements of the attributes (characteristics) of entities, such as people, places, things, and events.

Information:- Is processed data, which has been placed in a meaningful and useful context for an end user. Data is subjected to a "value-added" process (data processing or information processing) where:

- Its form is aggregated, manipulated, and organized.
- Its content is analyzed and evaluated.
- It is placed in a proper context for a human user.

Functional Management Information System (MIS)

Management information system provide decision-makers information and feedback on daily operations. Additionally, management information system can be used strategically, often incorporating Web technology.

Marketing MIS: Marketing Management Information System (MIS) supports managerial activities in product development, distribution, pricing decisions, promotional effectiveness and sales forecasting.

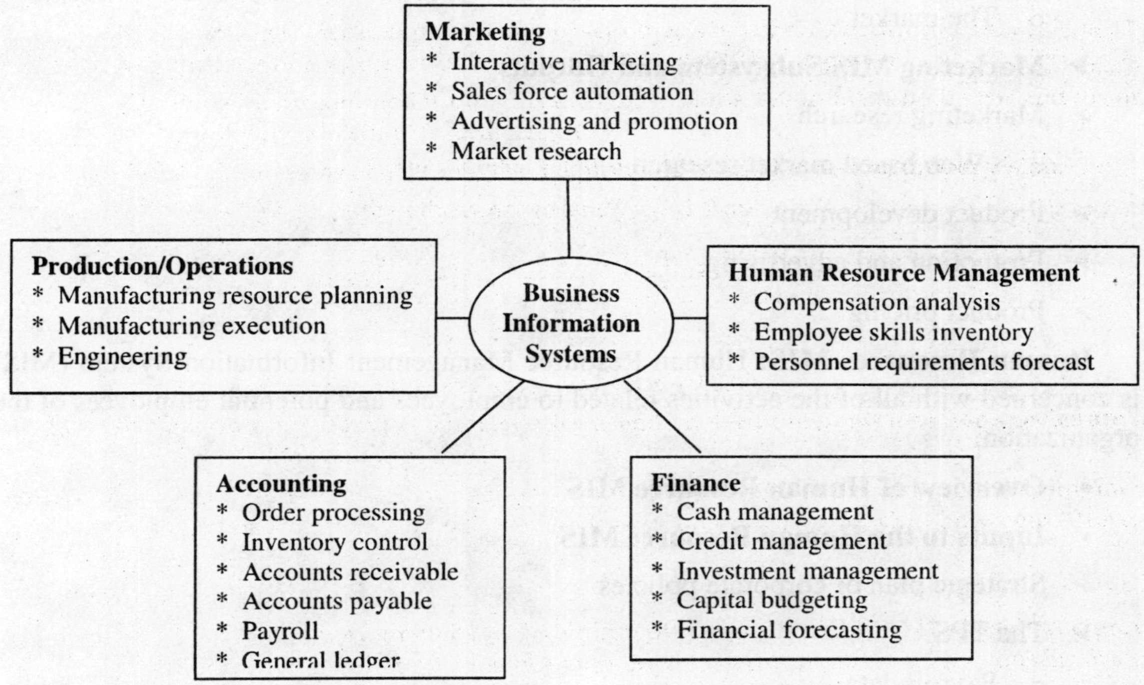

Cross Functional Information System

A cross-functional information system is the third era of information system, after calculations system and functional system.

Cross-functional system were designed to integrate the activities of the entire business process, and are called so because they 'cross' departmental boundaries.

Changing over to a cross-functional system from a functional one can be problematic at times, as it involves the coordination of activities across multiple departments, with the users changing the way that they work. There is no clear line of authority, and fierce peer competition can often lead to interdepartmental rivalries that hinder the development of the new system.

Overview of Marketing Management Information System (MIS)

Inputs to Marketing MIS

- Strategic plan and corporate policies

- The TPS
- External sources:
  - The competition
  - The market
- **Marketing MIS Subsystem and Outputs**
- Marketing research
  - Web based market research
- Product development
- Promotion and advertising
- Product pricing

Human Resources MIS: Human Resource Management Information System (MIS) is concerned with all of the activities related to employees and potential employees of the organization.

- **Overview of Human Resource MIS**
- ✓ **Inputs to the Human Resource MIS**
- Strategic plan or corporate policies
- The TPS:
  - Payroll data
  - Order processing data
  - Personnel data
- External sources
- ✓ **Human Resource MIS Subsystem and Outputs**
- Human resource planning
- Personnel selection and recruiting
- Training and skills inventory
- Scheduling and job placement
- Wage and salary administration

❖ Other MISs

➢ Accounting MISs

- o Provides aggregated information on accounts payable, accounts receivable, payroll, and other applications.

➢ Geographic information system (GISs)

- o Enables managers to pair pre-drawn maps or map outlines with tabular data to describe aspects of a particular geographic region.

Exercise

Q. 1. Explain the concept of Management Information System. Describe the relationship between Management Accounting and Management Information System.

Q. 2. Explain the concept of Information. Discuss the features and dimensions of Information.

Q. 3. Write short notes on any three of the following:

- Operations Data System.
- MIS in Marketing.
- MIS Issues in a Multinational Organization.
- Pyramid Structure of MIS.

Q. 4. Explain the evolution of Management Information System. Describe the stages theory of Management Information System.

Q. 5. Discuss the various concepts of Information. Explain the features and dimensions of Information.

Q. 6. Describe briefly the characteristics of Information for different management levels. Also state the need and importance of quality of Information.

Q. 7. Discuss the evolution of Management Information System. Also explain how management theories are useful in MIS.

Q. 8. Write short notes on the following:

- o Explain the steps involved in implementing a new IS.
- o Explain various control measures in the IS.
- o With block diagram explain different phases of building and maintaining IT based system.
- o Explain six basic data processing functions.

Q. 9. What are the key issues of five perspectives in viewing a work system? Explain.

Q. 10. Explain why knowledge of information system is important for business professionals and identify five areas of information system knowledge they need.

Q. 11. Give examples to illustrate how the business applications of information system can support a firm's business processes, managerial decision-making, and strategies for competitive advantage.

Q. 12. Provide examples of several major types of information system from your experiences with business organizations in the real world.

Q. 13. Identify several challenges that a business manager might face in managing the successful and ethical development and use of information technology in a business.

Question with Answer

Foundation Concepts: Information System and Technologies

Why Information System are Important?

An understanding of the effective and responsible use and management of information system is important for managers and other business knowledge workers in today's global information society. Information system and technologies have become a vital component of successful businesses and organizations. Information system constitute an essential field of study in business administration and management, as they are considered a major functional area in business operations.

What is an Information System?

An ***information system*** **(IS)** can be any organized combination of people, hardware, software, communications networks, and data resources that collect, transforms, and disseminate information in an organization.

What is Information Technologies?

Business professionals rely on many types of information system that use a variety of information technologies.

For example:

Types of IS

- Manual (paper-and-pencil) information system
- Informal (word-of-mouth) information system

- Formal (written procedures) information system
- Computer-based information system

Computer-based ***Information System*** (IS) use hardware, software, the Internet, and other telecommunications networks, computer-based data resource management techniques, and other forms of *Information Technologies (IT)* to transform data resources into a variety of information products for consumers and business professionals.

An ***information system model*** expresses a fundamental conceptual framework for the major components and activities of information system. An information system depends on the resources of people, hardware, software, data, and networks to perform input, processing, output, storage, and control activities that convert data resources into information products. The information system model outlined in the text emphasizes four major concepts that can be applied to all types of information system:

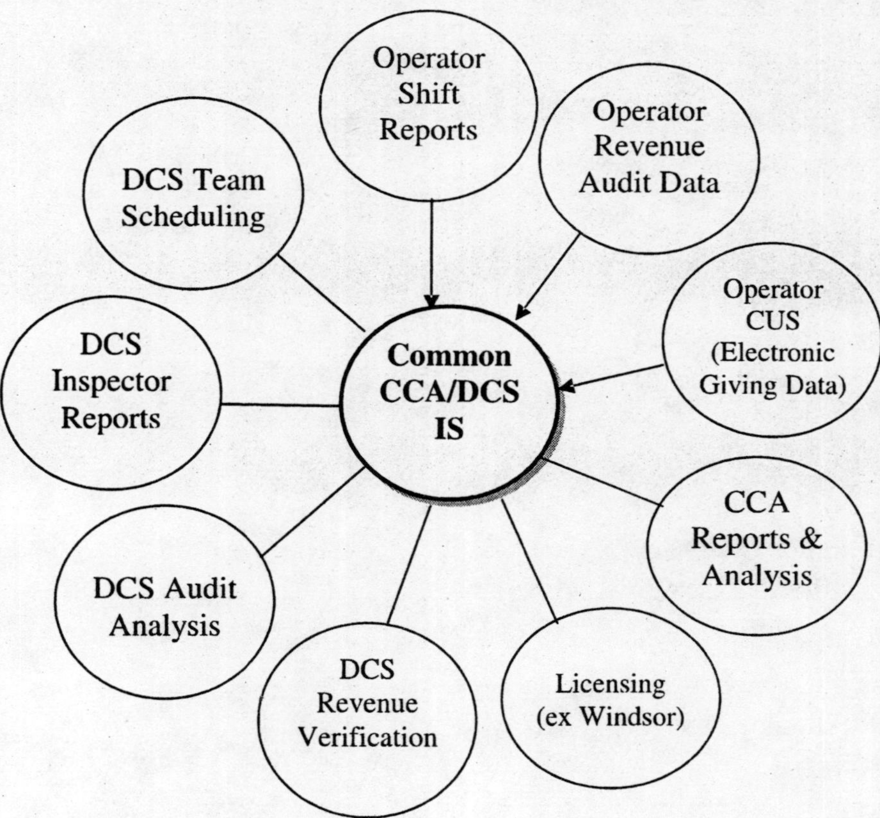

People, hardware, software, data, and networks, are the five basic resources of information system.

A people resource include end users and IS specialists, hardware resources consist of machines and media, software resources include both programs and procedures, data resources can include data and knowledge bases, and network resources include communications media and networks.

Data resources are transformed by information processing activities into a variety of information products for end users.

Information processing consists of input, processing, output, storage, and control activities.

❧

2 CLASSIFICATION OF SYSTEM

What is a system?

The term "system" originates from the Greek term system, which means to "place together." Multiple business and engineering domains have definitions of a system. This text defines a system as:

System An integrated set of interoperable elements, each with explicitly specified and bounded capabilities, working synergistically to perform value-added processing to enable a User to satisfy mission-oriented operational needs in a prescribed operating environment with a specified outcome and probability of success.

You need at least four types of agreement on working level definitions of a system:

1. A personal understanding
2. A program team consensus
3. An organizational (e.g., system developer) consensus, and
4. Most important, a contractual consensus with your customer.

System Concepts – A system is a group of interrelated components working toward the attainment of a common goal by accepting inputs and producing outputs in an organized transformation process. Feedback is data about the performance of a system. Control is the component that monitors and evaluates feedback and makes any necessary adjustments to the input and processing components to ensure that proper output is produced.

The simple diagram presented in Figure 1 represents a system. However, from an analytical perspective, the diagram is missing critical information that relates to how the system operates and performs within its operating environment. Therefore, we expand the diagram to identify these missing elements. The result is shown in Figure 2. The attributes of the construct—which include desirable/undesirable inputs, stakeholders, and desirable/undesirable outputs—serve as a key checklist to ensure that all contributory factors are duly considered when specifying, designing, and developing a system.

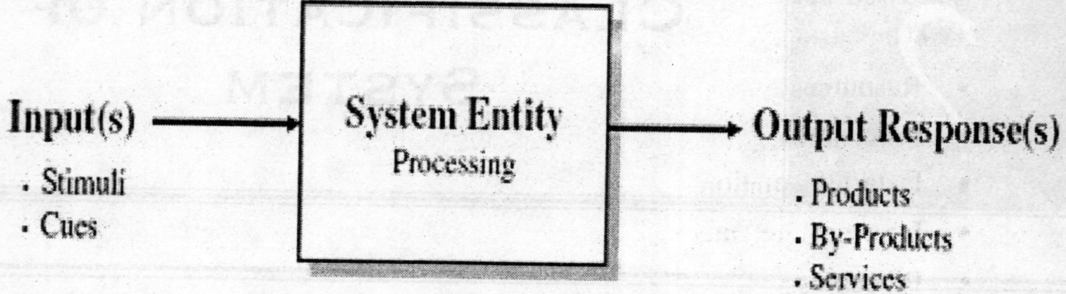

Figure 1 - Basic System Entity Construct

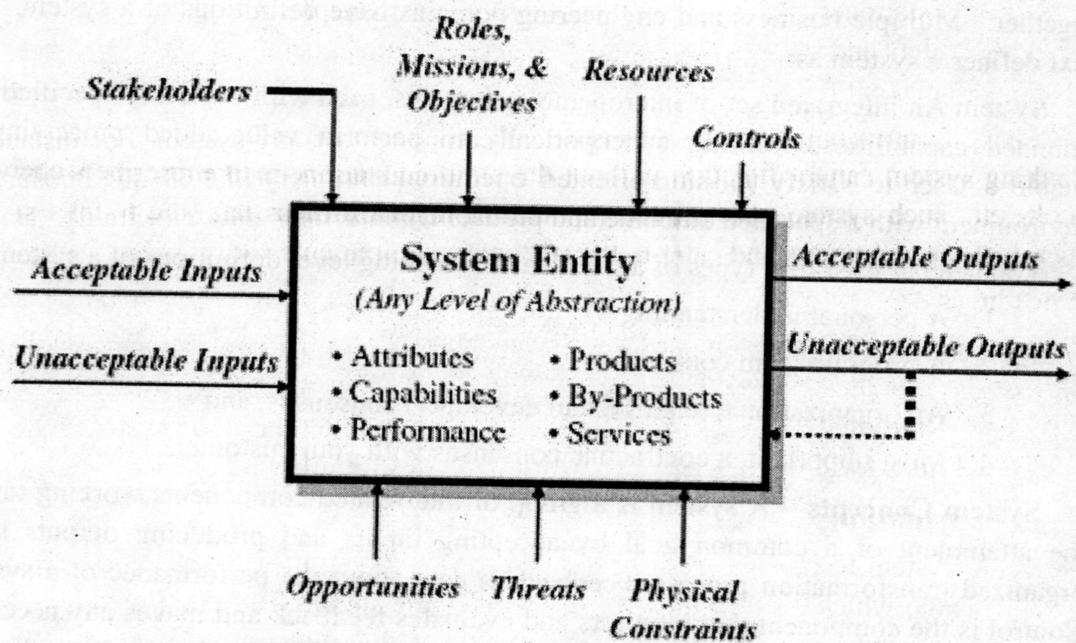

Figure 2 - Analytical System Entity Construct

A big system may be seen as a set of interacting smaller system known as subsystem or functional units each of which have its defined tasks. All these work in coordination to achieve the overall objective of the system. System engineering requires development of a strong foundation in understanding how to characterize a system, product, or service in terms of its attributes, properties, and performance.

As discussed above, a system is a set of components working together to achieve some goal. The basic elements of the system may be listed as:

- Resources
- Procedures
- Data/Information
- Intermediate Data
- Processes

Resources

Every system requires certain resources for the system to exist. Resources can be hardware, software or liveware. Hardware resources may include the computer, its peripherals, stationery etc. Software resources would include the programs running on these computers and the liveware would include the human beings required to operate the system and make it functional.

Thus, these resources make an important component of any system. For instance, a Banking system cannot function without the required stationery like cheque books, pass books etc. such system also need computers to maintain their data and trained staff to operate these computers and cater to the customer requirements.

Procedures

Every system functions under a set of rules that govern the system to accomplish the defined goal of the system. This set of rules defines the procedures for the system to Chapter 1 - Introduction to System operates. For instance, the Banking system have their predefined rules for providing interest at different rates for different types of accounts.

Data/Information

Every system has some predefined goal. For achieving the goal the system requires certain inputs, which are converted into the required output. The main objective of the System is to produce some useful output. Output is the outcome of processing. Output can be of any nature e.g. goods, services or information.

However, the Output must conform to the customer's expectations. Inputs are the elements that enter the system and produce Output. Input can be of various kinds, like material, information, etc.

Intermediate Data

Various processes process system's Inputs. Before it is transformed into Output, it goes through many intermediary transformations. Therefore, it is very important to identify the Intermediate Data. For example, in a college when students register for a new semester, the initial form submitted by student goes through many departments. Each department adds their validity checks on it.

Finally, the form gets transformed and the student gets a slip that states whether the student has been registered for the requested subjects or not. It helps in building the System in a better way. Intermediate forms of data occur when there is a lot of processing on the input data. So, intermediate data should be handled as carefully as other data since the output depends upon it.

Processes

The system have some processes that make use of the resources to achieve the set goal under the defined procedures. These processes are the operational element of the system.

For instance in a Banking system there are several processes that are carried out. Consider for example the processing of a cheque as a process. A cheque passes through several stages before it actually gets processed and converted. These are some of the processes of the Banking system. All these components together make a complete functional system.

System also exhibit certain features and characteristics, some of which are:

- Objective
- Standards
- Environment
- Feedback
- Boundaries and interfaces

Objective

Every system has a predefined goal or objective towards which it works. A system cannot exist without a defined objective. For example, an organization would have an objective of earning maximum possible revenues, for which each department and each individual has to work in coordination.

Standards

It is the acceptable level of performance for any system. System should be designed to meet standards. Standards can be business specific or organization specific.

For example take a sorting problem. There are various sorting algorithms. But each has its own complexity. So such algorithm should be used that gives most optimum efficiency. So there should be a standard or rule to use a particular algorithm. It should be seen whether that algorithm is implemented in the system.

Environment

Every system whether it is natural or manmade co-exists with an environment. It is very important for a system to adapt itself to its environment. Also, for a system to exist it should change according to the changing environment. For example, we humans live in a particular environment. As we move to other places, there are changes in the surroundings but our body gradually adapts to the new environment. If it were not the case, then it would have been very difficult for human to survive for so many thousand years.

Another example can be Y2K problem for computer system. Those system, which are not Y2K compliant, will not be able to work properly after year 2000. For computer system to survive it are important these system are made Y2K compliant or Y2K ready.

Feed-back

Feedback is an important element of system. The output of a system needs to be observed and feedback from the output taken so as to improve the system and make it achieve the laid standards. In fig 1.1, it is shown that a system takes input. It then transforms it into output. Also some feedback can come from customer (regarding quality) or it can be some intermediate data (the output of one process and input for the other) that is required to produce final output.

Boundaries and Interfaces

Every system has defined boundaries within which it operates. Beyond these limits the system has to interact with the other system. For instance, Personnel system in an organization has its work domain with defined procedures. If the financial details of an employee are required, the system has to interact with the Accounting system to get the required details.

Interfaces are another important element through which the system interacts with the outside world. System interacts with other system through its interfaces. Users of the system also interact with it through interfaces. Therefore, these should be customized to the user needs. These should be as user friendly as possible.

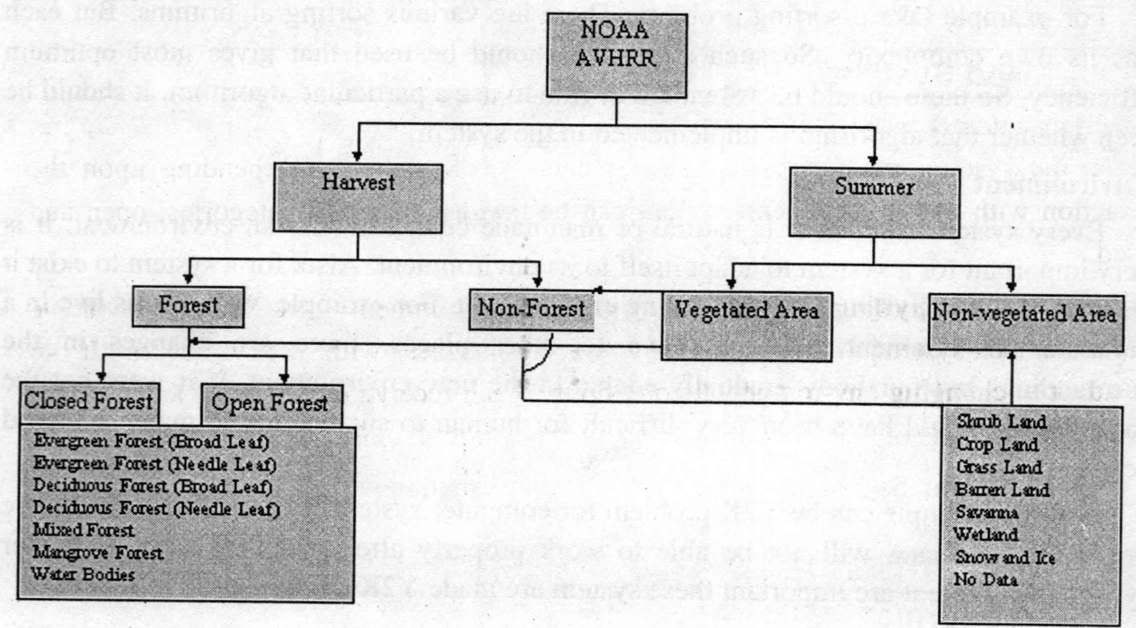

Classification of a System

From previous section we have a firm knowledge of various system components and its characteristics. There are various types of system. To have a good understanding of these system, these can be categorized in many ways. Some of the categories are open or closed, physical or abstract and natural or manmade information system, which are explained next.

Classification of system can be done in many ways.

Physical or Abstract System

Physical system are tangible entities that we can feel and touch. These may be static or dynamic in nature. For example, take a computer center. Desks and chairs are the static parts, which assist in the working of the center. Static parts don't change. The dynamic system are constantly changing. Computer system are dynamic system. Programs, data, and applications can change according to the user's needs.

Abstract system are conceptual. These are not physical entities. They may be formulas, representation or model of a real system.

Open Closed System

System interact with their environment to achieve their targets. Things that are not part of the system are environmental elements for the system. Depending upon the interaction with the environment, system can be divided into two categories, open and closed.

Open system: System that interact with their environment. Practically most of the system are open system. An open system has many interfaces with its environment. It can also adapt to changing environmental conditions. It can receive inputs from, and delivers output to the outside of system. An information system is an example of this category.

Closed system: System that don't interact with their environment. Closed system exist in concept only.

Man made Information System

The main purpose of information system is to manage data for a particular organization. Maintaining files, producing information and reports are few functions. An information system produces customized information depending upon the needs of the organization. These are usually formal, informal, and computer based.

Formal Information System: It deals with the flow of information from top management to lower management. Information flows in the form of memos, instructions, etc. But feedback can be given from lower authorities to top management.

Informal Information system: Informal system are employee based. These are made to solve the day to day work related problems. Computer-Based Information System: This class of system depends on the use of computer for managing business applications. These system are discussed in detail in the next section.

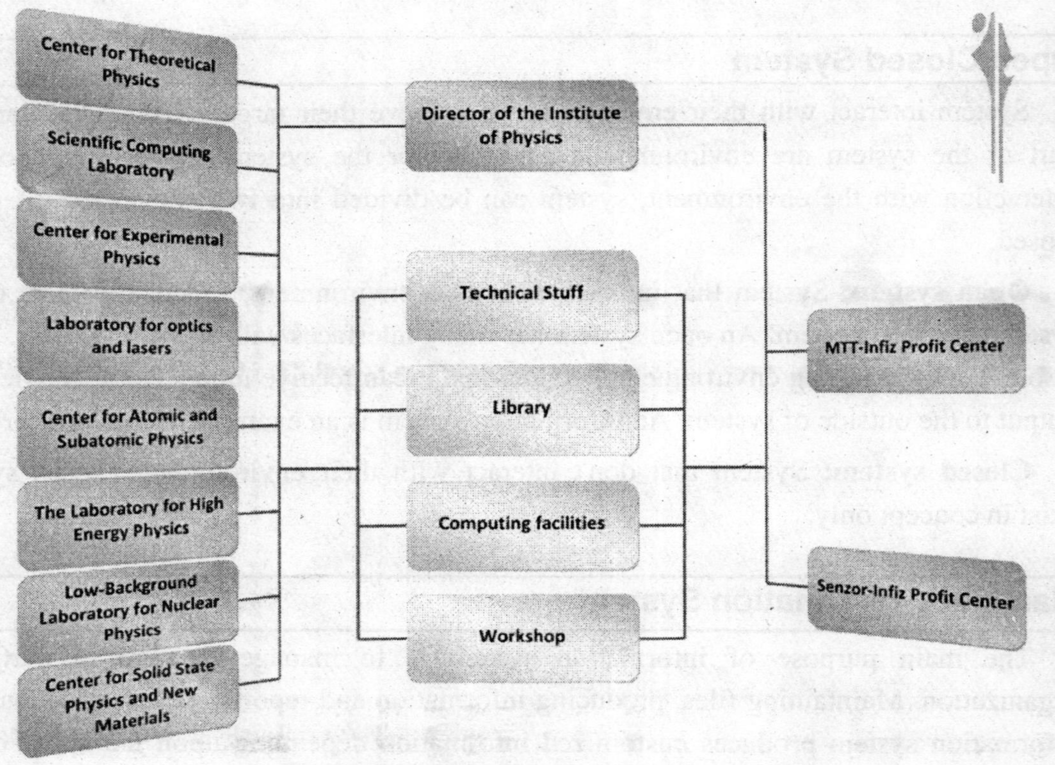

College Management System

Enterprise Resource Planning

Enterprise resource planning (ERP) is an integrated computer-based system used to manage internal and external resources, including tangible assets, financial resources, materials, and human resources. It is a software architecture whose purpose is to facilitate the flow of information between all business functions inside the boundaries of the organization and manage the connections to outside stakeholders. Built on a centralized database and normally utilizing a common computing platform, ERP system consolidate all business operations into a uniform and enterprise-wide system environment.

An ERP system can either reside on a centralized server or be distributed across modular hardware and software units that provide "services" and communicate on a local area network. The distributed design allows a business to assemble modules from different vendors without the need for the placement of multiple copies of complex and expensive computer system in areas which will not use their full capacity.

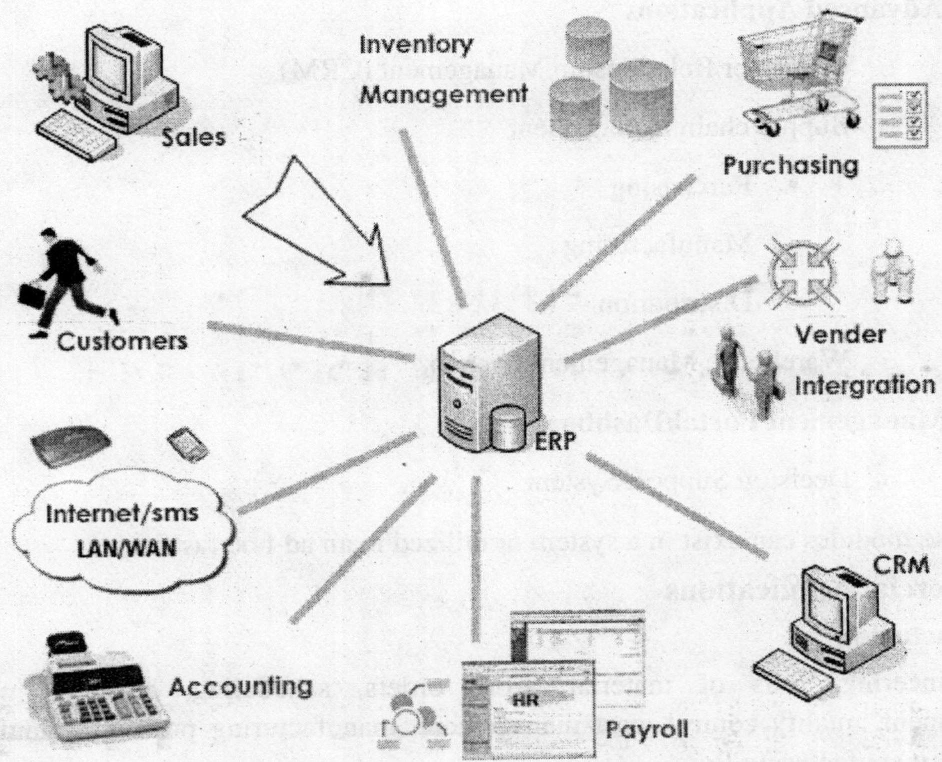

To be considered an ERP system, a software package should have the following traits:

- Should be integrated and operate in real time with no periodic batch updates.
- All applications should access one database to prevent redundant data and multiple data definitions.
- All modules should have the same look and feel.
- Users should be able to access any information in the system without needing integration work on the part of the IS department.
- Components
    - Financials
- Transactional Backbone
    - Distribution
    - Human Resources
    - Product lifecycle management

- **Advanced Applications**
  - Customer Relationship Management (CRM)
  - Supply chain management
    - Purchasing
    - Manufacturing
    - Distribution
  - Warehouse Management System
- **Management Portal/Dashboard**
  - Decision Support System

These modules can exist in a system or utilized in an ad-hoc fashion.

Commercial Applications

Manufacturing

Engineering, bills of material, work orders, scheduling, capacity, workflow management, quality control, cost management, manufacturing process, manufacturing projects, manufacturing flow.

Supply chain management

Order to cash, inventory, order entry, purchasing, product configuration, supply chain planning, supplier scheduling, and inspection of goods, claim processing, and commission calculation.

Financials

General ledger, cash management, accounts payable, accounts receivable, fixed assets.

Project management

Costing, billing, time and expense, performance units, activity management.

Human resources

Human resources, payroll, training, time and attendance, roistering, benefits.

Customer relationship management

Sales and marketing, commissions, service, customer contact, call-center support.

Data services

Various "self-service" interfaces for customers, suppliers and/or employees.

Access control

Management of user privileges for various processes ERP system are cross-functional and enterprise-wide. All functional departments that are involved in operations or production are integrated in one system. In addition to areas such as manufacturing, warehousing, logistics, and information technology, this typically includes accounting, human resources, marketing and strategic management.

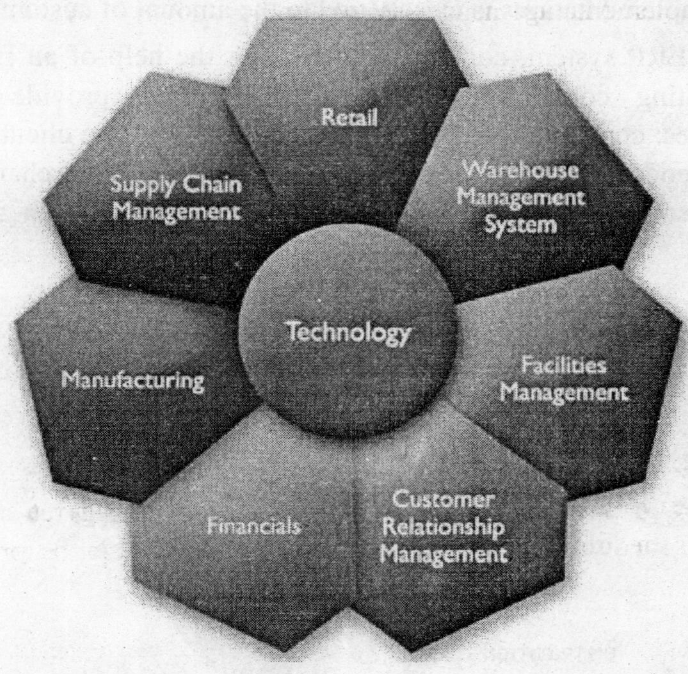

ERP Component

Implementation

Businesses have a wide scope of applications and processes throughout their functional units; producing ERP software system that are typically complex and usually impose significant changes on staff work practices.

Implementing ERP software is typically too complex for "in-house" skill, so it is desirable and highly advised to hire outside consultants who are professionally trained to implement these system. This is typically the most cost effective way. There are three types of services that may be employed for - Consulting, Customization, Support.

The length of time to implement an ERP system depends on the size of the business, the number of modules, the extent of customization, and the scope of the change and the willingness of the customer to take ownership for the project. ERP system are modular, so they don't all need be implemented at once. It can be divided into various stages, or phase-ins. The typical project is about 14 months and requires around 150 consultants. A small project (e.g., a company of less than 100 staff) can be planned and delivered within 3–9 months; however, a large, multi-site or multi-country implementation can take years the length of the implementations is closely tied to the amount of customization desired.

To implement ERP system, companies often seek the help of an ERP vendor or of third-party consulting companies. These firms typically provide three areas of professional services: consulting; customization; and support. The client organization can also employ independent program management, business analysis, change management, and UAT specialists to ensure their business requirements remain a priority during implementation.

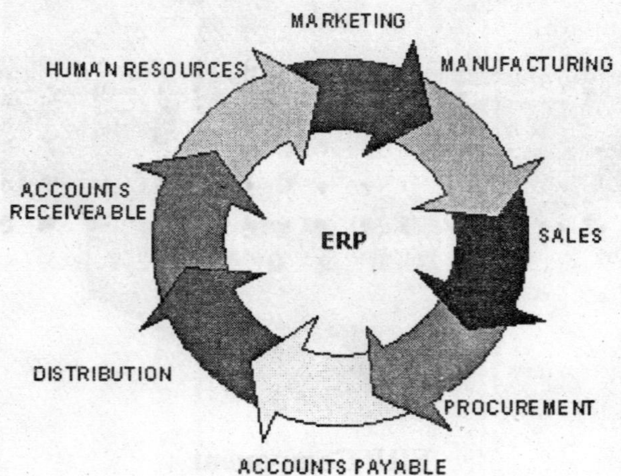

Data Migration

Data migration is one of the most important activities in determining the success of an ERP implementation. Since many decisions must be made before migration, a significant amount of planning must occur. Unfortunately, data migration is the last activity before the production phase of an ERP implementation, and therefore receives minimal attention due to time constraints. The following are steps of a data migration strategy that can help with the success of an ERP implementation:

Identifying the data to be migrated

1. Determining the timing of data migration
2. Generating the data templates
3. Freezing the tools for data migration
4. Deciding on migration related setups
5. Deciding on data archiving

Process preparation

ERP vendors have designed their system around standard business processes, based upon best business practices. Different vendor(s) have different types of processes but they are all of a standard, modular nature. Firms that want to implement ERP system are consequently forced to adapt their organizations to standardized processes as opposed to adapting the ERP package to the existing processes.

Research indicates that the risk of business process mismatch is decreased by:

- linking each current organizational process to the organization's strategy;
- analyzing the effectiveness of each process in light of its current related business capability;
- Understanding the automated solutions currently implemented.

A disadvantage usually attributed to ERP is that business process redesign to fit the standardized ERP modules can lead to a loss of competitive advantage. While documented cases exist where this has indeed materialized, other cases show that following thorough process preparation ERP system can actually increase sustainable competitive advantage.

Configuration

Configuring an ERP system is largely a matter of balancing the way you want the system to work with the way the system lets you work. Begin by deciding which modules to install, and then adjust the system using configuration tables to achieve the best possible fit in working with your company's processes.

Modules — Most system are modular simply for the flexibility of implementing some functions but not others. Some common modules, such as finance and accounting are adopted by nearly all companies implementing enterprise system; others however such as human resource management are not needed by some companies and therefore not adopted. A service company for example will not likely need a module for manufacturing. Other times companies will not adopt a module because they already have their own proprietary system they believe to be superior. Generally speaking the greater number of modules selected, the greater the integration benefits, but also the increase in costs, risks and changes involved.

Configuration Tables – A configuration table enables a company to tailor a particular aspect of the system to the way it chooses to do business. For example, an organization can select the type of inventory accounting – FIFO or LIFO – it will employ or whether it wants to recognize revenue by geographical unit, product line, or distribution channel.

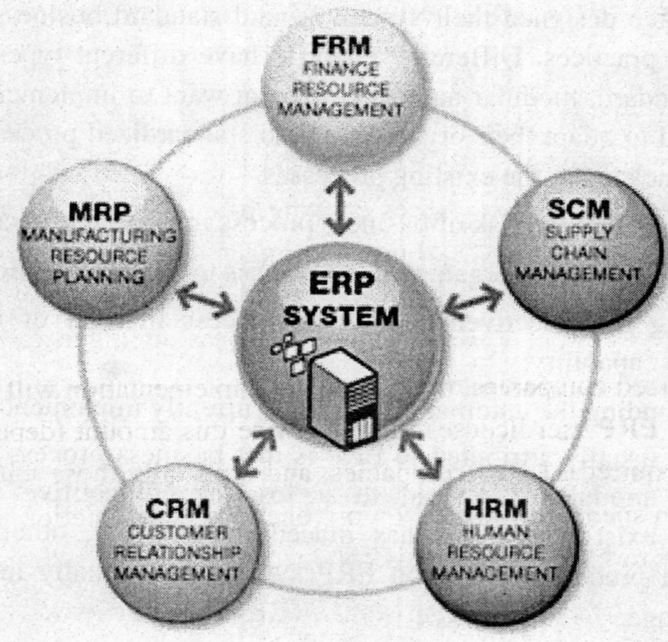

Enterprise Resource Planning (ERP)

So, what happens when the options the system allows just aren't good enough? At this point a company has two choices, both of which are not ideal. It can re-write some of the enterprise system's code, or it can continue to use an existing system and build interfaces between it and the new enterprise system. Both options will add time and cost to the implementation process. Additionally, they can dilute the system's integration benefits. The more customized the system becomes the less possible seamless communication between suppliers and customers.

Consulting services

Many organizations do not have sufficient internal skills to implement an ERP project. This results in many organizations offering consulting services for ERP implementation. Typically, a consulting team is responsible for the entire ERP implementation including.

1. Selecting
2. Planning
3. Training
4. Testing
5. Implementation
6. Delivery of Any Customized Modules.

Examples of customization includes creating processes and reports for compliance, additional product training; creation of process triggers and workflow; specialist advice to improve how the ERP is used in the business; system optimization; and assistance writing reports, complex data extracts or implementing Business Intelligence.

For most mid-sized companies, the cost of the implementation will range from around the list price of the ERP user licenses to up to twice this amount (depending on the level of customization required). Large companies, and especially those with multiple sites or countries, will often spend considerably more on the implementation than the cost of the user licenses—three to five times more is not uncommon for a multi-site implementation.

Unlike most single-purpose applications, ERP packages have historically included full source code and shipped with vendor-supported team IDEs for customizing and extending the delivered code. During the early years of ERP the guarantee of mature tools and support for extensive customization was an important sales argument when a potential customer was considering developing their own unique solution in-house, or assembling a cross-functional solution by integrating multiple "best of breed" applications.

Expert system

An **expert system** is software that attempts to provide an answer to a problem, or clarify uncertainties where normally one or more human experts would need to be consulted. Expert system are most common in a specific problem domain, and is a traditional application and/or subfield of artificial intelligence.

A wide variety of methods can be used to simulate the performance of the expert however common to most or all are 1) the creation of a so-called "knowledgebase" which uses some knowledge representation formalism to capture the Subject Matter Expert's (SME) knowledge and 2) a process of gathering that knowledge from the SME and codifying it according to the formalism, which is called knowledge engineering. Expert system may or may not have learning components but a third common element is that once the system is developed it is proven by being placed in the same real world problem solving situation as the human SME, typically as an aid to human workers or a supplement to some information system.

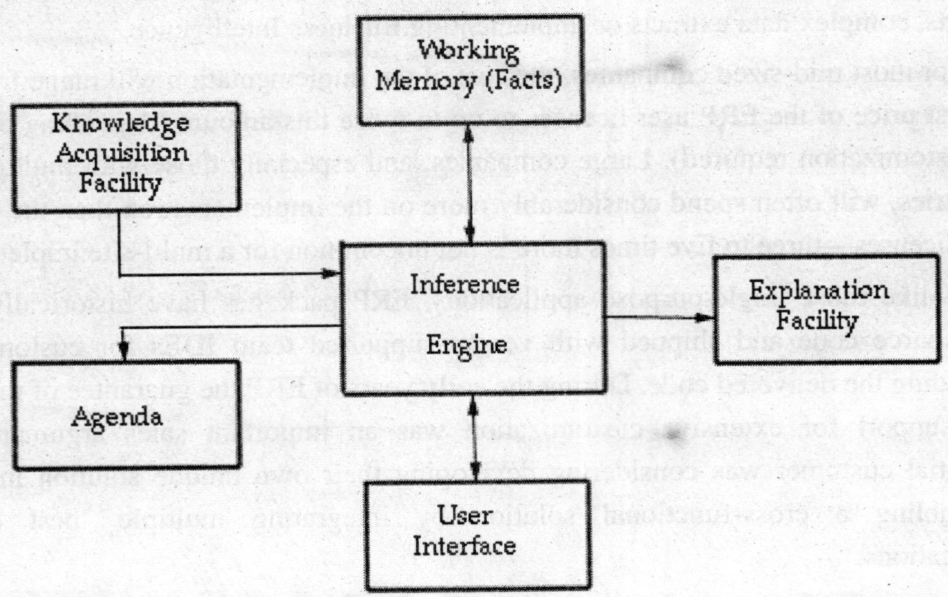

Components of an Expert System

As a premiere application of computing and artificial intelligence, the topic of expert system has many points of contact with general system theory, operations research, business process reengineering and various topics in applied mathematics and management science.

Expert System Part

Chaining

There are two main methods of reasoning when using inference rules: backward chaining and forward chaining.

Forward chaining starts with the data available and uses the inference rules to conclude more data until a desired goal is reached. An inference engine using forward chaining searches the inference rules until it finds one in which the *if* clause is known to be true. It then concludes the *then* clause and adds this information to its data. It would continue to do this until a goal is reached. Because the data available determines which inference rules are used, this method is also called *data driven*.

Backward chaining starts with a list of goals and works backwards to see if there is data which will allow it to conclude any of these goals. An inference engine using backward chaining would search the inference rules until it finds one which has a *then* clause that matches a desired goal. If the *if* clause of that inference rule is not known to be true, then it is added to the list of goals. For example, suppose a rule base contains:

1. If Fritz is green then Fritz is a frog.
2. If Fritz is a frog then Fritz hops.

Suppose a goal is to conclude that Fritz hops. The rule base would be searched and rule (2) would be selected because its conclusion (the *then* clause) matches the goal. It is not known that Fritz is a frog, so this "if" statement is added to the goal list. The rule base is again searched and this time rule (1) is selected because its then clause matches the new goal just added to the list. This time, the *if* clause (Fritz is green) is known to be true and the goal that Fritz hops is concluded. Because the list of goals determines which rules are selected and used, this method is called *goal driven*.

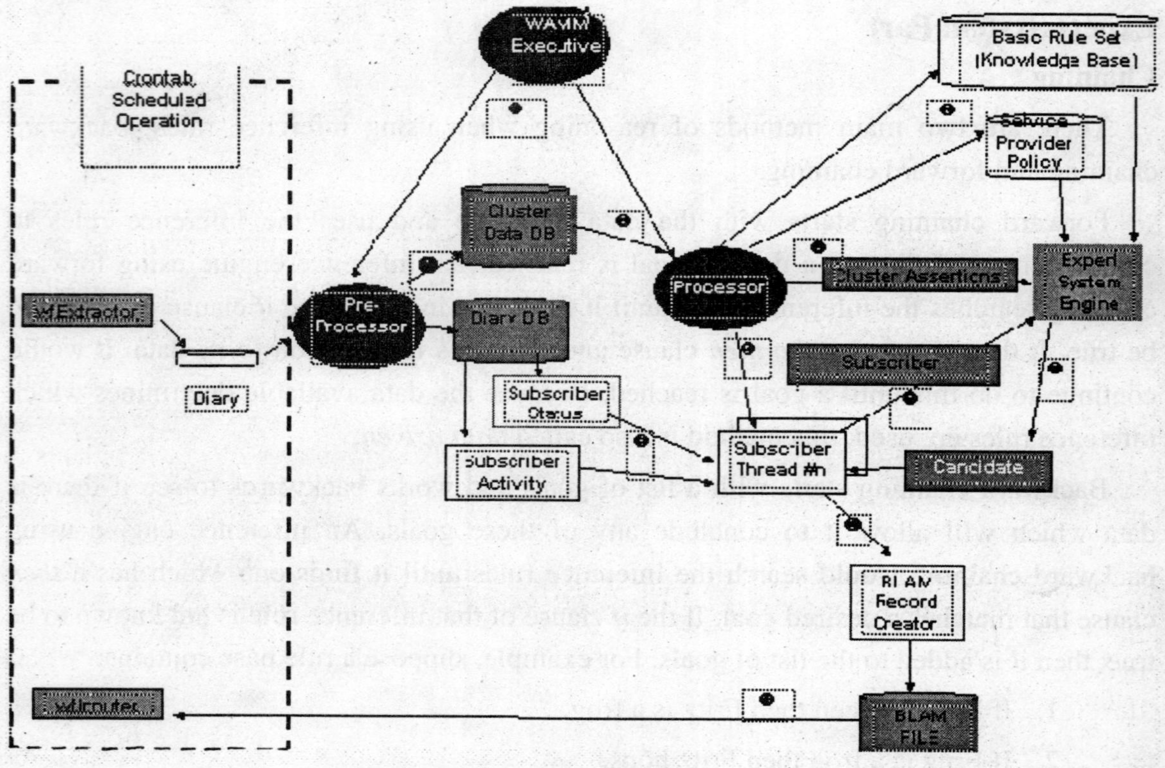

Certainty factors

One advantage of expert system over traditional methods of programming is that they allow the use of "confidences", also known as **certainty factors**. A human, when reasoning, does not always conclude things with 100% confidence: he might venture, "If Fritz is green, then he is probably a frog" (after all, he might be a chameleon). This type of reasoning can be imitated by using numeric values called *confidences*. For example, if it is known that Fritz is green, it might be concluded with 0.85 confidences that he is a frog; or, if it is known that he is a frog, it might be concluded with 0.95 confidences that he hops. These numbers are similar in nature to probabilities, but they are not the same: they are meant to imitate the confidences humans use in reasoning rather than to follow the mathematical definitions used in calculating probabilities.

Expert System Architecture

The following general points about expert system and their architecture have been illustrated.

1. The sequence of steps taken to reach a conclusion is dynamically synthesized with each new case. It is not explicitly programmed when the system is built.
2. Expert system can process multiple values for any problem parameter. This permits more than one line of reasoning to be pursued and the results of incomplete (not fully determined) reasoning to be presented.
3. Problem solving is accomplished by applying specific knowledge rather than specific technique. This is a key idea in expert system technology. It reflects the belief that human experts do not process their knowledge differently from others, but they do possess different knowledge. With this philosophy, when one finds that their expert system does not produce the desired results, work begins to expand the knowledge base, not to re-program the procedures.

There are various expert system in which a rule base and an inference engine cooperate to simulate the reasoning process that a human expert pursues in analyzing a problem and arriving at a conclusion. In these system, in order to simulate the human reasoning process, a vast amount of knowledge needed to be stored in the knowledge base. Generally, the knowledge base of such an expert system consisted of a relatively large number of "if then" type of statements that were interrelated in a manner that, in theory at least, resembled the sequence of mental steps that were involved in the human reasoning process.

Because of the need for large storage capacities and related programs to store the rule base, most expert system have, in the past, been run only on large information handling system. Recently, the storage capacity of personal computers has increased to a point where it is becoming possible to consider running some types of simple expert system on personal computers.

In some applications of expert system, the nature of the application and the amount of stored information necessary to simulate the human reasoning process for that application is just too vast to store in the active memory of a computer.

In other applications of expert system, the nature of the application is such that not all of the information is always needed in the reasoning process. An example of this latter type application would be the use of an expert system to diagnose a data processing system comprising many separate components, some of which are optional. When that type of expert system employs a single integrated rule base to diagnose the minimum system configuration of the data processing system, much of the rule base is not required since many of the components which are optional units of the system will not be present in the system. Nevertheless, earlier expert system require the entire rule base to be stored since all the rules were, in effect, chained or linked together by the structure of the rule base.

When the rule base is segmented, preferably into contextual segments or units, it is then possible to eliminate portions of the Rule base containing data or knowledge that is not needed in a particular application. The segmenting of the rule base also allows the expert system to be run with system or on system having much smaller memory capacities than was possible with earlier arrangements since each segment of the rule base can be paged into and out of the system as needed.

The segmenting of the rule base into contextual segments requires that the expert system manage various inter segment relationships as segments are paged into and out of memory during execution of the program. Since the system permits a rule base segment to be called and executed at any time during the processing of the first rule base, provision must be made to store the data that has been accumulated up to that point so that at some time later in the process, when the system returns to the first segment, it can proceed from the last point or rule node that was processed. Also, provision must be made so that data that has been collected by the system up to that point can be passed to the second segment of the rule base after it has been paged into the system and data collected during the processing of the second segment can be passed to the first segment when the system returns to complete processing that segment.

The user interface and the procedure interface are two important functions in the information collection process.

End user

The end-user usually seen an expert system through an interactive dialog, an example of which follows:

Q. Do you know which restaurant you want to go to?

A. No

Q. Is there any kind of food you would particularly like?

A. No

Q. Do you like spicy food?

A. No

Q. Do you usually drink wine with meals?

A. Yes

Q. When you drink wine, is it French wine?

A. Yes

As can be seen from this dialog, the system is leading the user through a set of questions, the purpose of which is to determine a suitable set of restaurants to recommend. This dialog begins with the system asking if the user already knows the restaurant choice (a common feature of expert system) and immediately illustrates a characteristic of expert system; users may choose not to respond to any question. In expert system, dialogs are not pre-planned. There is no fixed control structure. Dialogs are synthesized from the current information and the contents of the knowledge base. Because of this, not being able to supply the answer to a particular question does not stop the consultation.

Explanation system

Another major distinction between expert system and traditional system is illustrated by the following answer given by the system when the user answers a question with another question, "Why", as occurred in the above example. The answer is:

A. I am trying to determine the type of restaurant to suggest. So far Chinese is not a likely choice. It is possible that French is a likely choice. I know that if the diner is a wine drinker, and the preferred wine is French, then there is strong evidence that the restaurant choice should include French.

It is very difficult to implement a general explanation system (answering questions like "Why" and "How") in a traditional computer program. An expert system can generate an explanation by retracing the steps of its reasoning. The response of the expert system to the question WHY is an exposure of the underlying knowledge structure. It is a rule; a set of antecedent conditions which, if true, allow the assertion of a consequent. The rule references values, and tests them against various constraints or asserts constraints onto them. This, in fact, is a significant part of the knowledge structure.

There are values, which may be associated with some organizing entity. For example, the individual diner is an entity with various attributes (values) including whether they drink wine and the kind of wine. There are also rules, which associate the currently known values of some attributes with assertions that can be made about other attributes. It is the orderly processing of these rules that dictates the dialog itself.

Expert System versus Problem-Solving System

The principal distinction between expert system and traditional problem solving programs is the way in which the problem related expertise is coded. In traditional applications, problem expertise is encoded in both program and data structures. In the expert system approach all of the problem related expertise is encoded in data structures only; no problem-specific information is encoded in the program structure. This organization has several benefits.

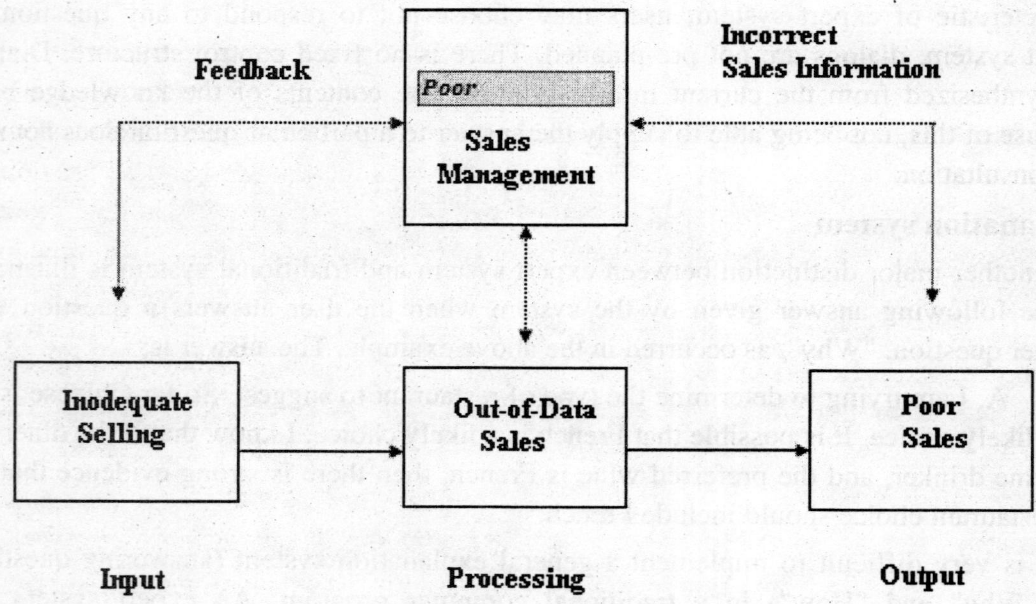

An example may help contrast the traditional problem solving program with the expert system approach. The example is the problem of tax advice. In the traditional approach, data structures describe the taxpayer and tax tables, and a program in which there are statements representing an expert tax consultant's knowledge, such as statements which relate information about the taxpayer to tax table choices. It is this representation of the tax expert's knowledge that is difficult for the tax expert to understand or modify.

In the expert system approach, the information about taxpayers and tax computations is again found in data structures, but now the knowledge describing the relationships between them is encoded in data structures as well.

The programs of an expert system are independent of the problem domain (taxes) and serve to process the data structures without regard to the nature of the problem area they describe. For example, there are programs to acquire the described data values through user interaction, programs to represent and process special organizations of description, and programs to process the declarations that represent semantic relationships within the problem domain and an algorithm to control the processing sequence and focus.

The general architecture of an expert system involves two principal components: a problem dependent set of data declarations called the knowledge base or rule base, and a problem independent (although highly data structure dependent) program which is called the inference engine.

Individuals Involved With Expert System

There are generally three individuals having an interaction with expert system. Primary among these is the end-user; the individual who uses the system for its problem solving assistance. In the building and maintenance of the system there are two other roles: the problem domain expert who builds and supplies the knowledge base providing the domain expertise, and a knowledge engineer who assists the experts in determining the representation of their knowledge, enters this knowledge into an explanation module and who defines the inference technique required to obtain useful problem solving activity. Usually, the knowledge engineer will represent the problem solving activity in the form of rules which is referred to as a rule-based expert system. When these rules are created from the domain expertise, the knowledge base stores the rules of the expert system.

Inference Rule

An understanding of the "inference rule" concept is important to understand expert system. An inference rule is a statement that has two parts, an *if* clause and a *then* clause. This rule is what gives expert system the ability to find solutions to diagnostic and prescriptive problems. An example of an inference rule is:

> If the restaurant choice includes French, and the occasion is romantic,
>
> Then the restaurant choice is definitely Paul Bocuse.

An expert system's rule base is made up of many such inference rules. They are entered as separate rules and it is the inference engine that uses them together to draw conclusions. Because each rule is a unit, rules may be deleted or added without affecting other rules (though it should affect which conclusions are reached). One advantage of inference rules over traditional programming is that inference rules use reasoning which more closely resemble human reasoning.

Thus, when a conclusion is drawn, it is possible to understand how this conclusion was reached. Furthermore, because the expert system uses knowledge in a form similar to the expert, it may be easier to retrieve this information from the expert.

Procedure Node Interface

The function of the procedure node interface is to receive information from the procedures coordinator and create the appropriate procedure call. The ability to call a procedure and receive information from that procedure can be viewed as simply a generalization of input from the external world. While in some earlier expert system external information has been obtained, that information was obtained only in a predetermined manner so only certain information could actually be acquired. This expert system, disclosed in the cross-referenced application, through the knowledge base, is permitted to invoke any procedure allowed on its host system. This makes the expert system useful in a much wider class of knowledge domains than if it had no external access or only limited external access.

In the area of machine diagnostics using expert system, particularly self-diagnostic applications, it is not possible to conclude the current state of "health" of a machine without some information. The best source of information is the machine itself, for it contains much detailed information that could not reasonably be provided by the operator.

The knowledge that is represented in the system appears in the rule base. In the rule base described in the cross-referenced applications, there are basically four different types of objects, with associated information present.

1. **Classes**—these are questions asked to the user.
2. **Parameters**—a parameter is a place holder for a character string which may be a variable that can be inserted into a class question at the point in the question where the parameter is positioned.
3. **Procedures**—these are definitions of calls to external procedures.
4. **Rule Nodes**—The differencing in the system is done by a tree structure which indicates the rules or logic which mimics human reasoning. The nodes of these trees are called rule nodes. There are several different types of rule nodes.

The rule base comprises a forest of many trees. The top node of the tree is called the goal node, in that it contains the conclusion. Each tree in the forest has a different goal node. The leaves of the tree are also referred to as rule nodes, or one of the types of rule nodes. A leaf may be an evidence node, an external node, or a reference node.

An evidence node functions to obtain information from the operator by asking a specific question. In responding to a question presented by an evidence node, the operator is generally instructed to answer "yes" or "no" represented by numeric values 1 and 0 or provide a value of between 0 and 1, represented by a "maybe."

Questions which require a response from the operator other than yes or no or a value between 0 and 1 are handled in a different manner.

A leaf that is an external node indicates that data will be used which was obtained from a procedure call.

A reference node functions to refer to another tree or sub tree.

A tree may also contain intermediate or minor nodes between the goal node and the leaf node. An intermediate node can represent logical operations like And or.

The inference logic has two functions. It selects a tree to trace and then it traces that tree. Once a tree has been selected, that tree is traced, depth-first, left to right.

The word "tracing" refers to the action the system takes as it traverses the tree, asking classes (questions), calling procedures, and calculating confidences as it proceeds.

As explained in the cross-referenced applications, the selection of a tree depends on the ordering of the trees. The original ordering of the trees is the order in which they appear in the rule base. This order can be changed, however, by assigning an evidence node an attribute "initial" which is described in detail in these applications. The first action taken is to obtain values for all evidence nodes which have been assigned an "initial" attribute. Using only the answers to these initial evidences, the rules are ordered so that the most likely to succeed is evaluated first. The trees can be further re-ordered since they are constantly being updated as a selected tree is being traced.

It has been found that the type of information that is solicited by the system from the user by means of questions or classes should be tailored to the level of knowledge of the user. In many applications, the group of prospective uses is nicely defined and the knowledge level can be estimated so that the questions can be presented at a level which corresponds generally to the average user. However, in other applications, knowledge of the specific domain of the expert system might vary considerably among the group of prospective users.

One application where this is particularly true involves the use of an expert system, operating in a self-diagnostic mode on a personal computer to assist the operator of the personal computer to diagnose the cause of a fault or error in either the hardware or software. In general, asking the operator for information is the most straightforward way for the expert system to gather information assuming, of course, that the information is or should be within the operator's understanding. For example, in diagnosing a personal computer, the expert system must know the major functional components of the system. It could ask the operator, for instance, if the display is a monochrome or color display. The operator should, in all probability, be able to provide the correct answer 100% of the time. The expert system could, on the other hand, cause a test unit to be run to determine the type of display. The accuracy of the data collected by either approach in this instance probably would not be that different so the knowledge engineer could employ either approach without affecting the accuracy of the diagnosis. However, in many instances, because of the nature of the information being solicited, it is better to obtain the information from the system rather than asking the operator, because the accuracy of the data supplied by the operator is so low that the system could not effectively process it to a meaningful conclusion.

In many situations the information is already in the system, in a form of which permits the correct answer to a question to be obtained through a process of inductive or deductive reasoning. The data previously collected by the system could be answers provided by the user to less complex questions that were asked for a different reason or results returned from test units that were previously run.

User Interface

The function of the user interface is to present questions and information to the user and supply the user's responses to the inference engine.

Any values entered by the user must be received and interpreted by the user interface. Some responses are restricted to a set of possible legal answers, others are not. The user interface checks all responses to insure that they are of the correct data type. Any responses that are restricted to a legal set of answers are compared against these legal answers. Whenever the user enters an illegal answer, the user interface informs the user that his answer was invalid and prompts him to correct it.

Application of Expert System

Expert system are designed and created to facilitate tasks in the fields of accounting, medicine, process control, financial service, production, human resources etc. Indeed, the foundation of a successful expert system depends on a series of technical procedures and development that may be designed by certain technicians and related experts.

A good example of application of expert system in banking area is expert system for mortgages. Loan departments are interested in expert system for mortgages because of the growing cost of labour which makes the handling and acceptance of relatively small loans less profitable. They also see in the application of expert system a possibility for standardized, efficient handling of mortgage loan, and appreciate that for the acceptance of mortgages there are hard and fast rules which do not always exist with other types of loans.

While expert system have distinguished themselves in AI research in finding practical application, their application has been limited. Expert system are notoriously narrow in their domain of knowledge—as an amusing example, a researcher used the "skin disease" expert system to diagnose his rust bucket car as likely to have developed measles—and the system were thus prone to making errors that humans would easily spot. Additionally, once some of the mystique had worn off, most programmers realized that simple expert system were essentially just slightly more elaborate versions of the decision logic they had already been using. Therefore, some of the techniques of expert system can now be found in most complex programs without any fuss about them.

An example, and a good demonstration of the limitations of, an expert system used by many people is the Microsoft Windows operating system troubleshooting software located in the "help" section in the taskbar menu. Obtaining expert/technical operating system support is often difficult for individuals not closely involved with the development of the operating system. Microsoft has designed their expert system to provide solutions, advice, and suggestions to common errors encountered throughout using the operating system.

Another 1970s and 1980s application of expert system — which we today would simply call AI — was in computer games. For example, the computer baseball games Earl Weaver Baseball and Tony La Russa Baseball each had highly detailed simulations of the game strategies of those two baseball managers. When a human played the game against the computer, the computer queried the Earl Weaver or Tony La Russa Expert System for a decision on what strategy to follow. Even those choices where some randomness was part of the natural system (such as when to throw a surprise pitch-out to try to trick a runner trying to steal a base) were decided based on probabilities supplied by Weaver or La Russa. Today, we would simply say that "the game's AI provided the opposing manager's strategy."

Advantages and disadvantages

Advantages:

- Provides consistent answers for repetitive decisions, processes and tasks
- Holds and maintains significant levels of information

- Encourages organizations to clarify the logic of their decision-making
- Never "forgets" to ask a question, as a human might
- Can work round the clock
- Can be used by the user more frequently
- A multi-user expert system can serve more users at a time

Disadvantages:

- Lacks common sense needed in some decision making
- Cannot make creative responses as human expert would in unusual circumstances
- Domain experts not always able to explain their logic and reasoning
- Errors may occur in the knowledge base, and lead to wrong decisions
- Cannot adapt to changing environments, unless knowledge base is changed

Types of Problems Solved By Expert System

Expert system are most valuable to organizations that have a high-level of know-how experience and expertise that cannot be easily transferred to other members. They are designed to carry the intelligence and information found in the intellect of experts and provide this knowledge to other members of the organization for problem-solving purposes.

Typically, the problems to be solved are of the sort that would normally be tackled by a medical or other professional. Real experts in the problem domain (which will typically be very narrow, for instance "diagnosing skin conditions in human teenagers") are asked to provide "rules of thumb" on how they evaluate the problems, either explicitly with the aid of experienced system developers, or sometimes implicitly, by getting such experts to evaluate test cases and using computer programs to examine the test data and (in a strictly limited manner) derive rules from that. Generally, expert system are used for problems for which there is no single "correct" solution which can be encoded in a conventional algorithm — one would not write an expert system to find shortest paths through graphs, or sort data, as there are simply easier ways to do these tasks.

Simple system use simple true/false logic to evaluate data. More sophisticated system are capable of performing at least some evaluation, taking into account real-world uncertainties, using such methods as fuzzy logic. Such sophistication is difficult to develop and still highly imperfect.

Expert System Shells or Inference Engine

A shell is a complete development environment for building and maintaining knowledge-based applications. It provides a step-by-step methodology, and ideally a user-friendly interface such as a graphical interface, for a knowledge engineer that allows the domain experts themselves to be directly involved in structuring and encoding the knowledge. Many commercial shells are available, one example being eGanges which aims to remove the need for a knowledge engineer.

Knowledge Based System

Knowledge based system are artificial intelligent tools working in a narrow domain to provide intelligent decisions with justification. Knowledge is acquired and represented using various knowledge representation techniques rules, frames and scripts. The basic advantages offered by such system are documentation of knowledge, intelligent decision support, self learning, reasoning and explanation.

Knowledge-based system are system based on the methods and techniques of Artificial Intelligence. Their core components are:

- knowledge base
- acquisition mechanisms
- inference mechanisms

While for some author's expert system, case-based reasoning system and neural networks are all particular types of knowledge-based system, there are others who consider that neural networks are different, and exclude it from this category.

KBS is a frequently used abbreviation for **knowledge-based system**.

A knowledge-based system (KBS) is a system that uses artificial intelligence techniques in problem-solving processes to support human decision-making, learning, and action. Ideal for advanced-undergraduate and graduate students, as well as business professionals, this text is designed to help users develop an appreciation of KBS and their architecture and understand a broad variety of knowledge-based techniques for decision support and planning.

It assumes basic computer science skills and a math background that includes set theory, relations, elementary probability, and introductory concepts of artificial intelligence. Each of the 12 chapters is designed to be modular, providing instructors with the flexibility to model the book to their own course needs. Exercises are incorporated throughout the text to highlight certain aspects of the material presented and to simulate thought and discussion. A comprehensive text and resource, ***Knowledge-Based System*** provides access to the most current information in KBS and new artificial intelligences, as well as neural networks, fuzzy logic, genetic algorithms, and soft system.

INFORMATION PROCESSING SYSTEM

An **information processor** or **information processing system**, as its name suggests, is a system (be it electrical, mechanical or biological) which takes information (a sequence of enumerated states) in one form and processes (transforms) it into another form, e.g. to statistics, by an algorithmic process.

An information processing system is made up of four basic parts, or sub-system:

- input
- processor
- storage
- output

An object may be considered an information processor if it receives information from another object and in some manner changes the information before transmitting it. This broadly defined term can be used to describe every change which occurs in the universe. As an example, a falling rock could be considered an information processor due to the following observable facts:

First, information in the form of gravitational force from the earth serves as input to the system we call a rock. At a particular instant the rock is a specific distance from the surface of the earth traveling at a specific speed. Both the current distance and speed properties are also forms of information which for that instant only may be considered "stored" in the rock.

In the next instant, the distance of the rock from the earth has changed due to its motion under the influence of the Earth's gravity. Any time the properties of an object change a process has occurred meaning that a processor of some kind is at work. In addition, the rock's new position and increased speed is observed by us as it falls. These changing properties of the rock are its "output."

It could be argued that in this example both the rock and the earth are the information processing system being observed since both objects are changing the properties of each other over time. If information is not being processed no change would occur at all.

In computing, **input/output**, or **I/O**, refers to the communication between an information processing system (such as a computer), and the outside world possibly a human, or another information processing system. Inputs are the signals or data received by the system, and outputs are the signals or data sent from it. The term can also be used as part of an action; to "perform I/O" is to perform an input or output operation. I/O devices are used by a person (or other system) to communicate with a computer. For instance, a keyboard or a mouse may be an input device for a computer, while monitors and printers are considered output devices for a computer. Devices for communication between computers, such as modems and network cards, typically serve for both input and output.

Note that the designation of a device as either input or output depends on the perspective. Mouse and keyboards take as input physical movement that the human user outputs and convert it into signals that a computer can understand. The output from these devices is input for the computer. Similarly, printers and monitors take as input signals that a computer outputs. They then convert these signals into representations that human users can see or read. For a human user the process of reading or seeing these representations is receiving input. These interactions between computers and humans is studied in a field called human–computer interaction.

In computer architecture, the combination of the CPU and main memory (i.e. memory that the CPU can read and write to directly, with individual instructions) is considered the brain of a computer, and from that point of view any transfer of information from or to that combination, for example to or from a disk drive, is considered I/O. The CPU and its supporting circuitry provide memory-mapped I/O that is used in low-level computer programming in the implementation of device drivers. An I/O algorithm is one designed to exploit locality and perform efficiently when data reside on secondary storage, such as a disk drive.

The **central processing unit (CPU)** is the portion of a computer system that carries out the instructions of a computer program, and is the primary element carrying out the computer's functions. The central processing unit carries out each instruction of the program in sequence, to perform the basic arithmetical, logical, and input/output operations of the system. This term has been in use in the computer industry at least since the early 1960s. The form, design and implementation of CPUs have changed dramatically since the earliest examples, but their fundamental operation remains much the same.

Early CPUs were custom-designed as a part of a larger, sometimes one-of-a-kind, and computer. However, this costly method of designing custom CPUs for a' particular application has largely given way to the development of mass-produced processors that are made for one or many purposes. This standardization trend generally began in the era of discrete transistor mainframes and minicomputers and has rapidly accelerated with the popularization of the integrated circuit (IC). The IC has allowed increasingly complex CPUs to be designed and manufactured to tolerances on the order of nanometers. Both the miniaturization and standardization of CPUs have increased the presence of these digital devices in modern life far beyond the limited application of dedicated computing machines. Modern microprocessors appear in everything from automobiles to cell phones and children's toys.

Computer data storage, often called **storage** or **memory**, refers to computer components and recording media that retain digital data used for computing for some interval of time. Computer data storage provides one of the core functions of the modern computer, that of information retention. It is one of the fundamental components of all modern computers, and coupled with a central processing unit (CPU, a processor), implements the basic computer model used since the 1940s.

In contemporary usage, memory usually refers to a form of semiconductor storage known as random-access memory, typically DRAM (Dynamic-RAM) but many times other forms of fast but temporary storage. Similarly, storage today more commonly refers to storage devices and their media not directly accessible by the CPU (secondary or tertiary storage) — typically hard disk drives, optical disc drives, and other devices slower than RAM but more permanent.[1] Historically, memory has been called main memory, real storage or internal memory while storage devices have been referred to as secondary storage, external memory or auxiliary/peripheral storage).

In computing, **input/output**, or **I/O**, refers to the communication between an information processing system (such as a computer), and the outside world possibly a human, or another information processing system. Inputs are the signals or data received by the system, and outputs are the signals or data sent from it. The term can also be used as part of an action; to "perform I/O" is to perform an input or output operation. I/O devices are used by a person (or other system) to communicate with a computer. For instance, a keyboard or a mouse may be an input device for a computer, while monitors and printers are considered output devices for a computer. Devices for communication between computers, such as modems and network cards, typically serve for both input and output.

Programmed Decision Making

Programmed decision making is a repetitive decision that can be handled by a routine approach and is not new. In this decision making process you has set procedure, rules and policiés to follow. Whereas, in **Non-programmed decision making**: It is a unique decision that needs a custom made solution. In, this you mostly deal with unstructured problem which are new or unusual and for which information is incomplete.

Office automation

Office automation refers to the varied computer machinery and software used to digitally create, collect, store, manipulate, and relay office information needed for accomplishing basic tasks and goals. Raw data storage, electronic transfer, and the management of electronic business information comprise the basic activities of an office automation system. Office automation helps in optimizing or automating existing office procedures.

The backbone of office automation is a LAN, which allows users to transmit data, mail and even voice across the network. All office functions, including dictation, typing, filing, copying, fax, Telex, microfilm and records management, telephone and telephone switchboard operations, fall into this category. Office automation was a popular term in the 1970s and 1980s as the desktop computer exploded onto the scene.

Business intelligence

Business intelligence (BI) refers to skills, technologies, applications and practices used to help a business acquire a better understanding of its commercial context. Business intelligence may also refer to the collected information itself.

BI technologies provide historical, current, and predictive views of business operations. Common functions of business intelligence technologies are reporting, OLAP, analytics, data mining, business performance management, benchmarking, text mining, and predictive analytics.

Business intelligence often aims to support better business decision-making. Thus, a BI system can be called a decision support system (DSS).

History

In a 1958 article, IBM researcher Hans Peter Luhn used the term business intelligence. He defined intelligence as: "the ability to apprehend the interrelationships of presented facts in such a way as to guide action towards a desired goal."

In 1989, Howard Dresner (later a Gartner Group analyst) proposed BI as an umbrella term to describe "concepts and methods to improve business decision making by using fact-based support system." It was not until the late 1990s that this usage was widespread.

Business Intelligence And Data Warehousing

Often BI applications use data gathered from a data warehouse or a data mart. However, not all data warehouses are used for business intelligence nor do all business intelligence applications require a data warehouse.

Business Intelligence And Business Analytics

Thomas Davenport has argued that business intelligence should be divided into querying, reporting, OLAP, an "alerts" tool, and business analytics.

Competitive Intelligence

The term business intelligence is often used as a synonym for competitive intelligence.

The future of business intelligence

A 2009 Gartner paper predicted these developments in business intelligence market.

- Because of lack of information, processes, and tools, through 2012, more than 35 per cent of the top 5,000 global companies will regularly fail to make insightful decisions about significant changes in their business and markets.
- By 2012, business units will control at least 40 per cent of the total budget for business intelligence.
- By 2010, 20 per cent of organizations will have an industry-specific analytic application delivered via software as a service as a standard component of their business intelligence portfolio.
- In 2009, collaborative decision making will emerge as a new product category that combines social software with business intelligence platform capabilities.
- By 2012, one-third of analytic applications applied to business processes will be delivered through coarse-grained application mashups.

Information System Careers

Information System have a number of different areas of work:

- Information system strategy
- Information system management
- Information system development
- Information system security

There are a wide variety of career paths in the information system discipline. "Workers with specialized technical knowledge and strong communications skills will have the best prospects. People with management skills and an understanding of business practices and principles will have excellent opportunities, as companies are increasingly looking to technology to drive their revenue."

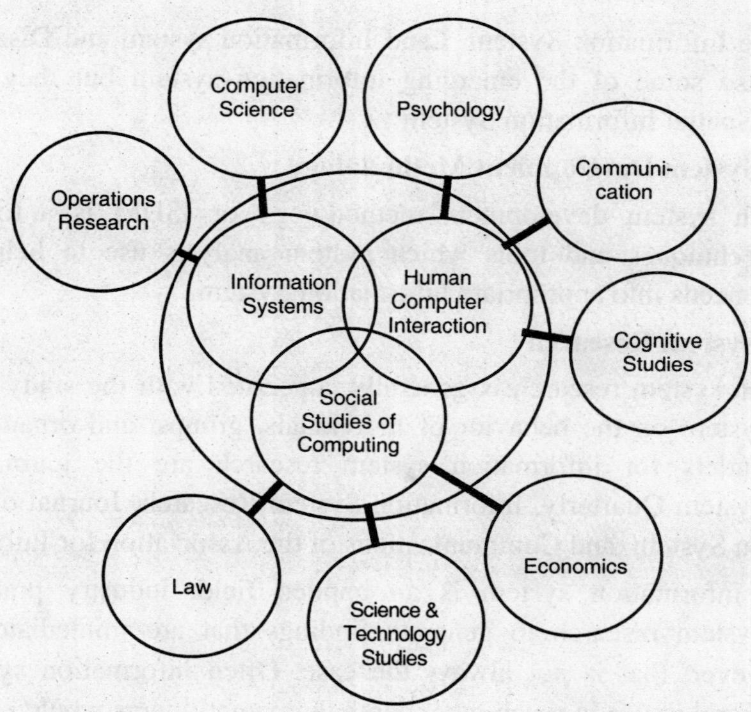

Information System Development

Information technology departments in larger organizations tend to strongly influence information technology development, use, and application in the organizations, which may be a business or corporation. A series of methodologies and processes can be used in order to develop and use an information system. Many developers have turned and used a more engineering approach such as the System Development Life Cycle (SDLC) which is a systematic procedure of developing an information system through stages that occur in sequence. An Information system can be developed in house (within the organization) or outsourced. This can be accomplished by outsourcing certain components or the entire system. A specific case is the geographical distribution of the development team (Off shoring, Global Information System).

A computer based information system, following a definition of Langefors, is:

- a technologically implemented medium for recording, storing, and disseminating linguistic expressions,
- As well as for drawing conclusions from such expressions.

Which can be formulated as a generalized information system design mathematical program?

Geographic Information System, Land Information system and Disaster Information System are also some of the emerging information system but they can be broadly considered as Spatial Information System.

Information System Development Methodology

Information system development methodology or ISDM is a tool kit of ideas, approaches, techniques and tools which system analysts use to help them translate organizational needs into appropriate Information System.

Information System Research

Information system research is generally concerned with the study of the effects of information system on the behavior of individuals, groups, and organizations. Notable publication outlets for information system research are the journals Management Information System Quarterly, Information System Research, Journal of the Association for Information System, and Communications of the Association for Information System.

Since an information system is an applied field, industry practitioners expect information system research to generate findings that are immediately applicable in practice. However, that is not always the case. Often information system researchers explore behavioral issues in much more depth than practitioners would expect them to do. This may render information system research results difficult to understand, and has led to criticism. To study an information system itself, rather than its effects, information system models are used, such as EATPUT.

Problems in Information System Development

Though information has become one of the most valuable assets of modern corporations, development of information system (IS) faces many problems. Among the most important are low productivity, a large number of failures, and an inadequate alignment of ISs with business needs. The first problem, low productivity, has been recognized in the term "software crisis", as indicated by the development backlog and maintenance problems (cf. Brooks 1975, Boehm and Papaccio 1988, Jeffrey 1987). Simply, demands for building new or improved ISs have increased faster than our ability to develop them. Some reasons are: the increasing cost of software development (especially when compared to the decreasing cost of hardware), the limited supply of personnel and funding and only moderate productivity improvements.

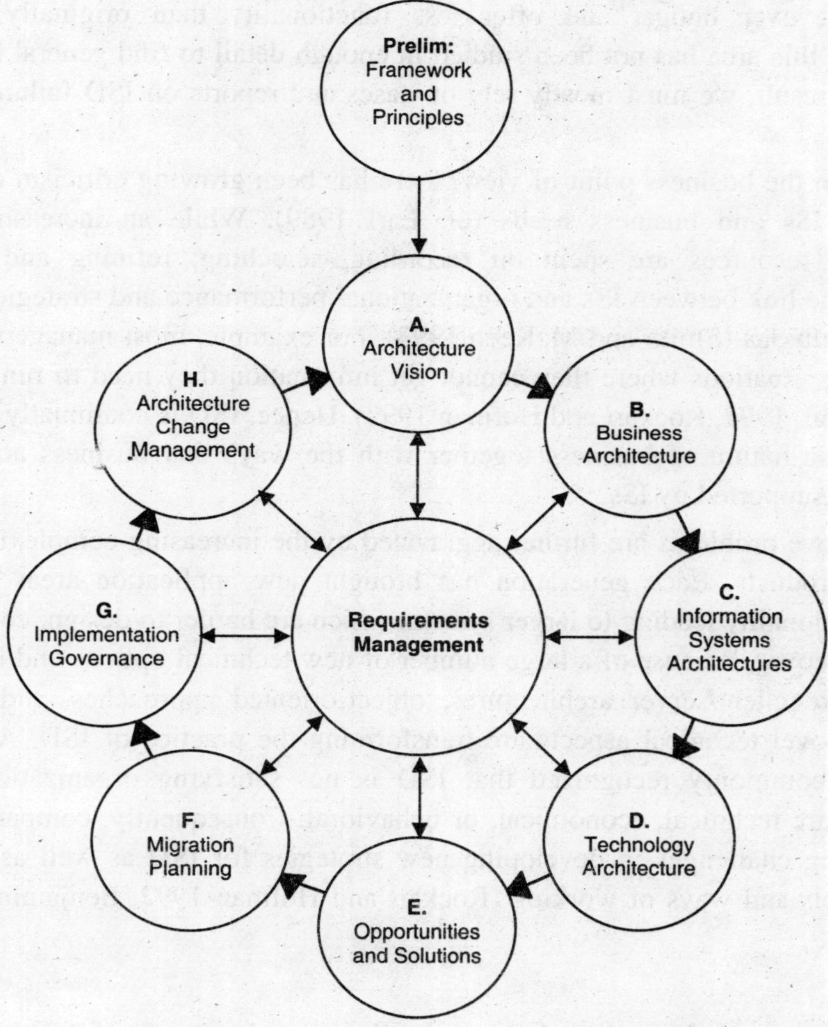

Second, IS development (ISD) efforts have resulted in a large number of outright failures (cf. Lyytinen and Hirschheim 1987, Charette 1989). These failures are sometimes due to economical mismatches, such as budget and schedule overruns, but surprisingly often due to poor product quality and insufficient user satisfaction. For example, one survey (Gladden 1982) estimates that 75% of IS developments undertaken are never completed, or the resulting system is never used. According to the Standish Group (1995) only 16% of all projects are delivered on time and within their budget. This study, conducted as a survey among 365 information technology managers, also reveals that 31% of ISD projects were canceled prior to completion and the majority, 53%, are completed but over budget and offer less functionality than originally specified. Unfortunately, this area has not been studied in enough detail to find general reasons for failures. As a result, we must mostly rely on cases and reports on ISD failures (e.g. Oz 1994).

Third, from the business point of view, there has been growing criticism of the poor alignment of ISs and business needs (cf. Earl 1989). While an increasing part of organizations' resources are spent on recording, searching, refining and analyzing information, the link between ISs and organizational performance and strategies has been shown to be dubious (Smith and McKeen 1993). For example, most managers and users are still facing situations where they cannot get information they need to run their units (Davenport et al. 1992, Rockart and Hofman 1992). Hence, ISD is continually challenged by the dynamic nature of business together with the ways that business activities are organized and supported by ISs.

All the above problems are further aggravated by the increasing complexity and size of software products. Each generation has brought new application areas as well as extended functionality leading to larger system, which are harder to design, construct and maintain. Moreover, because of a large number of new technical options and innovations available - like client/server architectures, object-oriented approaches, and electronic commerce - novel technical aspects are transforming the practice of ISD. All in all, it seems to be commonly recognized that ISD is not satisfying organizations' needs, whether they are technical, economical, or behavioral. Consequently, companies world-wide are facing challenges in developing new strategies for ISD as well as in finding supporting tools and ways of working (Rockart and Hofman 1992, Benjamin and Blunt 1992).

Summary

Introduction to Information System in Business-A variety of factors influence Information System Engineering, ranging from high level strategic to detailed technical issues. The following factors are considered, however the list is by no means exhaustive and you may well care to add your own:-

- Strategic Information System Planning
- Corporate Data Management,
- Business Process Re-Engineering,
- The Technical Environment,

- Models & Methodologies,
- Socio-Behavioral Development,
- Supporting Tools,
- Quality Assurance,
- Project Management,
- Human Resources,
- End-User System Development.

Introduction to System Analysis and Design

2.1 Introduction

System are created to solve problems. One can think of the system approach as an organized way of dealing with a problem. In this dynamic world, the subject System Analysis and Design mainly deals with the software development activities.

2.2 Objectives

After going through this lesson, you should be able to:

- understand a system
- understand the different phases of system developments life cycle
- know the components of system analysis
- know the components of system designing

2.3 Defining a System

A collection of components that work together to realize some objective forms a system. Basically, there are three major components in every system, namely input, processing and output.

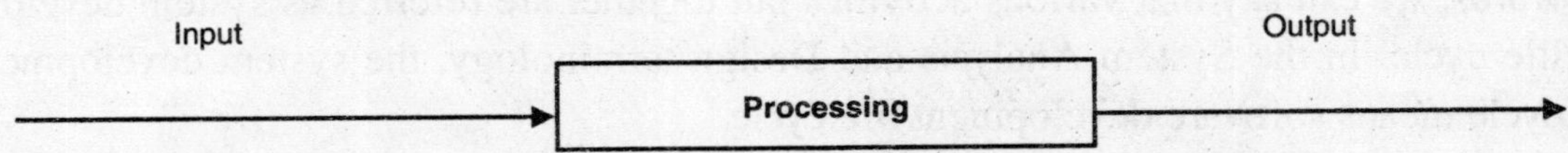

In a system, the different components are connected with each other and they are interdependent. For example, Human body represents a complete natural system. We are also bound by many national system such as political system, economic system, educational system and so forth. The objective of the system demands that some output is produced as a result of processing the suitable inputs.

2.4 System Life Cycle

System life cycle is an organizational process of developing and maintaining system. It helps in establishing a system project plan, because it gives overall list of processes and sub-processes required developing a system.

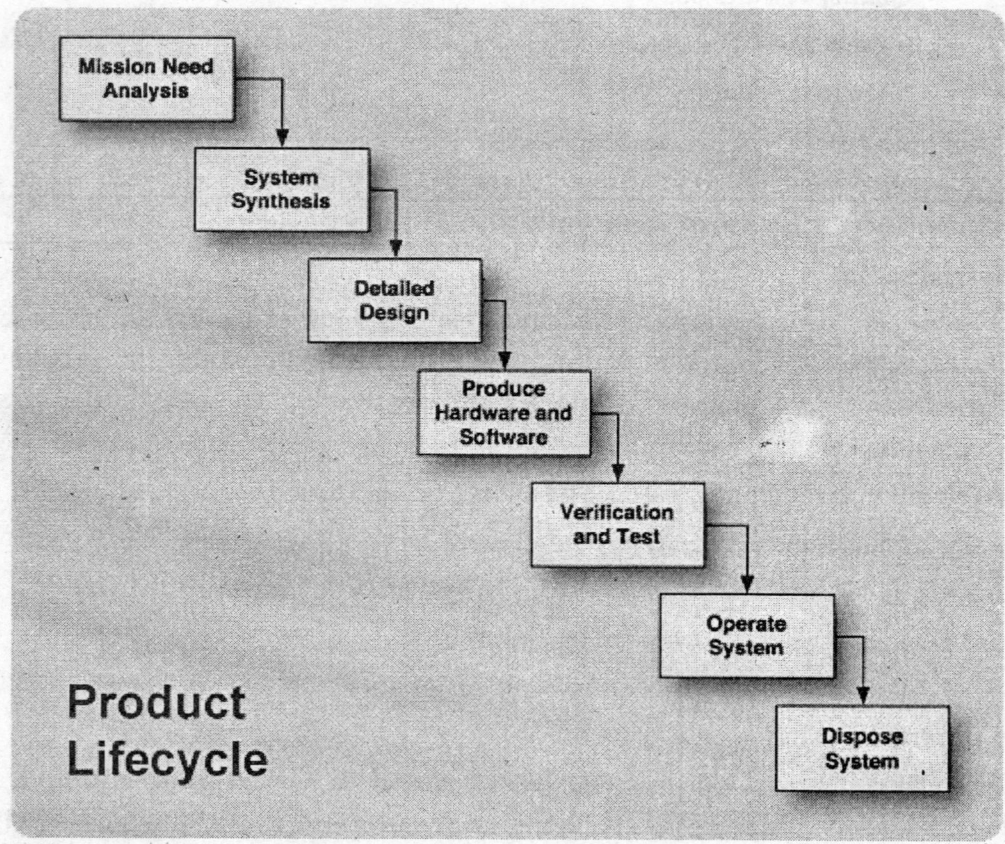

System development life cycle means combination of various activities. In other words, we can say that various activities put together are referred as system development life cycle. In the System Analysis and Design terminology, the system development life cycle means software development life cycle.

Following are the different phases of software development cycle:

- System study
- Feasibility study
- System analysis
- System design

- Coding
- Testing
- Implementation
- Maintenance

The different phases of software development life cycle is shown in Fig.2.1

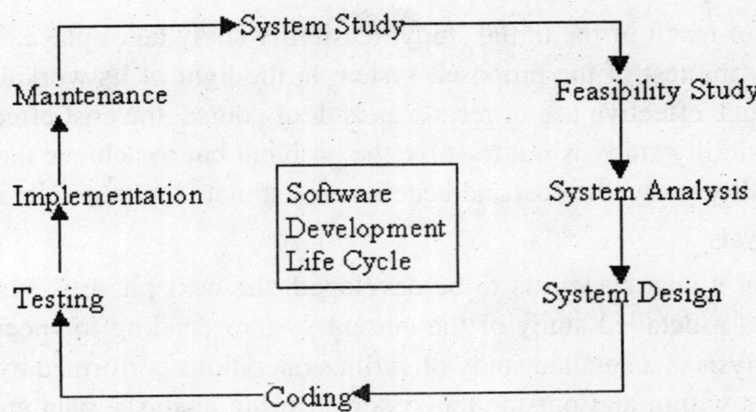

Fig. 2.1 Different phases of Software development Life Cycle

2.5 Phases of System Development Life Cycle

Let us now describe the different phases and the related activities of system development life cycle in detail.

(*a*) System Study

System study is the first stage of system development life cycle. This gives a clear picture of what actually the physical system is? In practice, the system study is done in two phases. In the first phase, the preliminary survey of the system is done which helps in identifying the scope of the system.

The second phase of the system study is more detailed and in-depth study in which the identification of user's requirement and the limitations and problems of the present system are studied. After completing the system study, a system proposal is prepared by the System Analyst (who studies the system) and placed before the user. The proposed system contains the findings of the present system and recommendations to overcome the limitations and problems of the present system in the light of the user's requirements.

To describe the system study phase more analytically, we would say that system study phase passes through the following steps:

- problem identification and project initiation
- background analysis
- inference or findings

(*b*) Feasibility Study

On the basis of result of the initial study, feasibility study takes place. The feasibility study is basically the test of the proposed system in the light of its workability, meeting user's requirements, effective use of resources and .of course, the cost effectiveness. The main goal of feasibility study is not to solve the problem but to achieve the scope. In the process of feasibility study, the cost and benefits are estimated with greater accuracy.

(*c*) System Analysis

Assuming that a new system is to be developed, the next phase is system **analysis**. Analysis involved a detailed study of the current system, leading to specifications of a new system. Analysis is a detailed study of various operations performed by a system and their relationships within and outside the system. During analysis, data are collected on the available files, decision points and transactions handled by the present system. Interviews, on-site observation and questionnaire are the tools used for system analysis. Using the following steps it becomes easy to draw the exact boundary of the new system under consideration:

- Keeping in view the problems and new requirements
- Workout the pros and cons including new areas of the system

All procedures, requirements must be analyzed and documented in the form of detailed data flow diagrams (DFDs), data dictionary, logical data structures and miniature specifications. System Analysis also includes sub-dividing of complex process involving the entire system, identification of data store and manual processes.

The main points to be discussed in system analysis are:

- Specification of what the new system is to accomplish based on the user requirements.
- Functional hierarchy showing the functions to be performed by the new system and their relationship with each other.
- Function network which are similar to function hierarchy but they highlight the functions which are common to more than one procedure.

- List of attributes of the entities - these are the data items which need to be held about each entity (record)?

(*d*) System Design

Based on the user requirements and the detailed analysis of a new system, the new system must be designed. This is the phase of **system designing**. It is a most crucial phase in the development of a system. Normally, the design proceeds in two stages:

- Preliminary or general design
- Structure or detailed design

Preliminary or general design: In the preliminary or general design, the features of the new system are specified. The costs of implementing these features and the benefits to be derived are estimated. If the project is still considered to be feasible, we move to the detailed design stage.

Structure or Detailed design: In the detailed design stage, computer oriented work begins in earnest. At this stage, the design of the system becomes more structured. Structure design is a blue print of a computer system solution to a given problem having the same components and inter-relationship among the same components as the original problem. Input, output and processing specifications are drawn up in detail. In the design stage, the programming language and the platform in which the new system will run are also decided.

There are several tools and techniques used for designing. These tools and techniques are:

- Flowchart
- Data flow diagram (DFDs)
- Data dictionary
- Structured English
- Decision table
- Decision tree

Each of the above tools for designing will be discussed in detailed in the next lesson.

(*e*) Coding

After designing the new system, the whole system is required to be converted into computer understanding language. **Coding** the new system into computer programming language does this. It is an important stage where the defined procedure is transformed into control specifications by the help of a computer language. This is also called the programming phase in which the programmer converts the program specifications into computer instructions, which we refer as **programs**. The programs coordinate the data movements and control the entire process in a system.

It is generally felt that the programs must be modular in nature. This helps in fast development, maintenance and future change, if required.

(*f*) Testing

Before actually implementing the new system into operations, a test run of the system is done removing all the bugs, if any. It is an important phase of a successful system. After codifying the whole programs of the system, a test plan should be developed and run on a given set of test data. The output of the test run should match the expected results.

Using the test data following test run are carried out:

- Unit test
- System test
- **Unit test:** When the programs have been coded and compiled and brought to working conditions, they must be individually tested with the prepared test data. Any undesirable happening must be noted and debugged (error corrections).
- **System Test:** After carrying out the unit test for each of the programs of the system and when errors are removed, then system test is done. At this stage the test is done on actual data. The complete system is executed on the actual data. At each stage of the execution, the results or output of the system is analyzed. During the result analysis, it may be found that the outputs are not matching the expected out of the system. In such case, the errors in the particular programs are identified and are fixed and further tested for the expected output.

When it is ensured that the system is running error-free, the users are called with their own actual data so that the system could be shown running as per their requirements.

(*g*) Implementation

After having the user acceptance of the new system developed, the implementation phase begins. Implementation is the stage of a project during which theory is turned into practice. During this phase, all the programs of the system are loaded onto the user's computer. After loading the system, training of the users starts. Main topics of such type of training are:

- How to execute the package

- How to enter the data
- How to process the data (processing details)
- How to take out the reports

After the users are trained about the computerized system, manual working has to shift from manual to computerized working. The following two strategies are followed for running the system:

(*i*) **Parallel run:** In such run for a certain defined period, both the system i.e. computerized and manual are executed in parallel. This strategy is helpful because of the following:

- o Manual results can be compared with the results of the computerized system.
- o Failure of the computerized system at the early stage, does not affect the working of the organization, because the manual system continues to work, as it used to do.

(*ii*) **Pilot run:** In this type of run, the new system is installed in parts. Some part of the new system is installed first and executed successfully for considerable time period. When the results are found satisfactory then only other parts are implemented. This strategy builds the confidence and the errors are traced easily.

(*h*) Maintenance

Maintenance is necessary to eliminate errors in the system during its working life and to tune the system to any variations in its working environment. It has been seen that there are always some errors found in the system that must be noted and corrected. It also means the review of the system from time to time. The review of the system is done for:

- knowing the full capabilities of the system
- knowing the required changes or the additional requirements
- studying the performance

If a major change to a system is needed, a new project may have to be set up to carry out the change. The new project will then proceed through all the above life cycle phases.

What You Have Learnt

In this lesson systematic approach of any given problem is explained. Computer based system are defined. System development life cycle is discussed in detail. The different phases of the development of system life cycle are explained in detail.

System Design: Input, Output, User Interface

Input Design

- A source document differs from a turnaround document in that the former contains data that change the status of a resource while the latter is a machine readable document.
- **Transaction *throughput* is the number of error-free transactions entered during a specified time period.**
- A document should be concise because longer documents contain more data and so take longer to enter and have a greater chance of data entry errors.
- Numeric coding substitutes numbers for character data (e.g., 1=male, 2=female); mnemonic coding represents data in a form that is easier for the user to understand and remember. (e.g., M=male, F=female).

Mnemonic vs. Numeric codes

Numeric (arbitrary)

1 = Male	2 = Male	4 = Male
2 = Female	1 = Female	7 = Female

Mnemonic

M = Male

F = Female

- The more quickly an error is detected, the closer the error is to the person who generated it and so the error is more easily corrected.
- An example of an illogical combination in a payroll system would be an option to eliminate federal tax withholding.
- By "multiple levels" of messages, Shneiderman means allowing the user to obtain more detailed explanations of an error by using a help option, but not forcing a lengthy message on a user who does not want it.
- An error suspense record would include the following fields: data entry operator identification, transaction entry date, transaction entry time, transaction type,

transaction image, fields in error, error codes, date transaction reentered successfully.

- A data input specification is a detailed description of the individual fields (data elements) on an input document together with their characteristics (i.e., type and length).

Error Messages to be displayed for the end user

- Be specific and precise, not general, ambiguous, or vague. (BAD: Syntax error, Invalid entry, General Failure)
- Don't JUST say what's wrong---- Be constructive; suggest what needs to be done to correct the error condition.
- Top of Form
- Bottom of Form
- Be positive; Avoid condemnation. Possibly even to the point of avoiding pejorative terms such as "invalid", "illegal" or "bad."
- Top of Form
- Bottom of Form
- Be user-centric and attempt to convey to the user that he or she is in control by replacing imperatives such as "Enter date" with wording such as "Ready for date."
- Consider multiple message levels: the initial or default error message can be brief but allow the user some mechanism to request additional information.
- Consistency in terminology and wording.
  - o place error messages in the same place on the screen
  - o Use consistent display characteristics (blinking, color, beeping, etc.)

Interactive Screen Design

The primary differences between an *interactive* and *batch* environment are:

- interactive processing is done during the organization's prime work hours
- interactive system usually have multiple, simultaneous users
- the experience level of users runs from novice to highly experienced

- Developers must be good communicators because of the need to design system with error messages, help text, and requests for user responses.

The seven step path that marks the structure of an interactive system is

1. Greeting screen (e.g., company logo)
2. Password screen -- to prevent unauthorized use
3. Main menu -- allow choice of several available application
4. Intermediate menus -- further delineate choice of functions
5. Function screens -- updating or deleting records
6. Help screens -- how to perform a task
7. Escape options -- from a particular screen or the application

- An intermediate menu and a function screen differ in that the former provides choices from a set of related operations while the latter provides the ability to perform tasks such as updates or deletes.
- The difference between inquiry and command language dialogue modes is that the former asks the user to provide a response to a simple question (e.g., "Do you really want to delete this file?") where the latter requires that the user know what he or she wants to do next (e.g., MS-DOS C:> prompt; VAX/VMS $ prompt; Unix shell prompt). GUI Interface (Windows, Macintosh) provide Dialog Boxes to prompt user to input required information/parameters.
- **Directions for designing form-filling screens**
  - o Fields on the screen should be in the same sequence as on the source document.
  - o Use cuing to provide the user with information such as field formats (e.g., dates)?
  - o Provide default values.
  - o Edit all entered fields for transaction errors.
  - o Move the cursor automatically to the next entry field.
  - o Allow entry to be free-form (e.g., do not make the user enter leading zeroes).
  - o Consider having all entries made at the same position on the screen.
- A *default* value is a value automatically supplied by the application when the user leaves a field blank. For example, at SXU the screen on which student names and addresses are entered has a default value of "IL" for State since the

majority of students have addresses in Illinois. At one time "312" was a default value for Area Code, but with the additional Area Codes now in use (312, 773, 708, 630, and 847) providing a default value for this field is no longer as useful.

- **The eight parts of an interactive screen menu are:**
    1. Locator -- what application the user is currently in
    2. Menu ID -- allows the more experienced user access without going through the entire menu tree.
    3. Title
    4. User instructions
    5. Menu list
    6. Escape option
    7. User response area
    8. System messages (e.g., error messages)
- Highlighting should be used for gaining attention and so should be limited to critical information, unusual values, high priority messages, or items that must be changed.
- Potential problems associated with the overuse of color are:
    - o Colors have different meanings to different people and in different cultures.
    - o A certain percentage of the population is known to have color vision deficiency.
    - o Some color combinations may be disruptive.
- Information density is important because density that is too high makes it more difficult to discern the information presented on a screen, especially for novice users.
- **Rules for defining message content include:**
    - o Use active voice.
    - o Use short, simple sentences.
    - o Use affirmative statements.
    - o Avoid hyphenation and unnecessary punctuation.
    - o Separate text paragraphs with at least one blank line.

- Keep field width within 40 characters for easy reading.
- Avoid word contractions and abbreviations.
- Use nonthreatening language.
- Avoid godlike language.
- Do not patronize.
- Use mixed case (upper and lower case) letters.
- Use humor carefully.

• Symmetry is important to screen design because it is aesthetically pleasing and thus more comforting.

• Input verification is asking the user to confirm his or her most recent input (e.g., "Are you sure you want to delete this file?")

• Adaptive models are useful because they adapt to the user's experience level as he or she moves from novice to experience over time as experience with the system grows.

• "Within User" sources of variation include: warm up, fatigue, boredom, environmental conditions, and extraneous events.

• The elements of the adaptive model are:
  - Triggering question to determine user experience level
  - Differentiation among user experience
  - Alternative processing paths based on user level
  - Transition of casual user to experienced processing path
  - Transition of novice user to experienced processing path
  - Allowing the user to move to an easier processing path

• Interactive tasks can be designed for closure by providing the user with feedback indicating that a task has been completed.

• Internal locus of control is making users feel that they are in control of the system, rather than that the system is in control of them.

• Examples of distracting use of surprise are:
  - Highlighting
  - Input verification
  - Flashing messages
  - Auditory messages

- Losing the interactive user can be avoided by using short menu paths and "You are here" prompts.

Some common user shortcuts are: direct menu access, function keys, and shortened response time.

Output Design

Output is the primary purpose of any system.

These guidelines apply for the most part to both paper and screen outputs. Output design is often discussed before other aspects of design because, from the client's point of view, the output is the system. Output is what the client is buying when he or she pays for a development project. Inputs, databases, and processes exist to provide output.

- Problems often associated with business information output are information delay, information (data) overload, paper domination, excessive distribution, and no tailoring.
- Mainframe printers: high volume, high speed, located in the data center . Remote site printers: medium speed, close to end user.
- COM is Computer Output Microfilm. It is more compact than traditional output and may be produced as fast as non-impact printer output.
- Turnaround documents reduce the cost of internal information processing by reducing both data entry and associated errors.
- Periodic reports have set frequencies such as daily or weekly; ad hoc reports are produced at irregular intervals.
- Detail and summary reports differ in the the former support day-to-day operation of the business while the latter include statistics and ratios used by managers to assess the health of operations.
- Page breaks and control breaks allow for summary totals on key fields.
- Report requirements documents contain general report information and field specifications; print layout sheets present a picture of what the report will actually look like.
- Page decoupling is the separation of pages into cohesive groups.
- Two ways to design output for strategic purposes are (1) make it compatible with processes outside the immediate scope of the system, and (2) turn action documents into turnaround documents.

- People often receive reports they do not need because the number of reports received is perceived as a measure of power.
- Fields on a report should be selected carefully to provide uncluttered reports, facilitate 80-column remote printing, and reduce information (data) overload.
- The types of fields which should be considered for business output are: key fields for access to information, fields for control breaks, fields that change, and exception fields.
- Output may be designed to aid future change by stressing unstructured reports, defining field size for future growth, making field constants into variables, and leaving room on summary reports for added ratios and statistics.
- Output can now be more easily tailored to the needs of individual users because inquiry-based system allow users themselves to create ad hoc reports.
- An output intermediary can restrict access to key information and prevent unauthorized access.
- An information clearinghouse (or information center) is a service center that provides consultation, assistance, and documentation to encourage end-user development and use of applications.
- The specifications needed to describe the output of a system are: data flow diagrams, data flow specifications, data structure specifications, and data element specifications.

Output Documents

Printed Reports

- **External Reports:** for use or distribution outside the organization; often on preprinted forms.
- **Internal Reports:** for use within the organization; not as "pretty", stock paper, greenbar, etc.
- **Periodic Reports:** produced with a set frequency (daily, weekly, monthly, every fifth Tuesday, etc.)
- **Ad-Hoc (On Demand) Reports:** irregular interval; produced upon user demand.
- **Detail Reports:** one line per transaction.
- **Summary Reports:** an overview.

- **Exception Reports:** only shows errors, problems, out-of-range values, or unexpected conditions or events.

Terminal Question

Q. 1. Define a system. Explain the components of a system.

Q. 2. What do you understand by system development life cycle?

Q. 3. Discuss the importance of system analysis and design in the development of a system.

Q. 4. Explain with a block diagram system development life cycle.

Q. 5. Discuss, DSS and executive information system.

Q. 6. Explain the various components of an information system.

Q. 7. Explain with a block diagram system development life cycle.

Q. 8. Explain the term prototyping and computer aided system engineering.

3 Categories of MIS

Information system differ in their business needs. Also depending upon different levels in organization information system differ. Three major information system are:

1. Transaction processing system
2. Management information system
3. Decision support system

Figure 1.2 shows relation of information system to the levels of organization. The information needs are different at different organizational levels. Accordingly, the information can be categorized as:

- Strategic information
- Managerial information
- Operational information.

Strategic information is the information needed by top most management for decision making. For example, the trends in revenues earned by the organization are required by the top management for setting the policies of the organization. This information is not required by the lower levels in the organization. The information system that provide these kinds of information are known as Decision Support System.

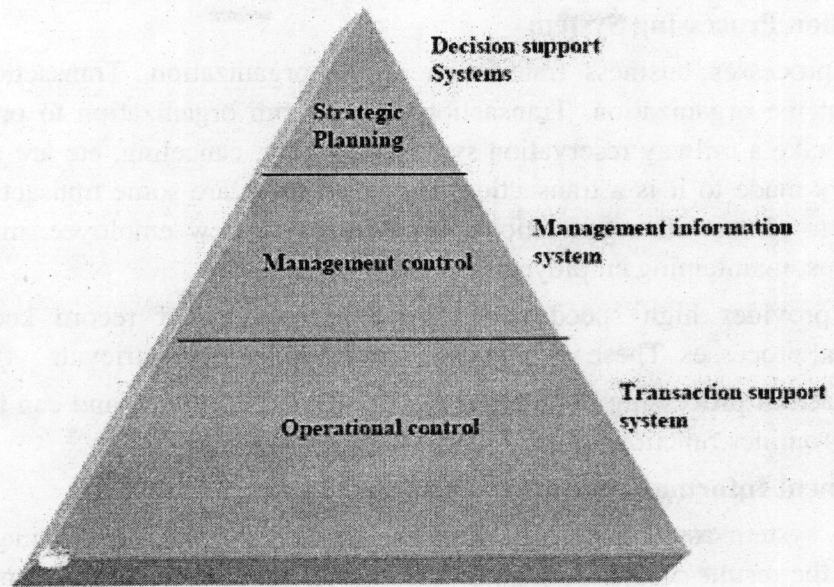

Figure 1.2 - Relation of information system to levels of organization

The second category of information required by the middle management is known as managerial information. The information required at this level is used for making short term decisions and plans for the organization. Information like sales analysis for the past quarter or yearly production details etc. fall under this category. Management information system (MIS) caters to such information needs of the organization.

Due to its capabilities to fulfill the managerial information needs of the organization, Management Information System have become a necessity for all big organizations. And due to its vastness, most of the big organizations have separate MIS departments to look into the related issues and proper functioning of the system.

The third category of information is relating to the daily or short term information needs of the organization such as attendance records of the employees. This kind of information is required at the operational level for carrying out the day-to-day operational activities. Due to its capabilities to provide information for processing transaction of the organization, the information system is known as Transaction Processing System or Data Processing System. Some examples of information provided by such system are processing of orders, posting of entries in bank, evaluating overdue purchaser orders etc.

Transaction Processing System

TPS processes business transaction of the organization. Transaction can be any activity of the organization. Transactions differ from organization to organization. For example, take a railway reservation system. Booking, canceling, etc are all transactions. Any query made to it is a transaction. However, there are some transactions, which are common to almost all organizations. Like employee new employee, maintaining their leave status, maintaining employees accounts, etc.

This provides high speed and accurate processing of record keeping of basic operational processes. These include calculation, storage and retrieval.

Transaction processing system provide speed and accuracy, and can be programmed to follow routines functions of the organization.

Management Information System

These system assist lower management in problem solving and making decisions. They use the results of transaction processing and some other information also. It is a set of information processing functions. It should handle queries as quickly as they arrive. An important element of MIS is database.

A database is a non-redundant collection of interrelated data items that can be processed through application programs and available to many users.

Decision Support System

These system assist higher management to make long term decisions. These type of system handle unstructured or semi structured decisions. A decision is considered unstructured if there are no clear procedures for making the decision and if not all the factors to be considered in the decision can be readily identified in advance.

These are not of recurring nature. Some recur infrequently or occur only once. A decision support system must very flexible. The user should be able to produce customized reports by giving particular data and format specific to particular situations.

Summary of Information System

Categories of Information System	Characteristics
Transaction Processing System	Substitutes computer-based processing for manual procedures. Deals with well-structured processes. Includes record keeping applications.
Management information system	Provides input to be used in the managerial

	decision process. Deals with supporting well structured decision situations. Typical information requirements can be anticipated.
Decision support system	Provides information to managers who must make judgments about particular situations. Supports decision-makers in situations that are not well structured.

Types of information system

As new information technologies are developed, new categories emerge that can be used to classify information system. Some examples are:

- Transaction processing system
- Management information system
- Global information system
- Decision support system
- Executive information system
- Expert system
- Office Automation
- Business intelligence

Transaction processing system

- Transaction processing system (TPS) automate the handling of data about business activities or transactions, which can be thought of as simple, discrete events in the life of an organization.
- Data about each transaction are captured, transactions are verified and accepted or rejected and validated transactions are stored for later aggregation. Reports may be produced immediately to provide standard summarizations of transactions and transactions may be moved from process to process in order to handle all aspects of the business activity.

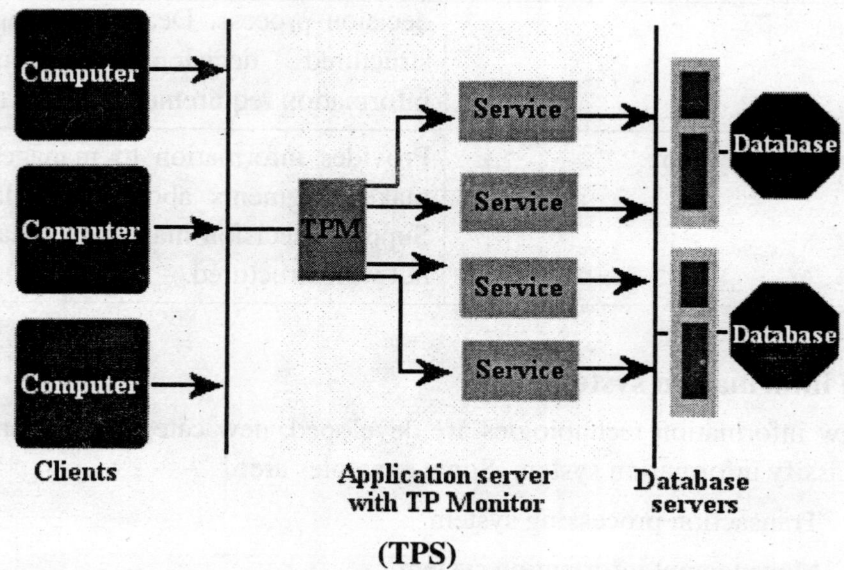

(TPS)

- The analysis and design of TPS means focusing on the firm's current procedures for processing transactions, whether those procedures are manual or automated. The focus on current procedures implies a careful tracking of data capture, flow, processing and output. The goal of TPS development is to improve transaction processing by speeding it up, using fewer people, improving efficiency and accuracy, integrating it with other organizational information system or providing information not previously available.

Management Information System

A management information system (MIS) is a subset of the overall internal controls of a business covering the application of people, documents, technologies, and procedures by management accountants to solve business problems such as costing a product, service or a business-wide strategy. Management information system are distinct from regular information system in that they are used to analyze other information system applied in operational activities in the organization.

Academically, the term is commonly used to refer to the group of information management methods tied to the automation or support of human decision making, e.g. Decision Support System, Expert system, and Executive information system. It has been described as, "MIS 'lives' in the space that intersects technology and business. MIS combines tech with business to get people the information they need to do their jobs better/faster/smarter. Information is the lifeblood of all organizations - now more than ever. MIS professionals work as system analysts, project managers, system administrators, etc., communicating directly with staff and management across the organization."

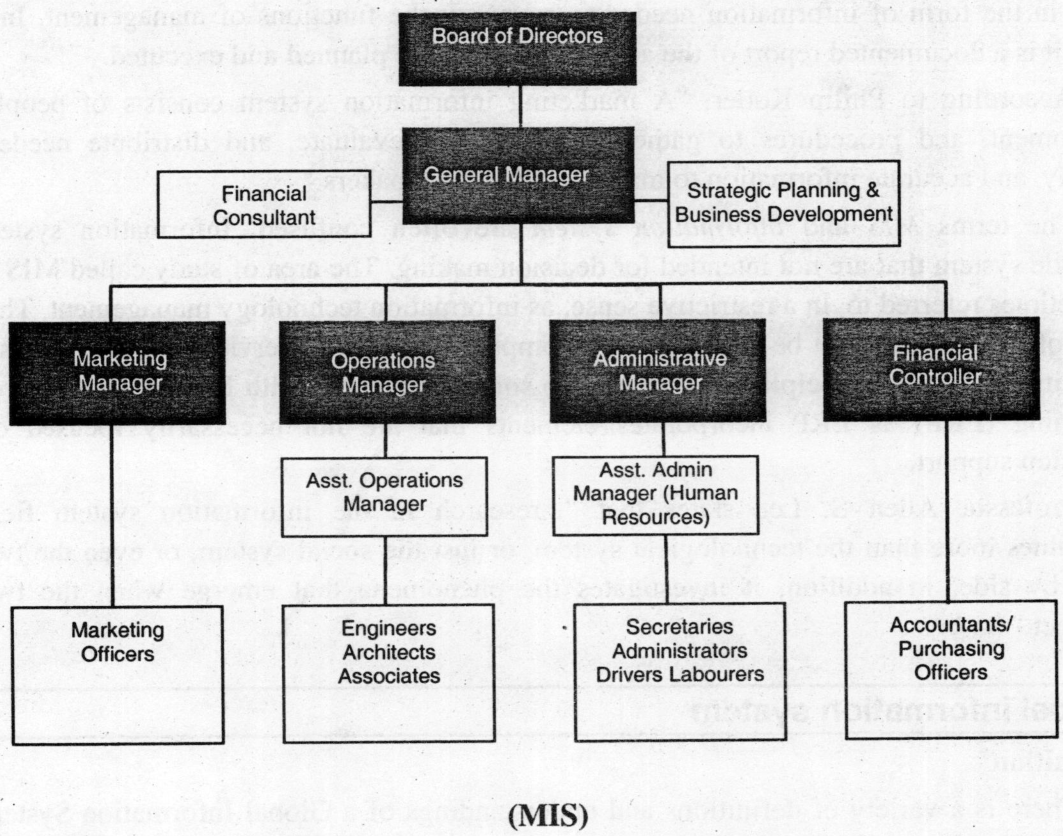

(MIS)

Overview

At the start, in businesses and other organizations, internal reporting was made manually and only periodically, as a by-product of the accounting system and with some additional statistics, and gave limited and delayed information on management performance.

In their infancy, business computers were used for the practical business of computing the payroll and keeping track of accounts payable and accounts receivable. As applications were developed that provided managers with information about sales, inventories, and other data that would help in managing the enterprise, the term "MIS" arose to describe these kinds of applications. Today, the term is used broadly in a number of contexts and includes (but is not limited to): decision support system, resource and people management applications, project management and database retrieval application.

Definition

An 'MIS' is a planned system of the collecting, processing, storing and disseminating data in the form of information needed to carry out the functions of management. In a way it is a documented report of the activities those were planned and executed.

According to Philip Kotler, "A marketing information system consists of people, equipment, and procedures to gather, sort, analyze, evaluate, and distribute needed, timely, and accurate information to marketing decision makers."

The terms *MIS* and *information system* are often confused. Information system include system that are not intended for decision making. The area of study called MIS is sometimes referred to, in a restrictive sense, as information technology management. That area of study should not be confused with computer science. IT service management is a practitioner-focused discipline. MIS has also some differences with Enterprise Resource Planning (ERP) as ERP incorporates elements that are not necessarily focused on decision support.

Professor Allen S. Lee states that "...research in the information system field examines more than the technological system, or just the social system, or even the two side by side; in addition, it investigates the phenomena that emerge when the two interact."

Global information system

Definition

There is a variety of definitions and understandings of a Global Information System (GIS, GLIS), such as

- A global information system (GLIS) is an information system which is developed and / or used in a global context.
- A global information system (GLIS) is any information system which attempts to deliver the totality of measurable data worldwide within a defined context. (USF)

The term Global Information System has the same acronym is the same, the meaning is different from the term Geographic Information System.

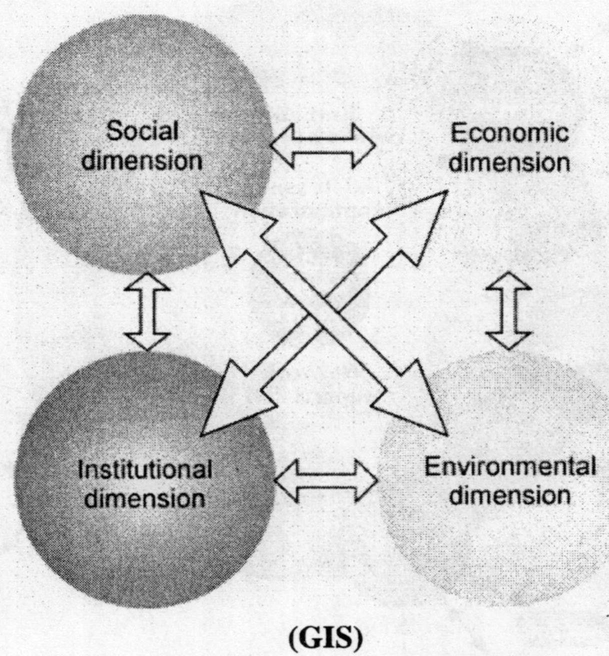

(GIS)

Common to this class of information system is that the context is a global setting, either for its use or development process. This means that it highly relates to distributed system / distributed computing where the distribution is global. The term also incorporates aspects of global software development and there outsourcing (when the outsourcing locations are globally distributed) and off shoring aspects. A specific aspect of global information system is the case (domain) of global software development . A main research aspect in this field concerns the coordination of and collaboration between virtual teams. Further, important aspects are the internationalization and localization of system components.

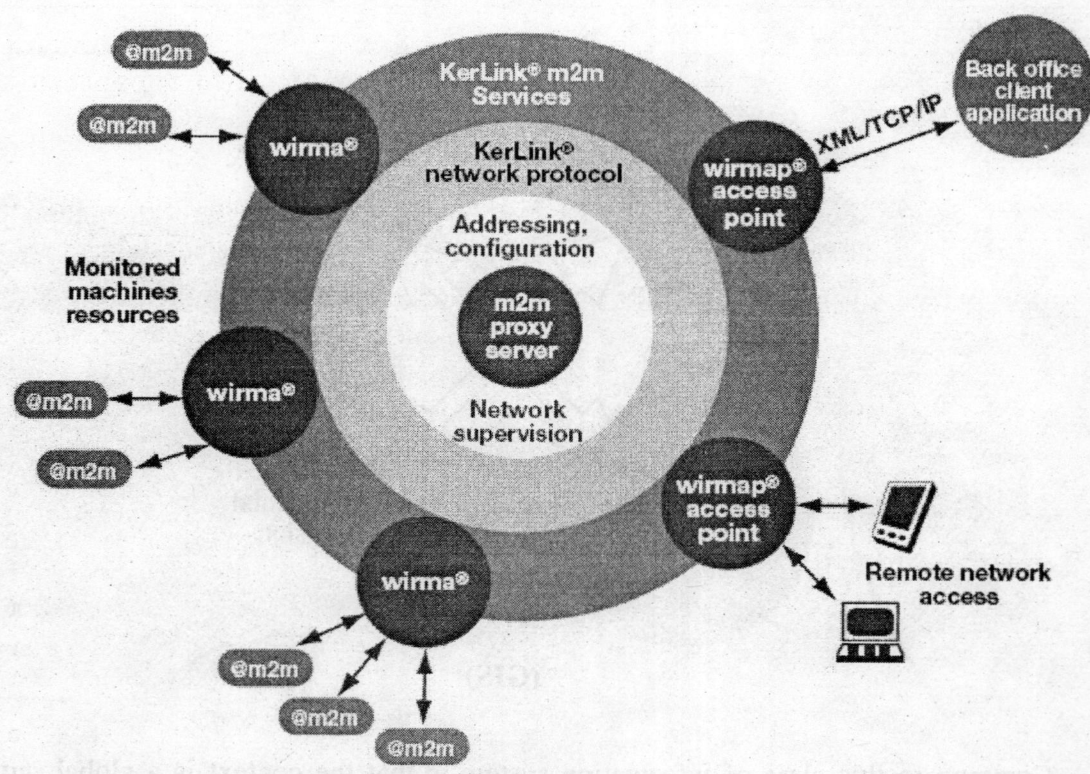

Tasks in Global Information System Design

Critical tasks in the design of Global Information System are:

- **Process and System Design:** How are the processes between distributed actors organized how are the system distributed / integrated.
- **Technical architecture:** What is the technical infrastructure enabling actor to collaborate?
- **Support mechanisms:** How are actors in the process of communication, collaboration, cooperation supported?

A variety of examples can be found - basically, every multi-lingual website can be seen as a global information system. However, mostly a GLIS is referred as a specific system developed or used in the global context.

Examples

Specific examples are:

- System developed for multinational users, e.g., SAP as a global ERP system
- Global Information System for Education: The Global Learning Objects Brokered Exchange
- Support system for global cooperation: System, e.g. Palantir

Decision Support System

Decision support system constitute a class of computer-based information system including knowledge-based system that support decision-making activities.

Overview

A Decision Support System (DSS) is a class of information system (including but not limited to computerized system) that support business and organizational decision-making activities. A properly designed DSS is an interactive software-based system intended to help decision makers compile useful information from a combination of raw data, documents, personal knowledge, or business models to identify and solve problems and make decisions.

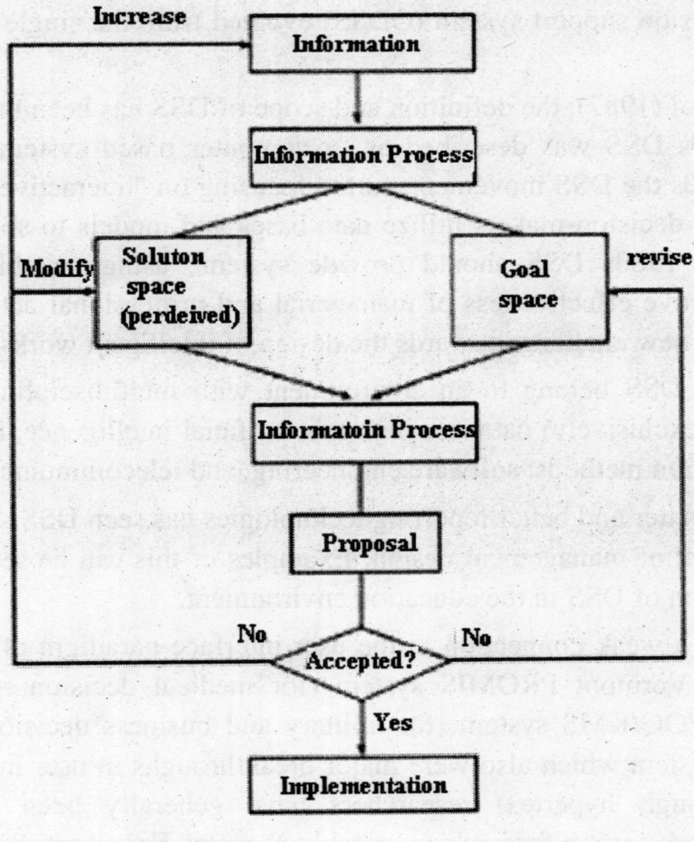

(DSS)

Typical information that a decision support application might gather and present are:

- An inventory of all of your current information assets (including legacy and relational data sources, cubes, data warehouses, and data marts),

- Comparative sales figures between one week and the next,
- Projected revenue figures based on new product sales assumptions.

History

According to Keen (1978), the concept of decision support has evolved from two main areas of research. The theoretical studies of organizational decision making done at the Carnegie Institute of Technology during the late 1950s and early 1960s, and the technical work on interactive computer system, mainly carried out at the Massachusetts Institute of Technology in the 1960s.

It is considered that the concept of DSS became an area of research of its own in the middle of the 1970s, before gaining in intensity during the 1980s. In the middle and late 1980s, executive information system (EIS), group decision support system (GDSS), and organizational decision support system (ODSS) evolved from the single user and model-oriented DSS.

According to Sol (1987), the definition and scope of DSS has been migrating over the years. In the 1970s DSS was described as "a computer based system to aid decision making". Late 1970s the DSS movement started focusing on "interactive computer-based system which help decision-makers utilize data bases and models to solve ill-structured problems". In the 1980s DSS should provide system "using suitable and available technology to improve effectiveness of managerial and professional activities", and end 1980s DSS faced a new challenge towards the design of intelligent workstations.

It is clear that DSS belong to an environment with multidisciplinary foundations, including (but not exclusively) database research, artificial intelligence, human-computer interaction, simulation methods, software engineering, and telecommunications.

The advent of better and better reporting technologies has seen DSS start to emerge as a critical component of management design. Examples of this can be seen in the intense amount of discussion of DSS in the education environment.

DSS also have a weak connection to the user interface paradigm of hypertext. Both the University of Vermont PROMIS system (for medical decision making) and the Carnegie Mellon ZOG/KMS system (for military and business decision making) were decision support system which also were major breakthroughs in user interface research. Furthermore, although hypertext researchers have generally been concerned with information overload, certain researchers, notably Douglas Engelbart, have been focused on decision makers in particular. There is no way to confirm/deny this.

Taxonomies

As with the definition, there is no universally-accepted taxonomy of DSS either. Different authors propose different classifications. Using the relationship with the user as the criterion, Haettenschwiler differentiates *passive*, *active*, and *cooperative DSS*. A *passive DSS* is a system that aids the process of decision making, but that cannot bring out explicit decision suggestions or solutions. An *active DSS* can bring out such decision suggestions or solutions. A *cooperative DSS* allows the decision maker (or its advisor) to modify, complete, or refine the decision suggestions provided by the system, before sending them back to the system for validation. The system again improves, completes, and refines the suggestions of the decision maker and sends them back to her for validation. The whole process then starts again, until a consolidated solution is generated.

Another taxonomy for DSS has been created by Daniel Power. Using the mode of assistance as the criterion, Power differentiates *communication-driven DSS*, *data-driven DSS*, *document-driven DSS*, *knowledge-driven DSS*, and *model-driven DSS*.

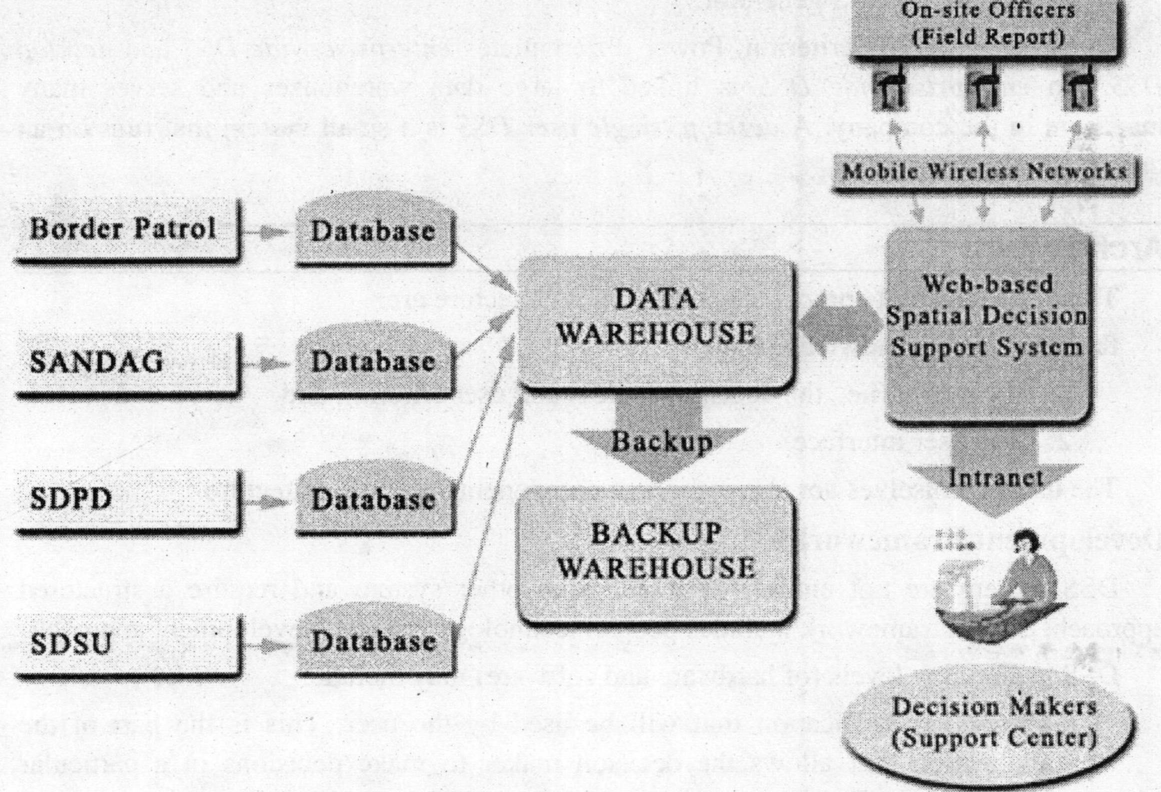

- A communication-driven DSS supports more than one person working on a shared task; examples include integrated tools like Microsoft's NetMeeting or Groove.
- A data-driven DSS or data-oriented DSS emphasizes access to and manipulation of a time series of internal company data and, sometimes, external data.
- A document-driven DSS manages, retrieves, and manipulates unstructured information in a variety of electronic formats.
- A knowledge-driven DSS provides specialized problem-solving expertise stored as facts, rules, procedures, or in similar structures.
- A model-driven DSS emphasizes access to and manipulation of a statistical, financial, optimization, or simulation model. Model-driven DSS use data and parameters provided by users to assist decision makers in analyzing a situation; they are not necessarily data-intensive. Dicodess is an example of an open source model-driven DSS generator.

Using scope as the criterion, Power differentiates *enterprise-wide DSS* and *desktop DSS*. An *enterprise-wide DSS* is linked to large data warehouses and serves many managers in the company. A *desktop, single-user DSS* is a small system that runs on an individual manager's PC.

Architecture

Three fundamental components of a DSS architecture are:

the database (or knowledge base),

1. the model (i.e., the decision context and user criteria), and
2. The user interface.

The users themselves are also important components of the architecture.

Development Frameworks

DSS system are not entirely different from other system and require a structured approach. Such a framework includes people, technology, and the development approach.

DSS technology levels (of hardware and software) may include:

1. The actual application that will be used by the user. This is the part of the application that allows the decision maker to make decisions in a particular problem area. The user can act upon that particular problem.

2. Generator contains Hardware/software environment that allows people to easily develop specific DSS applications. This level makes use of case tools or system such as Crystal, AIMMS, and think.
3. Tools include lower level hardware/software. DSS generators including special languages, function libraries and linking modules.

An iterative developmental approach allows for the DSS to be changed and redesigned at various intervals. Once the system is designed, it will need to be tested and revised for the desired outcome.

Classifying DSS

There are several ways to classify DSS applications. Not every DSS fits neatly into one category, but a mix of two or more architecture in one.

Holsapple and Whinston classify DSS into the following six frameworks: Text-oriented DSS, Database-oriented DSS, Spreadsheet-oriented DSS, Solver-oriented DSS, Rule-oriented DSS, and Compound DSS.

A compound DSS is the most popular classification for a DSS. It is a hybrid system that includes two or more of the five basic structures described by Holsapple and Whinston.

The support given by DSS can be separated into three distinct, interrelated categories: Personal Support, Group Support, and Organizational Support.

DSS Components May Be Classified as:

1. Inputs: Factors, numbers, and characteristics to analyze
2. User Knowledge and Expertise: Inputs requiring manual analysis by the user
3. Outputs: Transformed data from which DSS "decisions" are generated
4. Decisions: Results generated by the DSS based on user criteria

DSSs which perform selected cognitive decision-making functions and are based on artificial intelligence or intelligent agent's technologies are called Intelligent Decision Support System (IDSS).

The nascent field of Decision engineering treats the decision itself as an engineered object, and applies engineering principles such as Design and Quality assurance to an explicit representation of the elements that make up a decision.

Applications

As mentioned above, there are theoretical possibilities of building such system in any knowledge domain.

One example is the Clinical decision support system for medical diagnosis. Other examples include a bank loan officer verifying the credit of a loan applicant or an engineering firm that has bids on several projects and wants to know if they can be competitive with their costs.

DSS is extensively used in business and management. Executive dashboard and other business performance software allow faster decision making, identification of negative trends, and better allocation of business resources.

- A growing area of DSS application, concepts, principles, and techniques is in agricultural production, marketing for sustainable development. For example, the DSSAT4 package, developed through financial support of USAID during the 80's and 90's, has allowed rapid assessment of several agricultural production system around the world to facilitate decision-making at the farm and policy levels. There are, however, many constraints to the successful adoption on DSS in agriculture.
- DSS are also prevalent in forest management where the long planning time frame demands specific requirements. All aspects of Forest management, from log transportation, harvest scheduling to sustainability and ecosystem protection have been addressed by modern DSSs. A comprehensive list and discussion of all available system in forest management is being compiled under the COST action Forsys.
- A specific example concerns the Canadian National Railway system, which tests its equipment on a regular basis using a decision support system. A problem faced by any railroad is worn-out or defective rails, which can result in hundreds of derailments per year. Under a DSS, CN managed to decrease the incidence of derailments at the same time other companies were experiencing an increase.
- DSS has many applications that have already been spoken about. However, it can be used in any field where organization is necessary. Additionally, a DSS can be designed to help make decisions on the stock market, or deciding which area or segment to market a product toward.
- CACI has begun integrating simulation and decision support system. CACI defines three levels of simulation model maturity. "Level 1" models are traditional desktop simulation models that are executed within the native software package.

These often require a simulation expert to implement modifications, run scenarios, and analyze results. "Level 2" models embed the modeling engine in a web application that allows the decision maker to make process and parameter changes without the assistance of an analyst. "Level 3" models are also embedded in a web-based application but are tied to real-time operational data.

The execution of "level 3" models can be triggered automatically based on this real-time data and the corresponding results can be displayed on the manager's desktop showing the prevailing trends and predictive analytics given the current processes and state of the system. The advantage of this approach is that "level 1" models developed for the FDA projects can migrate to "level 2 and 3" models in support of decision support, production/operations management, process/work flow management, and predictive analytics. This approach involves developing and maintaining reusable models that allow decision makers to easily define and extract business level information (e.g., process metrics). "Level 1" models are decomposed into their business objects and stored in a database. All process information is stored in the database, including activity, resource, and costing data. The database becomes a template library that users can access to build, change, and modify their own unique process flows and then use simulation to study their performance in an iterative manner.

Benefits of DSS

1. Improves personal efficiency
2. Expedites problem solving (speed up the progress of problems solving in an organization)
3. Facilitates interpersonal communication
4. Promotes learning or training
5. Increases organizational control
6. Generates new evidence in support of a decision
7. Creates a competitive advantage over competition
8. Encourages exploration and discovery on the part of the decision maker
9. Reveals new approaches to thinking about the problem space
10. Helps automate the managerial processes.

Executive Information System

An Executive Information System (EIS) is a type of management information system intended to facilitate and support the information and decision-making needs of senior executives by providing easy access to both internal and external information relevant to meeting the strategic goals of the organization. It is commonly considered as a specialized form of a Decision Support System (DSS).

The emphasis of EIS is on graphical displays and easy-to-use user interfaces. They offer strong reporting and drill-down capabilities. In general, EIS are enterprise-wide DSS that help top-level executives analyze, compare, and highlight trends in important variables so that they can monitor performance and identify opportunities and problems. EIS and data warehousing technologies are converging in the marketplace.

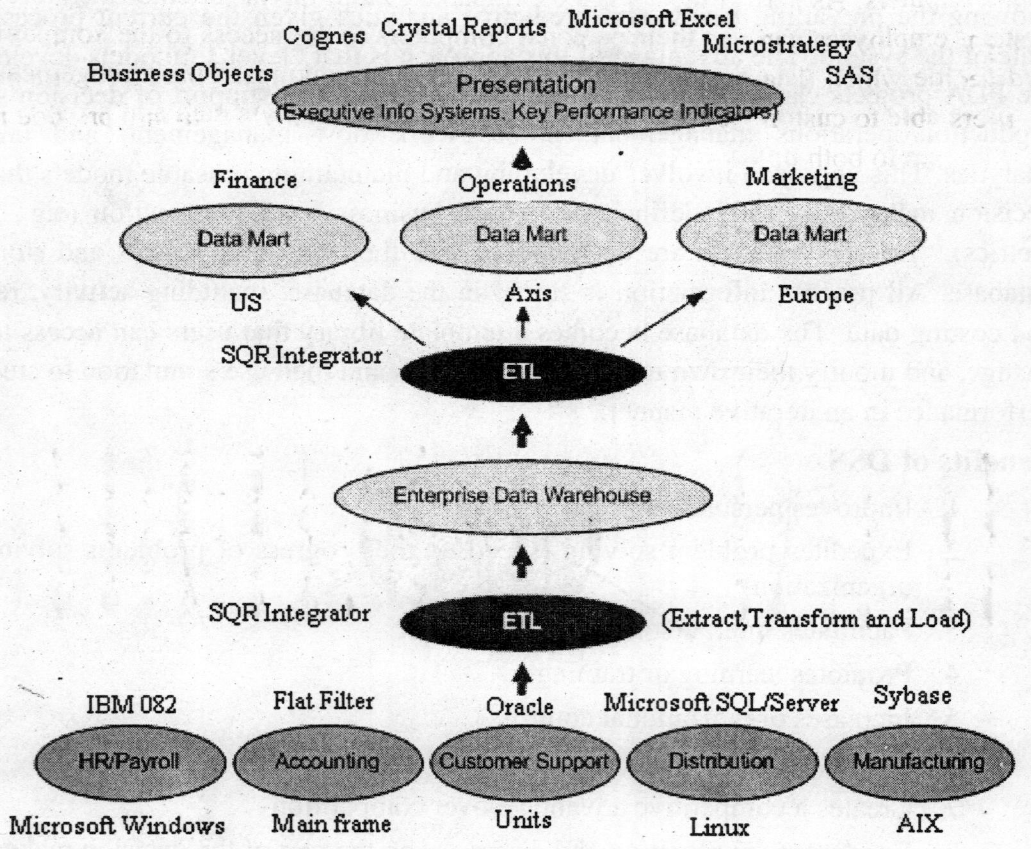

In recent years, the term EIS has lost popularity in favour of Business Intelligence (with the sub areas of reporting, analytics, and digital dashboards).

History

Traditionally, executive information system were developed as mainframe computer-based programs. The purpose was to package a company's data and to provide sales performance or market research statistics for decision makers, such as financial officers, marketing directors, and chief executive officers, who were not necessarily well acquainted with computers. The objective was to develop computer applications that would highlight information to satisfy senior executives' needs. Typically, an EIS provides data that would only need to support executive level decisions instead of the data for all the company.

Today, the application of EIS is not only in typical corporate hierarchies, but also at personal computers on a local area network. EIS now cross computer hardware platforms and integrate information stored on mainframes, personal computer system, and minicomputers. As some client service companies adopt the latest enterprise information system, employees can use their personal computers to get access to the company's data and decide which data are relevant for their decision makings. This arrangement makes all users able to customize their access to the proper company's data and provide relevant information to both upper and lower levels in companies.

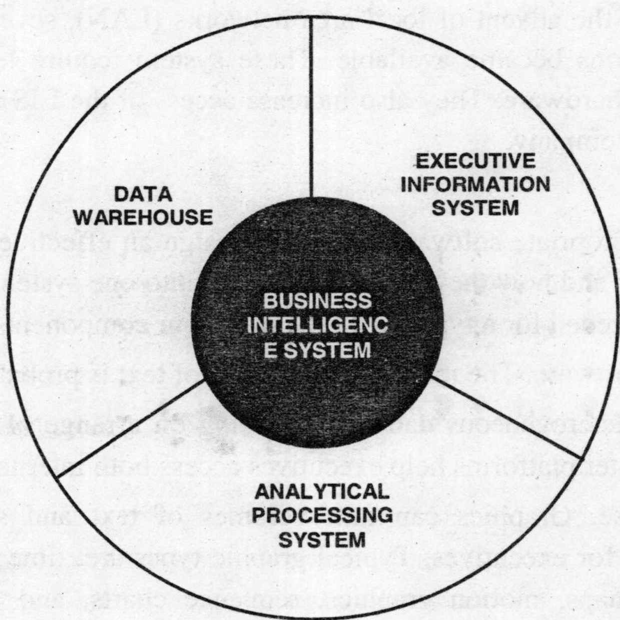

Components

The components of an EIS can typically be classified as:

Hardware

When talking about hardware for an EIS environment, we should focus on the hardware that meet the executive's needs. The executive must be put first and the executive's needs must be defined before the hardware can be selected. The basic computer hardware needed for a typical EIS includes four components:

1. Input data-entry devices. These devices allow the executive to enter, verify, and update data immediately;
2. The central processing unit (CPU), which is the kernel because it controls the other computer system components;
3. Data storage files. The executive can use this part to save useful business information, and this part also help the executive to search historical business information easily;
4. Output devices, which provide a visual or permanent record for the executive to save or read. This device refers to the visual output device or printer.

In addition, with the advent of local area networks (LAN), several EIS products for networked workstations became available. These system require less support and less expensive computer hardware. They also increase access of the EIS information to many more users within a company.

Software

Choosing the appropriate software is vital to design an effective EIS. Therefore, the software components and how they integrate the data into one system are very important. The basic software needed for a typical EIS includes four components:

1. Text base software. The most common form of text is probably documents;
2. Database. Heterogeneous databases residing on a range of vendor-specific and open computer platforms help executives access both internal and external data;
3. Graphic base. Graphics can turn volumes of text and statistics into visual information for executives. Typical graphic types are: time series charts, scatter diagrams, maps, motion graphics, sequence charts, and comparison-oriented graphs (i.e., bar charts);
4. Model base. The EIS models contain routine and special statistical, financial, and other quantitative analysis.

Perhaps a more difficult problem for executives is choosing from a range of highly technical software packages. Ease of use, responsiveness to executives' requests, and price are all reasonable considerations. Further, it should be considered whether the package can run on existing hardware.

User Interface

An EIS needs to be efficient to retrieve relevant data for decision makers, so the user interface is very important. Several types of interfaces can be available to the EIS structure, such as scheduled reports, questions/answers, menu driven, command language, natural language, and input/output.

It is crucial that the interface must fit the decision maker's decision-making style. If the executive is not comfortable with the information questions/answers style, the EIS will not be fully utilized. The ideal interface for an EIS would be simple to use and highly flexible, providing consistent performance, reflecting the executive's world, and containing help information.

Telecommunication

As decentralizing is becoming the current trend in companies, telecommunications will play a pivotal role in networked information system. Transmitting data from one place to another has become crucial for establishing a reliable network. In addition, telecommunications within an EIS can accelerate the need for access to distributed data.

Applications

EIS enables executives to find those data according to user-defined criteria and promote information-based insight and understanding. Unlike a traditional management information system presentation, EIS can distinguish between vital and seldom-used data, and track different key critical activities for executives, both which are helpful in evaluating if the company is meeting its corporate objectives. After realizing its advantages, people have applied EIS in many areas, especially, in manufacturing, marketing, and finance areas.

Manufacturing

Basically, manufacturing is the transformation of raw materials into finished goods for sale, or intermediate processes involving the production or finishing of semi-manufactures. It is a large branch of industry and of secondary production. Manufacturing operational control focuses on day-to-day operations, and the central idea of this process is effectiveness and efficiency.

To produce meaningful managerial and operational information for controlling manufacturing operations, the executive has to make changes in the decision processes. EIS provides the evaluation of vendors and buyers, the evaluation of purchased materials and parts, and analysis of critical purchasing areas. Therefore, the executive can oversee and review purchasing operations effectively with EIS. In addition, because production planning and control depends heavily on the plant's data base and its communications with all manufacturing work centers, EIS also provides an approach to improve production planning and control.

Marketing

In an organization, marketing executives' role is to create the future. Their main duty is managing available marketing resources to create a more effective future. For this, they need make judgments about risk and uncertainty of a project and its impact on the company in short term and long term. To assist marketing executives in making effective marketing decisions, an EIS can be applied. EIS provides an approach to sales forecasting, which can allow the market executive to compare sales forecast with past sales. EIS also offers an approach to product price, which is found in venture analysis. The market executive can evaluate pricing as related to competition along with the relationship of product quality with price charged. In summary, EIS software package enables marketing executives to manipulate the data by looking for trends, performing audits of the sales data, and calculating totals, averages, changes, variances, or ratios. All of these sales analysis functions help marketing executives to make final decisions.

Financial

A financial analysis is one of the most important steps to companies today. The executive needs to use financial ratios and cash flow analysis to estimate the trends and make capital investment decisions. An EIS is a responsibility-oriented approach that integrates planning or budgeting with control of performance reporting, and it can be extremely helpful to finance executives. Basically, EIS focuses on accountability of financial performance and it recognizes the importance of cost standards and flexible budgeting in developing the quality of information provided for all executive levels.

EIS enables executives to focus more on the long-term basis of current year and beyond, which means that the executive not only can manage a sufficient flow to maintain current operations but also can figure out how to expand operations that are contemplated over the coming years. Also, the combination of EIS and EDI environment can help cash managers to review the company's financial structure so that the best method of financing for an accepted capital project can be concluded. In addition, the EIS is a good tool to help the executive to review financial ratios, highlight financial trends and analyze a company's performance and its competitors.

- Advantages and Disadvantages
- Advantages
- Easy for upper-level executives to use, extensive computer experience is not required in operations

- Provides timely delivery of company summary information
- Information that is provided is better understood
- Filters data for management
- Improves to tracking information
- Offers efficiency to decision makers

Disadvantages

- Limited functionality, by design
- Information overload for some managers
- Benefits hard to quantify
- High implementation costs
- System may become slow, large, and hard to manage
- Need good internal processes for data management
- May lead to less reliable and less secure data
- System dependent

Future Trends

The future of executive info system will not be bound by mainframe computer system. This trend allows executives escaping from learning different computer operating system and substantially decreases the implementation costs for companies. Because utilizing existing software applications lies in this trend, executives will also eliminate the need to learn a new or special language for the EIS package.

Future executive information system will not only provide a system that supports senior executives, but also contain the information needs for middle managers. The future executive information system will become diverse because of integrating potential new applications and technology into the system, such as incorporating artificial intelligence (AI) and integrating multimedia characteristics and ISDN technology into an EIS.

4 CLASSIFICATION OF MIS

MIS is classified into various types. The classification depends on the following aspects:

(*a*) Functionality

(*b*) Utility

(*c*) Area of application

(*d*) Processing type

(*e*) Frequency of usage

(*a*) Functionality: Various management activities like the one which deals with scheduling, planning, resource allocation, product design, processes, and competitive strategy are the functional classification of MIS.

(*b*) Utility: Some of the processes like artificial intelligence, generating management related information, providing aid in decision making, necessary support system, and executive information system are the utility classification of MIS.

(*c*) Areas of Application: Depending upon the area where MIS could be used MIS is classified as Banking IS, Insurance IS, Production IS, Data warehouse IS, Public IS etc.

(*d*) Processing Type: Depending upon the type of management

Service in processing a data to generate information, MIS is classified into various processing types like:

- Online transactions
- Batch processing
- Distributed processing
- Multiprocessing etc.

(*e*) Frequency of usage: A MIS system is a system in which there is a constant need for review of the system. A mechanism can be built in the system to look into its performance and the outcome of such performed tasks may be assessed. This may be done periodically at fixed interval of time. Such mechanisms are categorized under MIS classification of frequency.

Though different types of IS exists in any organization, they are related to each other directly or indirectly. The information generated in one department may be used by another department to generate further information to be used by other departments and so on. Thus, there exists a relationship between various types of IS being used in any organization.

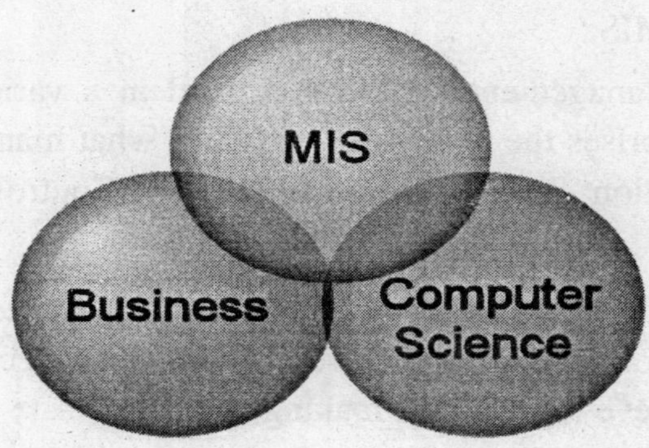

Predictive Information System

In technology-based enterprises, the achievement of networked and virtual organizations relies heavily upon the capability to develop suppliers and sub-contractors. While in many cases, suppliers are compliant and will embrace most initiatives in order to maintain contractual relationships, they often do so at additional cost to themselves. Traditional interventions such as second or third party audit, or other criteria-based assessments tend not to achieve genuine and sustained supplier improvement. Moreover, the more recent self-assessment movement is difficult to resource in many supplier organizations because of their (small) size and their remoteness of location.

To this end, the paper details the use of software system to act in quasi-consultancy mode, by predicting the likely organizational outcome of current management practices. Since the target users are senior managers in these small organizations, it is intended that the reflective style of the system will stimulate genuine learning. The paper discusses the process of developing the predictive system and the validation of predictions to-date in around 100 companies, predominantly employing less than 500 people. The current predictive accuracy of the system is over 80%. If companies were to heed these predictions there would be a marked change in their management practices and in the resultant competitiveness of the majority.

Decision Making Information System

Today's managers depend on information system for decision making. The managers have handful of data around them but manually they cannot process the data accurately and within the short period of time available to them due to heavy competition in modern world. Therefore mangers depend on information system.

- The concept of MIS:
- *Management:* Management has been defined in a variety of ways, but for our purposes it comprises the process or activities what managers do in the operation of their organization: Plan, Organize, Initiate and Control operations.

Information

Data are facts and figures that are not currently being used in a decision processes and usually take the form of historical records that are recorded and filed without immediate intent to retrieve for decision making.

Information consists of data that have been retrieved, processed or otherwise used for information or inference purposes, argument, or as a basis for forecasting or decision making.

System can be described simply as a set of elements joined together for a common objective. A subsystem is part of a larger system with which we are concerned. All system are part of larger system.

The objective of an MIS (Management Information System) is to provide information for decision making on planning, initiating, organizing, and controlling the operations of the subsystem of the form and to provide a synergetic organization in the process.

Decision Support System: It is sometimes described as the next evolutionary step after *Management Information System (MIS)*. MIS support decision making in both structured and unstructured problem environments. It supports decision making at all levels of the organization. IS (Information System) are intended to be woven into the fabric of the organizations, not standing alone. IS support all aspects of the decision making process. MIS are made of people, computers, procedures, databases, interactive query facilities and so on. They are intended to be evolutionary/adaptive and easy for people to use.

Methods of Decision Making

Type of Decision	Methods of decision making	
	OLD	**NEW**
Programmed Repetitive and Routine	Habit Standard operating procedure Organization structure, policy etc	Management Information System
Non-Programmed	Judgment, Intuition, Insight experience Training and Learning	Systematic Approach to problem solving & Decision making

MIS is a technique for making programmed decisions. If we include the computer and management science as integral parts or tools of computer –based information system, the prospects for a revolution in programmed decision making are very real. Just as a manufacturing process is becoming more and more automated so is the automation of programmed decisions increasing to support this production and other information needs throughout the organization.

Level of Management

The term **"Levels of Management"** refers to a line of demarcation between various managerial positions in an organization. The number of levels in management increases when the size of the business and work force increases and vice versa. The level of management determines a chain of command, the amount of authority & status enjoyed by any managerial position. The levels of management can be classified in three broad categories:

1. Top level / Administrative level
2. Middle level / Executory
3. Low level / Supervisory / Operative / First-line managers

Managers at all these levels perform different functions. The role of managers at all the three levels is discussed below:

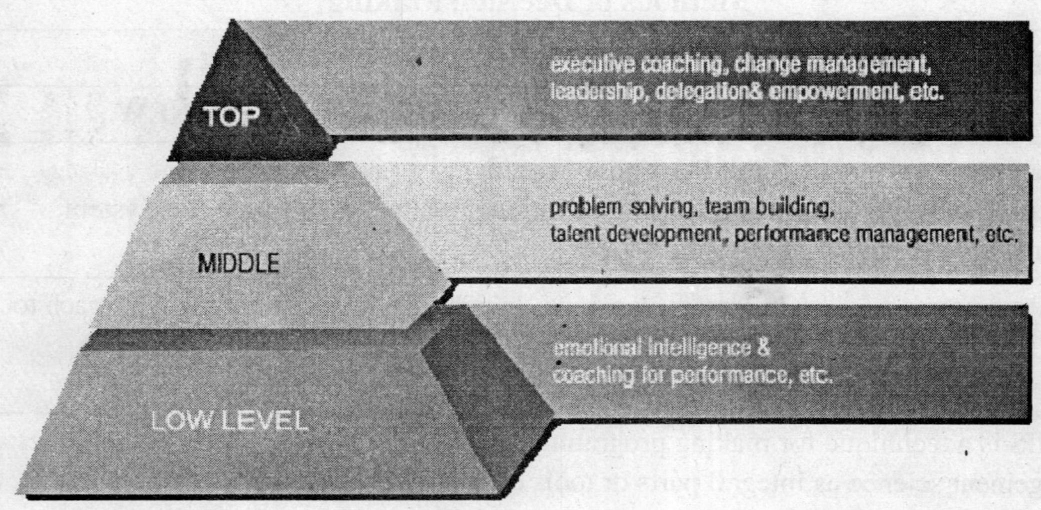

LEVEL OF MANAGEMENT

1. Top Level of Management

It consists of board of directors, chief executive or managing director. The top management is the ultimate source of authority and it manages goals and policies for an enterprise. It devotes more time on planning and coordinating functions.

The role of the top management can be summarized as follows –

- Top management lays down the objectives and broad policies of the enterprise.
- It issues necessary instructions for preparation of department budgets, procedures, schedules etc.
- It prepares strategic plans & policies for the enterprise.
- It appoints the executive for middle level i.e. departmental managers.
- It controls & coordinates the activities of all the departments.
- It is also responsible for maintaining a contact with the outside world.
- It provides guidance and direction.

- The top management is also responsible towards the shareholders for the performance of the enterprise.

2. Middle Level of Management

The branch managers and departmental managers constitute middle level. They are responsible to the top management for the functioning of their department. They devote more time to organizational and directional functions. In small organization, there is only one layer of middle level of management but in big enterprises, there may be senior and junior middle level management. Their role can be emphasized as –

- They execute the plans of the organization in accordance with the policies and directives of the top management.
- They make plans for the sub-units of the organization.
- They participate in employment & training of lower level management.
- They interpret and explain policies from top level management to lower level.
- They are responsible for coordinating the activities within the division or department.
- It also sends important reports and other important data to top level management.
- They evaluate performance of junior managers.
- They are also responsible for inspiring lower level managers towards better performance.

3. Lower Level of Management

Lower level is also known as supervisory / operative level of management. It consists of supervisors, foreman, section officers, superintendent etc. According to *R.C. Davis*, "Supervisory management refers to those executives whose work has to be largely with personal oversight and direction of operative employees". In other words, they are concerned with direction and controlling function of management. Their activities include–

- Assigning of jobs and tasks to various workers.
- They guide and instruct workers for day to day activities.
- They are responsible for the quality as well as quantity of production.
- They are also entrusted with the responsibility of maintaining good relation in the organization.

- They communicate workers problems, suggestions, and recommendatory appeals etc to the higher level and higher level goals and objectives to the workers.
- They help to solve the grievances of the workers.
- They supervise & guide the sub-ordinates.
- They are responsible for providing training to the workers.
- They arrange necessary materials, machines, tools etc for getting the things done.
- They prepare periodical reports about the performance of the workers.
- They ensure discipline in the enterprise.
- They motivate workers.
- They are the image builders of the enterprise because they are in direct contact with the workers.

The Main objectives of Management are:

- **Getting Maximum Results with Minimum Efforts** – The main objective of management is to secure maximum outputs with minimum efforts & resources. Management is basically concerned with thinking & utilizing human, material & financial resources in such a manner that would result in best combination. This combination results in reduction of various costs.
- **Increasing the Efficiency of factors of Production** – Through proper utilization of various factors of production, their efficiency can be increased to a great extent which can be obtained by reducing spoilage, wastages and breakage of all kinds, this in turn leads to saving of time, effort and money which is essential for the growth & prosperity of the enterprise.
- **Maximum Prosperity for Employer & Employees** – Management ensures smooth and coordinated functioning of the enterprise. This in turn helps in providing maximum benefits to the employee in the shape of good working condition, suitable wage system, incentive plans on the one hand and higher profits to the employer on the other hand.
- **Human betterment & Social Justice** – Management serves as a tool for the upliftment as well as betterment of the society. Through increased productivity & employment, management ensures better standards of living for the society. It provides justice through its uniform policies.

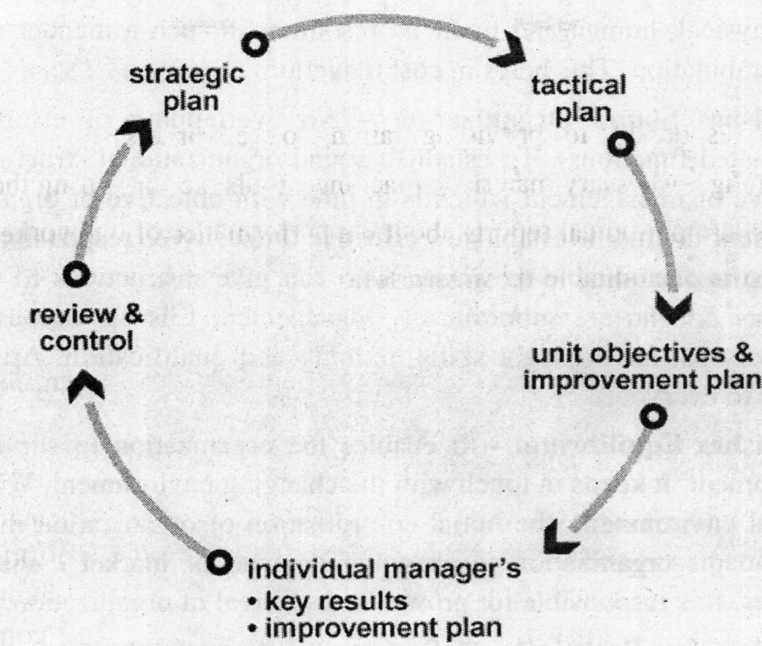

Management Objectives

- **IT helps in Achieving Group Goals –** It arranges the factors of production, assembles and organizes the resources, integrates the resources in effective manner to achieve goals. It directs group efforts towards achievement of pre-determined goals. By defining objective of organization clearly there would be no wastage of time, money and effort. Management converts disorganized resources of men, machines, money etc. into useful enterprise. These resources are coordinated, directed and controlled in such a manner that enterprise work towards attainment of goals.
- **Optimum Utilization of Resources –** Management utilizes all the physical & human resources productively. This leads to efficacy in management. Management provides maximum utilization of scarce resources by selecting its best possible alternate use in industry from out of various uses. It makes use of experts, professional and these services leads to use of their skills, knowledge, and proper utilization and avoids wastage. If employees and machines are producing its maximum there is no under employment of any resources.

- **Reduces Costs –** It gets maximum results through minimum input by proper planning and by using minimum input & getting maximum output. Management uses physical, human and financial resources in such a manner which results in best combination. This helps in cost reduction.
- **Establishes Sound Organization –** No overlapping of efforts (smooth and coordinated functions). To establish sound organizational structure is one of the objective of management which is in tune with objective of organization and for fulfillment of this, it establishes effective authority & responsibility relationship i.e. who is accountable to whom, who can give instructions to whom, who are superiors & who are subordinates. Management fills up various positions with right persons, having right skills, training and qualification. All jobs should be cleared to everyone.
- **Establishes Equilibrium –** It enables the organization to survive in changing environment. It keeps in touch with the changing environment. With the change is external environment, the initial co-ordination of organization must be changed. So it adapts organization to changing demand of market / changing needs of societies. It is responsible for growth and survival of organization.
- **Essentials for Prosperity of Society –** Efficient management leads to better economical production which helps in turn to increase the welfare of people. Good management makes a difficult task easier by avoiding wastage of scarce resource. It improves standard of living. It increases the profit which is beneficial to business and society will get maximum output at minimum cost by creating employment opportunities which generate income in hands. Organization comes with new products and researches beneficial for society.

According to *Theo Haimann*, "Administration means overall determination of policies, setting of major objectives, the identification of general purposes and lying down of broad programmers and projects". It refers to the activities of higher level. It lays down basic principles of the enterprise. According to Newman, "Administration means guidance, leadership & control of the efforts of the groups towards some common goals".

- Whereas, management involves conceiving, initiating and bringing together the various elements; coordinating, actuating, integrating the diverse organizational components while sustaining the viability of the organization towards some pre-determined goals. In other words, it is an art of getting things done through & with the people in formally organized groups.

The difference between **Management and Administration** can be summarized under 2 categories:

1. Functions
2. Usage / Applicability

On the Basis of Functions

Basis	Management	Administration
Meaning	Management is an art of getting things done through others by directing their efforts towards achievement of pre-determined goals.	It is concerned with formulation of broad objectives, plans & policies.
Nature	Management is an executing function.	Administration is a decision-making function.
Process	Management decides who should as it & how should he dot it.	Administration decides what is to be done & when it is to be done.
Function	Management is a doing function because managers get work done under their supervision.	Administration is a thinking function because plans & policies are determined under it.
Skills	Technical and Human skills	Conceptual and Human skills
Level	Middle & lower level function	Top level function

On the Basis of Usage

Basis	Management	Administration
Applicability	It is applicable to business concerns i.e. profit-making organization.	It is applicable to non-business concerns i.e. clubs, schools, hospitals etc.
Influence	The management decisions are influenced by the values, opinions, beliefs & decisions of the managers.	The administration is influenced by public opinion, govt. policies, religious organizations, customs etc.
Status	Management constitutes the employees of the organization who are paid remuneration (in the form of salaries & wages).	Administration represents owners of the enterprise who earn return on their capital invested & profits in the form of dividend.

Practically, there is no difference between management & administration. Every manager is concerned with both – administrative management function and operative management function as shown in the figure. However, the managers who are higher up in the hierarchy denote more time on administrative function & the lower level denote more time on directing and controlling worker's performance i.e. management.

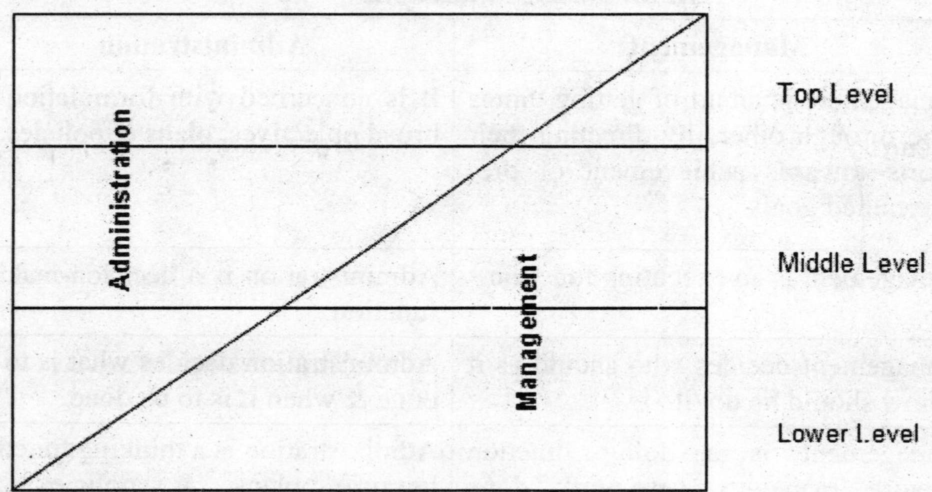

The Figure above clearly shows the degree of administration and management performed by the different levels of management.

Management has been described as a social process involving responsibility for economical and effective planning & regulation of operation of an enterprise in the fulfillment of given purposes. It is a dynamic process consisting of various elements and activities. These activities are different from operative functions like marketing, finance, purchase etc. Rather these activities are common to each and every manger irrespective of his level or status.

Different experts have classified functions of management. According to *George & Jerry*, "There are four fundamental functions of management i.e. planning, organizing, actuating and controlling". According to Henry Fayol, "To manage is to forecast and plan, to organize, to command, & to control". Whereas Luther Gullick has given a keyword '**POSDCORB**' where P stands for Planning, O for Organizing, S for Staffing, D for Directing, Co for Co-ordination, R for reporting & B for Budgeting. But the most widely accepted are functions of management given by KOONTZ and O'DONNEL i.e. **Planning**, **Organizing**, **Staffing**, **Directing** and **Controlling**.

For theoretical purposes, it may be convenient to separate the function of management but practically these functions are overlapping in nature i.e. they are highly inseparable. Each function blends into the other & each affects the performance of others.

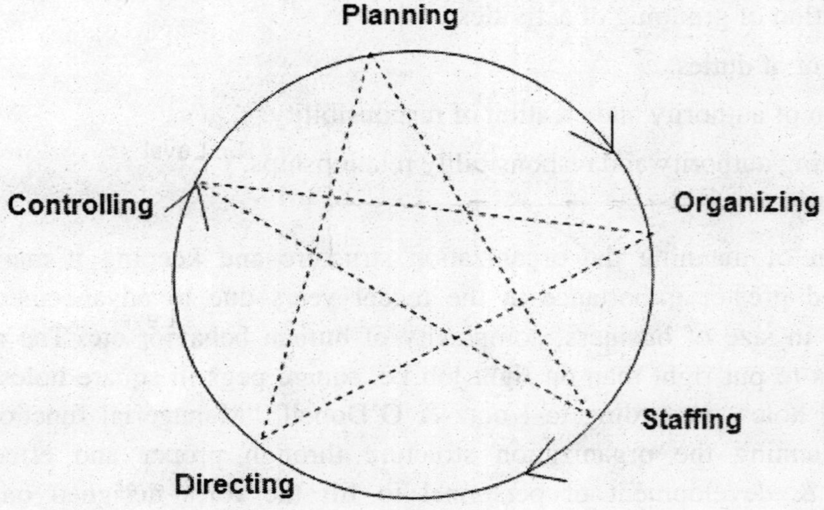

1. Planning

It is the basic function of management. It deals with chalking out a future course of action & deciding in advance the most appropriate course of actions for achievement of pre-determined goals. According to KOONTZ, "Planning is deciding in advance – what to do, when to do & how to do. It bridges the gap from where we are & where we want to be". A plan is a future course of actions. It is an exercise in problem solving & decision making. Planning is determination of courses of action to achieve desired goals. Thus, planning is a systematic thinking about ways & means for accomplishment of pre-determined goals. Planning is necessary to ensure proper utilization of human & non-human resources. It is all pervasive, it is an intellectual activity and it also helps in avoiding confusion, uncertainties, risks, wastages etc.

2. Organizing

It is the process of bringing together physical, financial and human resources and developing productive relationship amongst them for achievement of organizational goals. According to Henry Fayol, "To organize a business is to provide it with everything useful or its functioning i.e. raw material, tools, capital and personnel's". To organize a business involves determining & providing human and non-human resources to the organizational structure. Organizing as a process involves:

- Identification of activities.
- Classification of grouping of activities.
- Assignment of duties.
- Delegation of authority and creation of responsibility.
- Coordinating authority and responsibility relationships.

3. Staffing

It is the function of manning the organization structure and keeping it manned. Staffing has assumed greater importance in the recent years due to advancement of technology, increase in size of business, complexity of human behavior etc. The main purpose of staffing is to put right man on right job i.e. square pegs in square holes and round pegs in round holes. According to Kootz & O'Donell, "Managerial function of staffing involves manning the organization structure through proper and effective selection; appraisal & development of personnel to fill the roles designed on the structure". Staffing involves:

- Manpower Planning (estimating man power in terms of searching, choose the person and giving the right place).
- Recruitment, selection & placement.
- Training & development.
- Remuneration.
- Performance appraisal.
- Promotions & transfer.

4. Directing

It is that part of managerial function which actuates the organizational methods to work efficiently for achievement of organizational purposes. It is considered life-spark of the enterprise which sets it in motion the action of people because planning, organizing and staffing are the mere preparations for doing the work. Direction is that inter-personnel aspect of management which deals directly with influencing, guiding, supervising, motivating sub-ordinate for the achievement of organizational goals. Direction has following elements:

- Supervision
- Motivation

  - Leadership
  - Communication

- **Supervision-** implies overseeing the work of subordinates by their superiors. It is the act of watching & directing work & workers.
- **Motivation-** means inspiring, stimulating or encouraging the sub-ordinates with zeal to work. Positive, negative, monetary, non-monetary incentives may be used for this purpose.
- **Leadership-** may be defined as a process by which manager guides and influences the work of subordinates in desired direction.
- **Communications-** is the process of passing information, experience, opinion etc from one person to another. It is a bridge of understanding.

5. Controlling

It implies measurement of accomplishment against the standards and correction of deviation if any to ensure achievement of organizational goals. The purpose of controlling is to ensure that everything occurs in conformities with the standards. An efficient system of control helps to predict deviations before they actually occur. According to *Theo Haimann*, "Controlling is the process of checking whether or not proper progress is being made towards the objectives and goals and acting if necessary, to correct any deviation". According to Koontz & O'Donell, "Controlling is the measurement & correction of performance activities of subordinates in order to make sure that the enterprise objectives and plans desired to obtain them as being accomplished". Therefore controlling has following steps:

(*a*) Establishment of standard performance.

(*b*) Measurement of actual performance.

(*c*) Comparison of actual performance with the standards and finding out deviation if any.

(*d*) Corrective action.

Co-ordination is the unification, integration, synchronization of the efforts of group members so as to provide unity of action in the pursuit of common goals. It is a hidden force which binds all the other functions of management. According to *Mooney and Reelay*, "Co-ordination is orderly arrangement of group efforts to provide unity of action in the pursuit of common goals". According to *Charles Worth*, "Co-ordination is the integration of several parts into an orderly hole to achieve the purpose of understanding".

Management seeks to achieve co-ordination through its basic functions of planning, organizing, staffing, directing and controlling. That is why; co-ordination is not a separate function of management because achieving of harmony between individuals efforts towards achievement of group goals is a key to success of management. Co-ordination is the essence of management and is implicit and inherent in all functions of management.

A manager can be compared to an orchestra conductor since both of them have to create rhythm and unity in the activities of group members. Co-ordination is an integral element or ingredient of all the managerial functions as discussed below: -

(*a*) **Co-ordination through Planning –** Planning facilitates co-ordination by integrating the various plans through mutual discussion, exchange of ideas. e.g. - co-ordination between finance budget and purchases budget.

(*b*) **Co-ordination through Organizing –** Mooney considers co-ordination as the very essence of organizing. In fact when a manager groups and assigns various activities to subordinates, and when he creates department's co-ordination uppermost in his mind.

(*c*) **Co-ordination through Staffing –** A manager should bear in mind that the right no. of personnel in various positions with right type of education and skills are taken which will ensure right men on the right job.

(*d*) **Co-ordination through Directing –** The purpose of giving orders, instructions & guidance to the subordinates is served only when there is a harmony between superiors & subordinates.

(*e*) **Co-ordination through Controlling –** Manager ensures that there should be co-ordination between actual performance & standard performance to achieve organizational goals.

From above discussion, we can very much affirm that co-ordination is the very much essence of management. It is required in each & every function and at each & every stage & therefore it cannot be separated.

Co-ordination is an orderly arrangement of efforts to provide unity of action in the fulfillment of common objective whereas co-operation denotes collective efforts of persons working in an enterprise voluntarily for the achievement of a particular purpose. It is the willingness of individuals to help each other.

Co-ordination is an effort to integrate effectively energies of different groups whereas co-operation is sort to achieve general objectives of business.

Though these two are synonymous but they are different as below:

Differences between Co-ordination and Co-operation

Basis	Co-ordination	Co-operation
Meaning	It is an orderly arrangement of group efforts in pursuit of common goals.	It means mutual help willingly.
Scope	It is broader than co-operation which includes as well because it harmonizes the group efforts.	It is termed as a part of co-ordination.
Process	The function of co-ordination is performed by top management.	The functions of co-operation are prepared by persons at any level.
Requirements	Co-ordination is required by employees and departments at work irrespective of their work.	Co-operation is emotional in nature because it depends on the willingness of people working together.
Relationship	It establishes formal and informal relationships.	It establishes informal relationship.
Freedom	It is planned and entrusted by the central authority & it is essential.	It depends upon the sweet will of the individuals and therefore it is not necessary.
Support	It seeks wholehearted support from various people working at various levels.	Co-operation without co-ordination is fruitless & therefore it may lead to unbalanced developments.

Therefore, existence of co-operation may prove to be effective condition or requisite for co-ordination. But it does not mean that co-ordination originates automatically from the voluntary efforts of the group of members. It has to be achieved through conscious & deliberate efforts of managers, therefore to conclude we can say that co-operation without co-ordination has no fruit and co-ordination without co-operation has no root.

There are 14 Principles of Management described by Henri Fayol.

A principle refers to a fundamental truth. It establishes cause and effect relationship between two or more variables under given situation. They serve as a guide to thought & actions. Therefore, management principles are the statements of fundamental truth based on logic which provides guidelines for managerial decision making and actions. These principles are derived:

On the basis of observation and analysis i.e. practical experience of managers.

By conducting experimental studies.

1. Division of Labor

(*a*) Henry Fayol has stressed on the specialization of jobs.

(*b*) He recommended that work of all kinds must be divided & subdivided and allotted to various persons according to their expertise in a particular area.

(*c*) Subdivision of work makes it simpler and results in efficiency.

(*d*) It also helps the individual in acquiring speed, accuracy in his performance.

(*e*) Specialization leads to efficiency & economy in spheres of business.

2. Party of Authority & Responsibility

(*a*) Authority & responsibility are co-existing.

(*b*) If authority is given to a person, he should also be made responsible.

(*c*) In a same way, if anyone is made responsible for any job, he should also have concerned authority.

(*d*) Authority refers to the right of superiors to get exactness from their sub-ordinates whereas responsibility means obligation for the performance of the job assigned.

(*e*) There should be a balance between the two i.e. they must go hand in hand.

(*f*) Authority without responsibility leads to irresponsible behavior whereas responsibility without authority makes the person ineffective.

3. Principle of One Boss

(*a*) A sub-ordinate should receive orders and be accountable to one and only one boss at a time.

(*b*) In other words, a sub-ordinate should not receive instructions from more than one person because –

- It undermines authority
- Weakens discipline
- Divides loyalty
- Creates confusion
- Delays and chaos

- Escaping responsibilities
- Duplication of work
- Overlapping of efforts

(*c*) Therefore, dual sub-ordination should be avoided unless and until it is absolutely essential.

(*d*) Unity of command provides the enterprise a disciplined, stable & orderly existence.

(*e*) It creates harmonious relationship between superiors and sub-ordinates.

4. Unity of Direction

(*a*) Fayol advocates one head one plan which means that there should be one plan for a group of activities having similar objectives.

(*b*) Related activities should be grouped together. There should be one plan of action for them and they should be under the charge of a particular manager.

(*c*) According to this principle, efforts of all the members of the organization should be directed towards common goal.

(*d*) Without unity of direction, unity of action cannot be achieved.

(*e*) In fact, unity of command is not possible without unity of direction.

Basis	Unity of command	Unity of direction
Meaning	It implies that a sub-ordinate should receive orders & instructions from only one boss.	It means one head, one plan for a group of activities having similar objectives.
Nature	It is related to the functioning of personnel's.	It is related to the functioning of departments, or organization as a whole.
Necessity	It is necessary for fixing responsibility of each subordinate.	It is necessary for sound organization.
Advantage	It avoids conflicts, confusion & chaos.	It avoids duplication of efforts and wastage of resources.
Result	It leads to better superior sub-ordinate relationship.	It leads to smooth running of the enterprise.

Therefore, it is obvious that they are different from each other but they are dependent on each other i.e. unity of direction is a pre-requisite for unity of command. But it does not automatically come from the unity of direction.

5. Equity

(*a*) Equity means combination of fairness, kindness & justice.

(*b*) The employees should be treated with kindness & equity if devotion is expected of them.

(*c*) It implies that managers should be fair and impartial while dealing with the subordinates.

(*d*) They should give similar treatment to people of similar position.

(*e*) They should not discriminate with respect to age, caste, sex, religion, relation etc.

(*f*) Equity is essential to create and maintain cordial relations between the managers and sub-ordinate.

(*g*) But equity does not mean total absence of harshness.

(*h*) Fayol was of opinion that, "at times force and harshness might become necessary for the sake of equity".

5. Order

(*a*) This principle is concerned with proper & systematic arrangement of things and people.

(*b*) Arrangement of things is called material order and placement of people is called social order.

(*c*) Material order- There should be safe, appropriate and specific place for every article and every place to be effectively used for specific activity and commodity.

(*d*) Social order- Selection and appointment of most suitable person on the suitable job. There should be a specific place for everyone and everyone should have a specific place so that they can easily be contacted whenever need arises.

6. Discipline

(*a*) According to Fayol, "Discipline means sincerity, obedience, respect of authority & observance of rules and regulations of the enterprise".

(*b*) This principle applies that subordinate should respect their superiors and obey their order.

(*c*) It is an important requisite for smooth running of the enterprise.

(*d*) Discipline is not only required on path of subordinates but also on the part of management.

(*e*) Discipline can be enforced if –

- There are good superiors at all levels.
- There are clear & fair agreements with workers.
- Sanctions (punishments) are judiciously applied.

6. Initiative

(*a*) Workers should be encouraged to take initiative in the work assigned to them.

(*b*) It means eagerness to initiate actions without being asked to do so.

(*c*) Fayol advised that management should provide opportunity to its employees to suggest ideas, experiences & new method of work.

(*d*) It helps in developing an atmosphere of trust and understanding.

(*e*) People then enjoy working in the organization because it adds to their zeal and energy.

(*f*) To suggest improvement in formulation & implementation of place.

(*g*) They can be encouraged with the help of monetary & non-monetary incentives.

7. Fair Remuneration

(*a*) The quantum and method of remuneration to be paid to the workers should be fair, reasonable, satisfactory & rewarding of the efforts.

(*b*) As far as possible, it should accord satisfaction to both employer and the employees.

(*c*) Wages should be determined on the basis of cost of living, work assigned, financial position of the business, wage rate prevailing etc.

(*d*) Logical & appropriate wage rates and methods of their payment reduce tension & differences between workers & management creates harmonious relationship and pleasing atmosphere of work.

(*e*) Fayol also recommended provision of other benefits such as free education, medical & residential facilities to workers.

8. Stability of Tenure

(*a*) Fayol emphasized that employees should not be moved frequently from one job position to another i.e. the period of service in a job should be fixed.

(*b*) Therefore employees should be appointed after keeping in view principles of recruitment and selection but once they are appointed their services should be served.

(*c*) According to Fayol, "Time is required for an employee to get used to a new work and succeed to doing it well but if he is removed before that he will not be able to render worthwhile services".

(*d*) As a result, the time, effort and money spent on training the worker will go waste.

(*e*) Stability of job creates team spirit and a sense of belongingness among workers which ultimately increase the quality as well as quantity of work.

9. Scalar Chain

(*a*) Fayol defines scalar chain as "the chain of superiors ranging from the ultimate authority to the lowest".

(*b*) Every orders, instructions, messages, requests, explanation etc has to pass through Scalar chain.

(*c*) But, for the sake of convenience and urgency, this path can be cut shirt and this short cut is known as Gang Plank.

(*d*) A **Gang Plank** is a temporary arrangement between two different points to facilitate quick and easy communication as explained below:

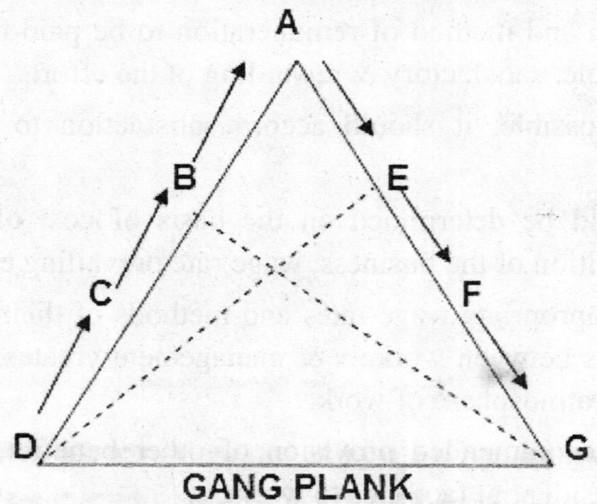

(*e*) In the figure given, if D has to communicate with G he will first send the communication upwards with the help of C, B to A and then downwards with the help of E and F to G which will take quite some time and by that time, it may not be worth therefore a gang plank has been developed between the two.

(*f*) **Gang Plank** clarifies that management principles are not rigid rather they are very flexible. They can be molded and modified as per the requirements of situations.

10. Sub-Ordination of Individual Interest to General Interest

(*a*) An organization is much bigger than the individual it constitutes, therefore interest of the undertaking should prevail in all circumstances.

(*b*) As far as possible, reconciliation should be achieved between individual and group interests.

(*c*) But in case of conflict, individual must sacrifice for bigger interests.

(*d*) In order to achieve this attitude, it is essential that–

- Employees should be honest and sincere.
- Proper and regular supervision of work.
- Reconciliation of mutual differences and clashes by mutual agreement.

For example, for change of location of plant, for change of profit sharing ratio, etc.

11. Espirit De' Corps (can be achieved through unity of command)

(*a*) It refers to team spirit, i.e., harmony in the work groups and mutual understanding among the members.

(*b*) Spirit De' Corps inspires workers to work harder.

(*c*) Fayol cautioned the managers against dividing the employees into competing groups because it might damage the moral of the workers and interest of the undertaking in the long run.

(*d*) To inculcate Espirit De' Corps following steps should be undertaken–

- There should be proper co-ordination of work at all levels.
- Subordinates should be encouraged to develop informal relations among themselves.
- Efforts should be made to create enthusiasm and keenness among subordinates so that they can work to the maximum ability.
- Efficient employees should be rewarded and those who are not up to the mark should be given a chance to improve their performance.
- Subordinates should be made conscious of that whatever they are doing is of great importance to the business and society.

(*e*) He also cautioned against the more use of Britain communication to the subordinates, i.e., face to face communication should be developed. The managers should infuse team spirit and belongingness. There should be no place for misunderstanding. People then enjoy working in the organization and offer their best towards the organization.

12. Centralization & De-Centralization

(*a*) Centralization means concentration of authority at the top level. In other words, centralization is a situation in which top management retains most of the decision making authority.

(*b*) Decentralization means disposal of decision making authority to all the levels of the organization. In other words, sharing authority downwards is decentralization.

(*c*) According to Fayol, "Degree of centralization or decentralization depends on no. of factors like size of business, experience of superiors, dependability & ability of subordinates etc.

(*d*) Anything which increases the role of subordinate is decentralization & anything which decreases it is centralization.

(*e*) Fayol suggested that absolute centralization or decentralization is not feasible. An organization should strike to achieve a lot between the two.

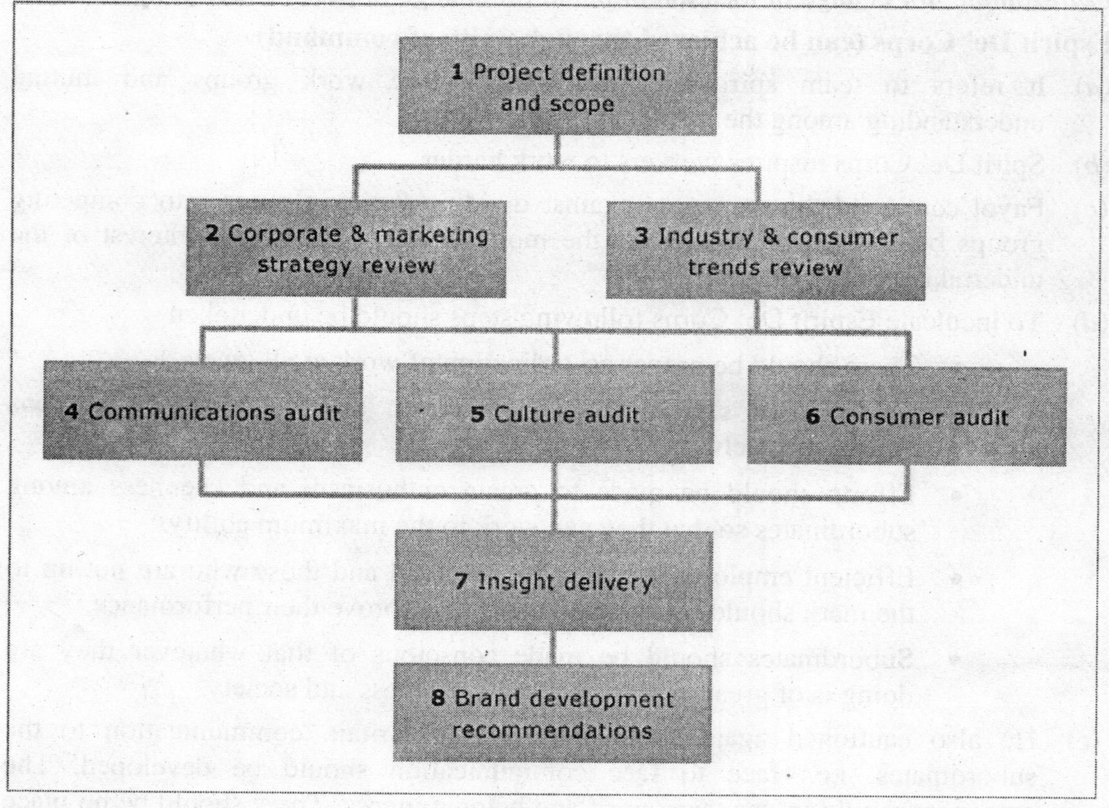

1. Principles of Management are *Universal*

(*a*) Management principles are applicable to all kinds of organizations business & non business.

(*b*) They are applicable to all levels of management.

(*c*) Every organization must make best possible use by the use of management principles.

(*d*) Therefore, they are universal or all pervasive.

2. Principles of Management are *Flexible*

(*a*) Management principles are dynamic guidelines and not static rules.

(*b*) There is sufficient room for managerial discretion i.e. they can be modified as per the requirements of the situation.

(*c*) Modification & improvement is a continuous phenomenon in case of principles of management.

3. Principles of Management have a *Cause & Effect Relationship*

(*a*) Principles of management indicate cause and effect relationship between related variables.

(*b*) They indicate what will be the consequence or result of certain actions. Therefore, if one is known, the other can be traced.

4. Principles of Management - Aims at Influencing Human Behavior

(*a*) Human behavior is complex and unpredictable.

(*b*) Management principles are directed towards regulating human behavior so that people can give their best to the organization.

(*c*) Management is concerned with integrating efforts and harmonizing them towards a goal.

(*d*) But in certain situations even these principles fail to understand human behavior.

5. Principles of Management are of *Equal Importance*

(*a*) All management principles are equally important.

(*b*) No particular principle has greater importance than the other.

(*c*) They are all required together for the achievement of organizational goals.

Principles of Management

Following are the main importance of the Principles of Management

1. Improves Understanding.
2. Direction for Training of Managers.
3. Role of Management.
4. Guide to Research in Management.

1. Improves Understanding: From the knowledge of principles managers get indication on how to manage an organization. The principles enable managers to decide what should be done to accomplish given tasks and to handle situations which may arise in management. These principles make managers more efficient.

2. Direction for Training of Managers: Principles of management provide understanding of management process what managers would do to accomplish what. Thus, these are helpful in identifying the areas of management in which existing & future managers should be trained.

3. Role of Management: Management principles makes the role of manager's concrete. Therefore, these principles act as ready reference to the managers to check whether their decisions are appropriate. Besides these principles define managerial activities in practical terms. They tell what a manager is expected to do in specific situation.

4. Guide to Research in Management: The body of management principles indicate lines along which research should be undertaken to make management practical and more effective. The principles guide managers in decision making and action. The researchers can examine whether the guidelines are useful or not. Anything which makes management research more exact & pointed will help improve management practice.

- *Fredrick Winslow Taylor (March 20, 1856 - March 21, 1915)* commonly known as 'Father of Scientific Management' started his career as an operator and rose to the position of chief engineer. He conducted various experiments during this process which forms the basis of scientific management. It implies application of scientific principles for studying & identifying management problems.
- According to Taylor, "Scientific Management is an art of knowing exactly what you want your men to do and seeing that they do it in the best and cheapest way". In Taylors view, if a work is analyzed scientifically it will be possible to find *one best way* to do it.
- Hence scientific management is a thoughtful, organized, dual approach towards the job of management against hit or miss or Rule of Thumb.

- According to *Drucker*, "The cost of scientific management is the organized study of work, the analysis of work into simplest element & systematic management of worker's performance of each element".

1. Development of Science for each part of men's job (replacement of rule of thumb)

a. This principle suggests that work assigned to any employee should be observed, analyzed with respect to each and every element and part and time involved in it.

b. This means replacement of odd rule of thumb by the use of method of enquiry, investigation, data collection, analysis and framing of rules.

c. Under scientific management, decisions are made on the basis of facts and by the application of scientific decisions.

2. Scientific Selection, Training & Development of Workers

a. There should be scientifically designed procedure for the selection of workers.

b. Physic[illegible], mental & other requirement should be specified for each and every job.

c. Workers should be selected & trained to make them fit for the job.

d. The management has to provide opportunities for development of workers having better capabilities.

e. According to Taylor efforts should be made to develop each employee to his greatest level and efficiency & prosperity.

3. Co-operation between Management & workers or Harmony not discord

a. Taylor believed in co-operation and not individualism.

b. It is only through co-operation that the goals of the enterprise can be achieved efficiently.

c. There should be no conflict between managers & workers.

d. Taylor believed that interest of employer & employees should be fully harmonized so as to secure mutually understanding relations between them.

4. Division of Responsibility

a. This principle determines the concrete nature of roles to be played by different level of managers & workers.

b. The management should assume the responsibility of planning the work whereas workers should be concerned with execution of task.

c. Thus planning is to be separated from execution.

5. Mental Revolution

a. The workers and managers should have a complete change of outlook towards their mutual relation and work effort.

b. It requires that management should create suitable working condition and solve all problems scientifically.

c. Similarly workers should attend their jobs with utmost attention, devotion and carefulness. They should not waste the resources of enterprise.

d. Handsome remuneration should be provided to workers to boost up their moral.

e. It will create a sense of belongingness among worker.

f. They will be disciplined, loyal and sincere in fulfilling the task assigned to them.

g. There will be more production and economical growth at a faster rate.

6. Maximum Prosperity for Employer & Employees

a. The aim of scientific management is to see maximum prosperity for employer and employees.

b. It is important only when there is opportunity for each worker to attain his highest efficiency.

c. Maximum output & optimum utilization of resources will bring higher profits for the employer & better wages for the workers.

d. There should be maximum output in place of restricted output.

e. Both managers & workers should be paid handsomely.

Exercise

Q. 1. What is management? Explain in brief the principles of management and discuss the contribution.

Q. 2. Explain of F.W. Taylor and Henri Fayol to the Management Thought.

Q. 3. Explain in brief the Leadership Styles. Also discuss which Leadership Style you would prefer if you are placed at the top level management of a large business concern. Give reasons for your choice.

Q. 4. What are essentials of an effective Control System in Management?

Q. 5. Explain how information technology can be applied in Controlling.

Q. 6. What is Management? Is Management a Science or an Art? Explain your point of view giving suitable examples.

5 Development of Information System

Aims and Objectives

The aim of this section is to introduce information system engineering in organizations. The following topics will be discussed:-

- The reasons why Information Technology and Information System are crucial to modern organizations and thus subject to professional management;
- The factors influencing information system engineering.

Some of the ideas and many of the references in this chapter are adopted from Avison & Fitzgerald's influential 'Information System Development: Methodologies, Techniques and Tools'. This is one of the recommended texts for the Information System in Business Degree in the School of Computing at the University of Glamorgan.

The Importance of Information Technology and Information System

All medium to large organizations depend on Information technology for their continued survival. Consider organizations like British Gas, British Telecom, the Power and Water companies having to manually calculate, millions of customer bills every month or quarter! Clearly the clerical effort involved would make it difficult if not impossible for the organization to make a profit. Similar arguments apply to many other organizations such as the high street banks, central and local government.

A recent article in the Daily Telegraph IT supplement suggested that many large organizations could last no longer than 24 hours without IT support! There should be little wonder that attitudes to the development of information system have changed over the years from an ad hoc almost cavalier 'approach to a professionally managed, disciplined, planned, and engineering approach.

Factors Influencing the System Development Effort

A variety of factors influence Information System Engineering, ranging from high level strategic to detailed technical issues. The following factors are considered, however the list is by no means exhaustive and you may well care to add your own:-

- Strategic Information System Planning
- Corporate Data Management,
- Business Process Re-Engineering,
- The Technical Environment,
- Models & Methodologies,
- Socio-Behavioral Development,
- Supporting Tools,
- Quality Assurance,
- Project Management,
- Human Resources,
- End-User System Development.

Strategic Information System Planning

Organizations typically develop rolling business plans, they are constructed by taking into account the current business, the external influences on the business (e.g. the economy, government policy and technological advances), and the aims and objectives of the most senior levels of management. The strategic business plan describes how the organization will strive to move from the current business to the target business.

Information System support is necessary to achieve the strategic business plan, so the business plan feeds into a Strategic Information System Plan (SISP), which describes how the current IT system are intended to evolve into the target IT system. A 'big bang' approach is infeasible; therefore a project based approach is used. The output of the SISP is a series of development projects which will either involve modifying existing system or developing new system (which are likely to have to interface or integrate with existing system).

In the past, information system were developed simply to improve the efficiency of specific business functions. More recently information system have been viewed as tools for obtaining competitive advantage. Avison and Fitzgerald (1995) have discussed the following ways in which information system can help to achieve competitive advantage:-

"Redefine the boundaries of particular industries,
Develop new products or services,
Change the relationships between suppliers and customers,
Establish barriers to deter new entrants to marketplaces."

Porter (1980) identifies five competitive forces that any organization needs to consider:-

1. Threat of new entrants.
2. Bargaining power of customers.
3. Threat of substitute products or services.
4. Bargaining power of suppliers.
5. Rivalry among existing firms.

Earl (1989) extends Porter's work by illustrating the strategic role that Information Technology (IT) can play in addressing these forces. The result of Earl's work is a 'multiple' methodology. The methodology adopts a three pronged approach to strategic information system development. The first prong involves the top-down analysis of business objectives using Critical Success Factors (CSF), SWOT (Strengths, Weaknesses, Opportunities, and Threats) analysis and Porter's five forces. The second prong involves bottom-up analysis of existing system and the third prong emphasizes the creative use of IT.

Bullen and Rockart (1984) have produced a strategic information system methodology based on CSF analysis. The methodology involves the analysis of business goals and objectives and the factors critical to achieving those objectives. The next stage is the identification of the information system required to support these CSFs.

The discussion so far has emphasized a holistic approach, looking at high level business objectives rather than detailed functional requirements. These approaches emphasize the importance of shared corporate data, an issue which will be discusses in detail in the next section.

Corporate Data Management

Organizations like British Gas, British Telecom and the NHS have come to realize that on a replacement cost basis their computerized databases are amongst their most valuable assets (consider how much it would cost for British Gas to recapture its customer database) and that as such they need to be professionally managed.

These companies have realized how important data accuracy and consistency is and have developed company system and data architectures. These are very high level models which describe the main processes the organization carries out and the main entities and relationships required to support these business processes. The development of application system is constrained by the need to be consistent with the overarching, high level, companywide view of its data. Chapter 5 discusses these issues in much greater depth.

Business Process Re-Engineering / Process Innovation

The idea of process innovation (Davenport and Short, 1990, Davenport, 1993) is closely linked with the techniques of Business Process Re-engineering. The argument is that computerizing existing system is only likely to yield marginal gains. In many cases the only means of achieving radical improvements is to radically re-engineer the business process itself and use IT to enable to re-engineered process. Process Innovation illustrates the main argument of the paper, i.e. that an effective methodology for ISE should adopt a rigorous, structured approach to data design and a dynamic approach to process design.

The Technical Environment

A company which has made a substantial investment in ICL hardware and the INGRES Relational Database Management System (RDBMS) does not decide to convert to IBM and DB2 lightly, so realistically the development is constrained by the existing technical environment.

Paradigms, Models & Methodologies

Structured Methodologies

The industry has realized that a standard approach using proven analysis and design techniques should improve the 'quality' of system. The standard methodology for the development of business information system in the UK is **Structured System Analysis and Design Methodology** (SSADM). However there are many other methodologies in use around the world such as Yourdon, Gane & Sarson, Hood and Information Engineering and DSDM (Dynamic System Development Methodology). A company which has adopted SSADM has chosen to constrain its system development activities in a particular way.

SSADM is an example of the waterfall model of information system engineering. SSADM covers the Feasibility, Analysis and Design stages of the waterfall project lifecycle

- **Feasibility:** Is the project likely to be cost effective?
- **Analysis:** What is required by the business?

- **Design:** How is the requirement going to be implemented?
- **Software Development:** Building and testing software.
- **Implementation:** Delivery and installation of new hardware/software system.
- **Maintenance:** The cycle continues ad infinitum at a lower level.

The whole process is circular and never ending because implemented system become part of the current set of IT system which feed into the on-going SISP exercise.

There are other non-monolithic models of information system engineering which are discussed at length in a paper by Graham entitled 'Incremental Development: review of non-monolithic life cycle development models' (Graham, 1989).

Decision Making

Decision making can be regarded as the mental processes (cognitive process) resulting in the selection of a course of action among several alternatives. Every decision making process produces a final choice. The output can be an action or an opinion of choice.

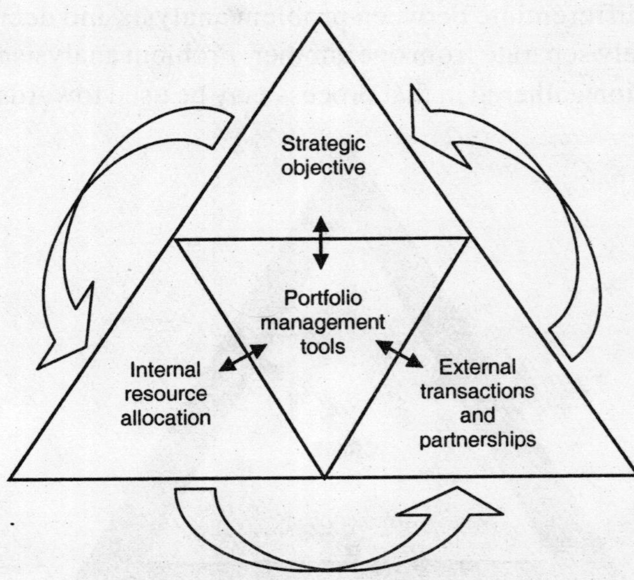

Overview

Human performance in decision making terms has been the subject of active research from several perspectives. From a psychological perspective, it is necessary to examine individual decisions in the context of a set of needs, preferences an individual has and values they seek. From a cognitive perspective, the decision making process must be regarded as a continuous process integrated in the interaction with the environment. From a normative perspective, the analysis of individual decisions is concerned with the logic of decision making and rationality and the invariant choice it leads to.

Logical decision making is an important part of all science-based professions, where specialists apply their knowledge in a given area to making informed decisions. For example, medical decision making often involves making a diagnosis and selecting an appropriate treatment. Some research using naturalistic methods shows, however, that in situations with higher time pressure, higher stakes, or increased ambiguities, experts use intuitive decision making rather than structured approaches, following a recognition primed decision approach to fit a set of indicators into the expert's experience and immediately arrive at a satisfactory course of action without weighing alternatives. Recent robust decision efforts have formally integrated uncertainty into the decision making process. However, Decision Analysis, recognized and included uncertainties with a structured and rationally justifiable method of decision making since its conception in 1964.

Problem Analysis vs. Decision Making

It's important to differentiate between problem analysis and decision making. The concepts are completely separate from one another. Problem analysis must be done first, and then the information gathered in that process may be used towards decision making.

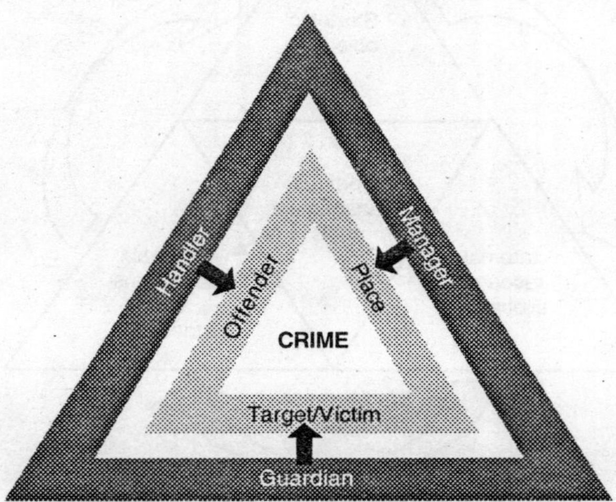

Problem Analysis

- Analyze performance, what should the results be against what they actually are
- Problems are merely deviations from performance standards

- Problem must be precisely identified and described
- Problems are caused by some change from a distinctive feature
- Something can always be used to distinguish between what has and hasn't been effected by a cause
- Causes to problems can be deducted from relevant changes found in analyzing the problem
- Most likely cause to a problem is the one that exactly explains all the facts

Decision Making

- Objectives must first be established
- Objectives must be classified and placed in order of importance
- Alternative actions must be developed
- The alternative must be evaluated against all the objectives
- The alternative that is able to achieve all the objectives is the tentative decision
- The tentative decision is evaluated for more possible consequences
- The decisive actions are taken, and additional actions are taken to prevent any adverse consequences from becoming problems and starting both system (problem analysis and decision making) all over again

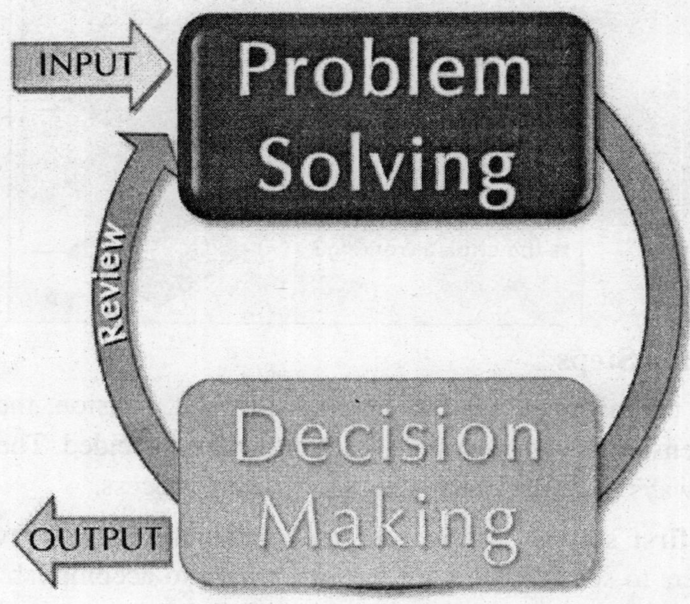

Decision-Making Stages

Developed by B. Aubrey Fisher, there are four stages that should be involved in all group decision making. These stages, or sometimes called phases, are important for the decision-making process to begin

- **Orientation stage**- This phase is where members meet for the first time and start to get to know each other.
- **Conflict stage**- Once group members become familiar with each other, disputes, little fights and arguments occur. Group members eventually work it out.
- **Emergence stage**- The group begins to clear up ambiguity in opinions is talked about.
- **Reinforcement stage**- Members finally make a decision, while justifying themselves that it was the right decision.

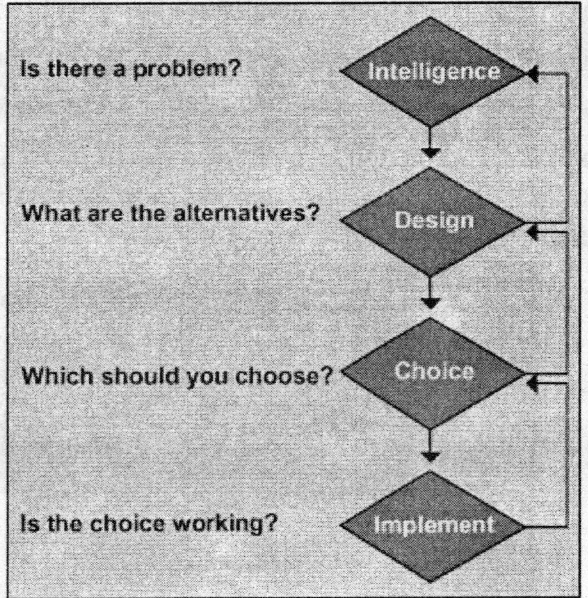

Decision-Making Steps

When in an organization and faced with a difficult decision, there are several steps one can take to ensure the best possible solutions will be decided. These steps are put into seven effective ways to go about this decision making process.

- The **first step** - Outline your goal and outcome. This will enable decision makers to see exactly what they are trying to accomplish and keep them on a specific path.

- The **second step** - Gather data. This will help decision makers have actual evidence to help them come up with a solution.
- The **third step** - Brainstorm to develop alternatives. Coming up with more than one solution ables you to see which one can actually work.
- The **fourth step** - List pros and cons of each alternative. With the list of pros and cons, you can eliminate the solutions that have more cons than pros, making your decision easier.
- The **fifth step** - Make the decision. Once you analyze each solution, you should pick the one that has many pros, and the one that everyone can agree with.
- The **sixth step** - Immediately take action. Once the decision is picked, you should implement it right away.

The **seventh step** - Learn from, and reflect on the decision making. This step allows you to see what you did right and wrong when coming up.

Decision Making Skills and Techniques

We use our decision making skills to solve problems by selecting one course of action from several possible alternatives. Decision making skills are also a key component of time management skills.

Decision making can be hard. Almost any decision involves some conflicts or dissatisfaction. The difficult part is to pick one solution where the positive outcome can outweigh possible losses. Avoiding decisions often seems easier. Yet, making your own decisions and accepting the consequences are the only way to stay in control of your time, your success, and your life. If you want to learn more on how to make a decision, here is some decision making tips to get you started.

A significant part of decision making skills is in knowing and practicing good decision making techniques. One of the most practical decision making techniques can be summarized in those simple decision making steps:

1. **Identify the purpose of your decision:** What is exactly the problem to be solved? Why it should be solved?
2. **Gather information:** What factors does the problem involve?
3. **Identify the principles to judge the alternatives:** What standards and judgment criteria should the solution meet?

4. **Brainstorm and list different possible choices:** Generate ideas for possible solutions. See more on extending your options for your decisions on my brainstorming tips page.
5. **Evaluate each choice in terms of its consequences:** Use your standards and judgment criteria to determine the cons and pros of each alternative.
6. **Determine the best alternative:** This is much easier after you go through the above preparation steps.
7. **Put the decision into action:** Transform your decision into specific plan of action steps. Execute your plan.
8. **Evaluate the outcome of your decision and action steps:** What lessons can be learnt? This is an important step for further development of your decision making skills and judgment.

Final remark. In everyday life we often have to make decisions fast, without enough time to systematically go through the above action and thinking steps. In such situations the most effective decision making strategy is to keep an eye on your goals and then let your intuition suggest you the right choice.

Decision Making Model in Five Steps

1. State The Problem: The first and arguably the most important step in the decision making model in five steps is to identifying the problem. Until you have a clear understanding of the problem or decision to be made, it is meaningless to proceed. If the problem is stated incorrectly or unclearly then your decisions will be wrong.

2. Identify Alternatives: Sometimes your only alternatives are to do it or don't do it. Most of the time you will have several feasible alternatives. It is worth doing research to ensure you have as many good alternatives as possible.

3. Evaluate The Alternatives: This is where the analysis begins. You must have some logical approach to rank the alternatives. Two such logical approaches are discussed at Example of a Decision Matrix and at Sample SWOT Analysis. It is important to realize that these analysis methods are only one of the five steps in the decision making model.

4. Make A Decision: You have evaluated your alternatives. Two or more of your high ranked alternatives may be very close in the evaluations. You should eliminate all of the alternatives that were low ranked. Now it is time to go back and examine the inputs you made to evaluation criteria for the close high ranked alternatives. Do you still feel comfortable with the inputs you made? When you have made any changes it is time for some subjection. You have eliminated the alternatives that do not make logical sense. Now it is time to let your subconscious work. Review all the details of the remaining high ranked close alternatives, so they are completely clear in your mind. Completely leave the project alone for a few days. When you return to the project, the decision will likely be very clear in your head. This only works if you have done your homework!

5. Implement Your Decision: A decision has no value unless you implement it. If you are not good with implementation, then find someone that is. Part of the implementation phase is the follow up. The follow up ensures that the implementation sticks.

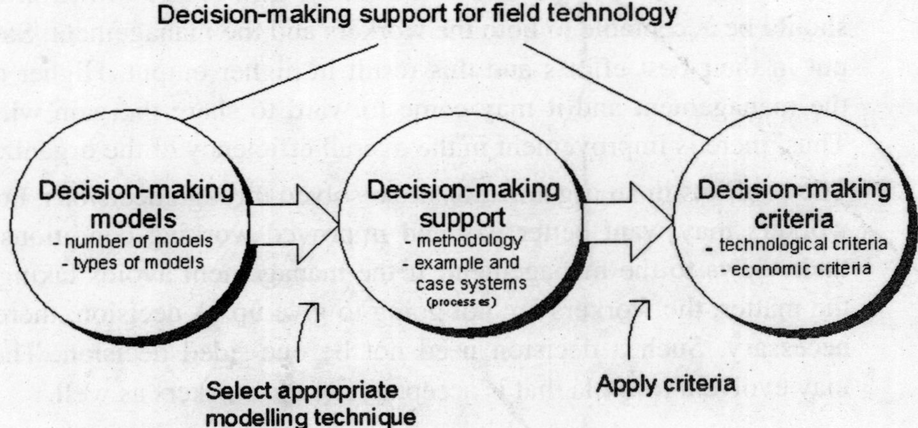

Summary

This decision making model in five steps shows a logical structured methodology for making a decision. The discipline that it provides will guide you to the goal of making good decisions.

"When there are different ways of performing a task, it becomes necessary to find out the best way and that is what decision-making is all about."

The need for decision-making may be stated as follows:

1. Decision-making makes it possible to adopt the best course of action in carrying out a given task. When there are different ways of performing a task, it becomes necessary to find out the best way and that is what decision-making is all about. The course of action finally selected should produce the best results.
2. By choosing the best method of doing any work, decision-making ensures optimum use of the enterprise resources, namely, men, machines, materials and

money. Resources are always scarce and therefore, it is necessary to make a proper use of the same.

3. Decision-making helps to find a solution to any problem in a work place. For example, if an organization faces the problem of low productivity, such a problem cannot be ignored and it becomes necessary to find a remedy. To find a remedy, the actual cause of the problem must be identified after which corrective action may be taken. If negative employee attitude is found to be the root cause of low productivity, the management may have to decide on the right course of action to be adopted to change such a negative attitude.
4. Decision-making helps to identify the best course of action in each given situation and thereby promotes efficiency. The course of action finally selected should be acceptable to both the workers and the management. Satisfied workers put in their best efforts and this result in higher output. Higher output satisfies the management and it may come forward to share the gain with the workers. Thus, there is improvement in the overall efficiency of the organization.
5. The conflicts in an organization are resolved through decisions. For example, the workers may want better pay and improved working conditions and put forth their views to the management. If the management avoids taking a decision on the matter, the workers are not going to give up. A decision, therefore, becomes necessary. Such a decision need not be one-sided decision. The management may evolve a formula that is acceptable to the workers as well.

Types of Decision Making

Structured Decision Making

Structured Decision Making, or SDM, is an organized approach to identifying and evaluating creative options and making choices in complex decision situations.

SDM is designed to **deliver insight to decision makers** about how well their objectives may be satisfied by potential alternative courses of action. It helps find 'win-win' solutions across groups, clarifies the irreducible trade-offs that may exist between alternate potential courses of action and helps to communicate how people view these various options.

SDM uses rigorous methods developed in the decision sciences

- SDM is particularly useful for decisions involving the integration of technical analysis with value-based deliberations

- SDM has been adapted for on-ground decisions and is helpful for facilitating multi-disciplinary technical planning and stakeholder involvement
- The goal of an SDM process is to inform difficult choices, and to make them more transparent and efficient

SDM Steps

Although their exact use in any situation may vary, certain stages of thinking and analysis are central to structured decision making. These stages are often introduced as a series of steps, worked through in a largely linear way but with iteration throughout.

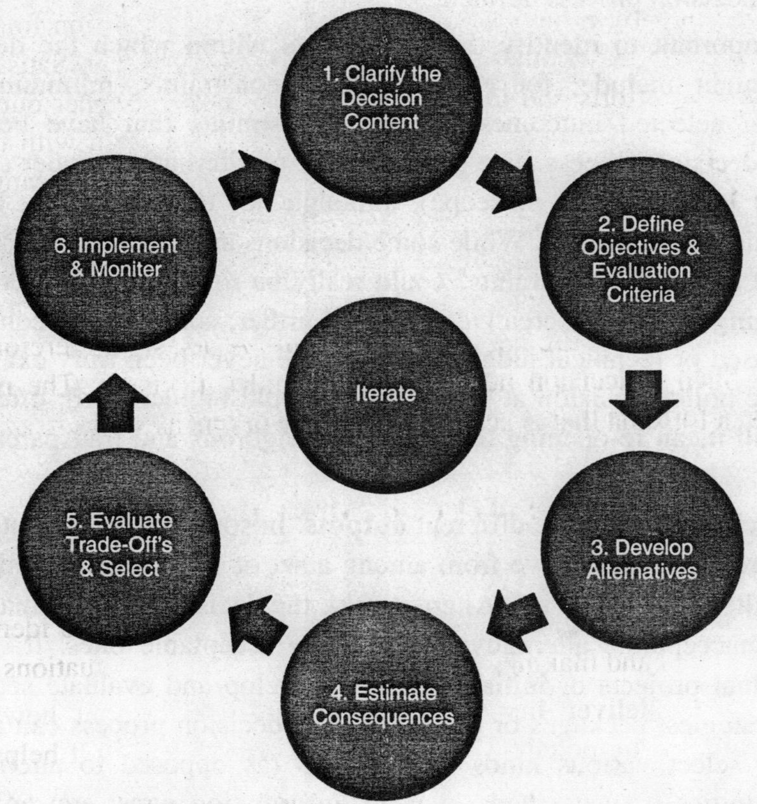

Step 1: Clarify the Decision Context

The first step in good decision making involves defining what question or problem is being addressed and why, identifying who needs to involved and how, establishing scope and bounds for the decision, and clarifying the roles and responsibilities of the decision team.

Clarifying the decision context involves defining **what decision is being made and why**, as well as its **relationship to other decisions** previously made or anticipated. If risks are being ranked, why? How will the information be used in future decisions? If a change in policy or management is under consideration, what are the key drivers of the change and what are the underlying policy objectives? What is the general scope of alternatives under consideration and why? Gaining a clear and common understanding the question is often harder than it seems, but is key to working on the answer.

Roles and responsibilities should be clearly established, including identification of the ultimate decision maker. Stakeholders and key technical experts are identified, and their role in the decision process defined.

It is also important to identify the **constraints** within which the decision will be made. These might include, for example, legal constraints, minimum performance requirements for selected outcomes, or other constraints that have been established through a prior decision process. The general range of alternatives under consideration is identified (what is in and out of scope), although not their specifics. Use caution in defining constraints at this stage. While some decisions are truly constrained by previous decisions, many apparent "constraints" could really be relaxed or dropped to facilitate a more wide-ranging search for creative options. Further, some policy constraints embed critical value-based or technical judgments that have never been truly examined, and are pivotal to public policy decision at hand. These should be identified; often reaching the best solution will mean re-opening these for more rigorous and transparent analysis and discussion.

Different decisions may have different **outputs**. In some cases, the output may be the selection of a preferred alternative from among a set of candidates. In others, it may be the ranking of alternatives in a set. Alternatively, the decision process may simply serve to screen out unacceptable alternatives or identify acceptable ones. It can be used to evaluate individual projects or initiatives, or to develop and evaluate sets of projects - often termed strategies, packages or portfolios. The decision process can also be used to screen, rank or select various kinds of problems (as opposed to alternatives) - e.g., hazards, communities or watersheds in need, information gaps, etc. as a step toward prioritizing where investments of time or resources should be made. In still other cases, what is important is timing, and the decision process will focus on strategies for making sequenced decisions. The output of the decision process should be established up front.

A great way to clarify the decision context is to hold a **"scoping" session** involving key people that quickly move through all the steps of the SDM process in a one-day or half-day workshop. This stage should culminate in a **decision charter** or project plan that summarizes the approach to planning and consultation that will be taken for the decision.

Prepare for the session

Spend some time preparing for the session:

- **Confirm the list of participants** to make sure all the relevant people will be involved.
- **Decide who should facilitate:** for internal scoping sessions, you may be able to do it yourself but for very controversial or complex decisions you may want someone more neutral.
- **Interview key people in advance**, in particular the project initiator and any key people who won't be able to attend.

Hold the session

The session could be anything from a couple of hours to a couple of days depending on the decision problem. You are essentially going to walk the group through a "rough cut" of Steps 1 to 3 with the goal of gaining a common understanding of the decision at hand, and preparing a decision charter to guide the process. Although, it will vary with the situation, you will want to cover most of the following topics at the session:

- **Introduce SDM:** Provide a short summary of the process and share some examples of how it has been applied so that people know what to expect.
- **Clarify the decision context:** What exactly is the decision that will be made? Who will make it: What are the key drivers of the decision process? How is it related to other decisions? What are the constraints on the process? Are they really constraints? Should the "constraints" be tested?
- **Identify objectives:** Brainstorm the issues or concerns people want to see addressed and help the group to turn a loose set of issues into a more concise set of objectives.
- **Identify the range of possible alternatives:** Not the details, but broadly, what is the range of things under consideration? What's in and what's out? Be practical, but also be careful not to be too limiting.
- **Identify information needs:** Sketch out a consequence table with the objectives and alternatives you've identified. You can leave it blank or fill it with plusses and minuses or check marks and Xs. How will you get the information you need to fill in the table. What data or modeling do you have?

What data or analytical capability do you need to gather or develop? Where could you rely on expert judgment?

- **Identify key trade-offs and uncertainties:** What are likely to be the key trade-offs or controversial issues? Where are the key uncertainties? Which ones seem most likely to affect the decision at hand? How could you address the data gaps?
- **Discuss roles and responsibilities:** Who should do what? What is the role of experts and stakeholder consultation? What resources do you need internally (people, timelines, money)? What are the next steps?

Document the Session

The outcomes of the scoping session can be documented in the form of a decision charter, or project plan that summarizes the approach to planning and consultation that will be taken for the decision, and that ensures that resources are allocated to the issues according to the extent to which they are expected to influence the decision.

A common mistake in decision making is to focus on the technical analysis of one or two key outcomes - usually the key drivers of the decision. Yet the driver of a decision - particularly complex resource management decisions - is only one of many important factors that will need careful analysis. A key to a good decision process is recognizing the multi-dimensional nature of the decision up-front and allocating resources to all dimensions of the problem.

Consider for example a species recovery plan. The plan is always driven primarily by concern for the conservation of the species at risk. Managers may be tempted to focus on the scientific analysis needed to assess biological or ecological impacts of proposed management actions on the species of concern. But the proposed actions are likely to have much more wide-ranging social and economic impacts, as well as impacts on other species. By clarifying the decision context early, these impacts will be identified, and resources can be allocated not just to biological studies, but also to a careful assessment of socio-economic impacts.

The outcomes of a scoping session can be summarized in a decision charter or project plan that concisely summarizes:

- The **decision** to be made and its relationship to other decisions or constraints;
- The **range of alternatives** to be considered;
- The **minimum objectives** that must be evaluated;

- **Uncertainties and trade-offs** that are expected to be central to the decision, with a view to prioritizing the allocation of analytical and consultation resources;
- **Other key issues** to be addressed, including institutional, logistical, policy, technical and consultation issues;
- The specific **responsibilities** of technical specialists, stakeholders and decision team members;
- The **role and responsibilities of decision makers** and key review points where their involvement will guide the process;
- The general nature of **technical analysts** expected and in some cases, general terms of reference for specific studies or modeling;
- The nature, scope and approach to **consultation**;
- An **implementation plan**, budget and schedule for the decision process.

The core of SDM is a set of well defined objectives and evaluation criteria. Together they define "what matters" about the decision, drive the search for creative alternatives, and become the framework for comparing alternatives.

Step 2: Define Objectives and Evaluation Criteria

The core of SDM is a set of well defined objectives and evaluation criteria. Together they define "what matters" about the decision, drive the search for creative alternatives, and become the framework for comparing alternatives.

Contents: Objectives

- Introduction
- Brainstorming Objectives
- Stating Objectives
- Separating Means from Ends
- Objectives Hierarchies
- Testing Objectives
- The Difference between Objectives and Targets

Step 3: Develop Alternatives

A range of creative policy or management alternatives designed to address the objectives is developed. Alternatives should reflect substantially different approaches to the problem or different priorities across objectives, and should present decision makers with real options and choices.

Good solutions are not possible without good alternatives. Yet we often move to a single solution, without truly exploring distinct and creative alternatives. Technical teams take on the task of delivering "recommendations" to decision makers. But often these recommendations encompass value judgments that are better made by decision makers. Usually, what decision makers need is good information about a small, carefully thought out set of alternatives - their consequences, key differences (trade-offs) in their consequences, and the response of key stakeholders with respect to these trade-offs. Generating good alternatives is a source of important insights both from a technical perspective and a values perspective.

Most often, an alternative is not a single action, but a set of actions - a 'portfolio', "strategy", or 'package' of individual elements that together provide a comprehensive approach to the decision situation.

In this section we explore:

- The characteristics of good alternatives
- Generating alternatives from objectives and criteria
- Screening
- Developing strategies or portfolios
- Refining

Characteristics of Good Alternatives

Developing good alternatives is an iterative task. Initially, the task is to generate a range of creative alternatives. These alternatives are carefully evaluated technically, in terms of their estimated consequences. They are also evaluated deliberatively, in terms of their relative desirability. New alternatives are generated, joint gains are found and the key trade-offs and uncertainties are highlighted. By the time alternatives are presented to decision makers, they should be:

- **Value-Focused**, meaning that they are explicitly designed to address the fundamental values or ends of the decision - the "things that matter" or "felt needs", as defined by the objectives and the evaluation criteria;
- **Technically Sound**, meaning that in developing alternatives for achieving the objectives, the project team has drawn on the best available information about cause and effect relationships and has designed creative and diverse alternatives based on sound analysis;

- **Clearly and Consistently Defined**, meaning that all alternatives are defined to a sufficient and consistent level of detail using logically consistent assumptions, and that a base case against which all alternatives can be compared has been clearly established;
- **Small in number and high in quality**, meaning that poor (dominated) alternatives have been eliminated and those remaining have been iteratively refined to incorporate new ideas and joint gains;
- **Comprehensive and mutually exclusive**, meaning that individual elements or components of a strategy are combined into complete packages, and that the packages are directly comparable;
- **Able to expose fundamental trade-offs**, meaning that they emphasize rather than hide difficult but unavoidable value-based trade-offs and present real choices for decision makers.
- **Developed collaboratively with the people most affected**, because difficult trade-offs are easier to make and to accept when people believe that a thorough search for good alternatives has been conducted and that the best alternatives are on the table.

Brainstorming Alternatives

The approach should be iterative. It's a mutual learning process. The basic approach involves:

Get the **right people** - Bring together people of all disciplines/backgrounds.

Start with **individual objectives** - For each objective, asks how it could be best supported or achieved. What alternatives look desirable from the perspective of that objective alone?

Then look for **win-wins** - -Logical combinations that meet multiple objectives at once.

Identify the "**givens**" - These are the things you're going to do no matter what - no-regrets, slam-dunks, policy directives…etc.

Examine and welcome trade-offs - There will be **trade-offs**: expose them by creating and evaluating alternatives that support different objectives to different degrees.

Refine the alternatives - the process is iterative. Don't expect to have the best alternatives in the first round. By evaluating the first set, you'll learn and start to develop better ones.

When you're brainstorming alternatives, the emphasis is on creativity and comprehensiveness. Some tips include:

- Ask "how"... how can we achieve the objectives we've set?
- List alternatives first, evaluate them later. Critiquing them as they are offered hinders creativity.
- Consider writing down ideas individually first, then reading them out to the group. This helps to avoid group-think and improves creativity.
- Challenge constraints. Some are real but some are only assumed. Try out alternatives that assume the constraint is not there. If the alternative looks great, start questioning the assumed constraint.
- For example, sometimes it's useful to isolate an objective as a means of removing implicit assumptions about what will be economically or politically feasible ... i.e., "if you were considering only the objective of x, what alternatives might you consider?"
- Ask yourself what others would think. If you presented this alternative to others, what concerns might they have? What alternatives can you think of to address these concerns?

Remember that there are **different kinds of alternatives**:

Process alternatives - rather than prescribing an outcome, prescribe the process and people for deciding the outcome **Information gathering** alternatives - if uncertainty is an issue, buying time to gather more information may be a good alternative.

Screening

Sometimes, it is useful to screen individual actions on the basis of some criterion. For example, if there is a suite of possible actions all of which deliver exactly the same sort of benefit, it may be helpful to screen them on the basis of cost. Emission reduction measures, for example, all delivering some incremental reduction in tonnes of say particulate emission (or for water management, say, TSS), could be screened on the basis of a pre-defined cost per tonne ceiling.

Use caution in screening however. The danger is in prematurely screening out candidate actions that seem unacceptable at first glance. In fact, once combined in a logical strategy, these actions might be completely viable. For example, strategies that involve slightly more risk in managing an endangered species might be unacceptable at first glance, but acceptable if complemented with more intensive monitoring; actions involving greater cost might be acceptable if complemented with appropriate cost-recovery mechanisms.

Some common screens include:

- technical feasibility
- uncertainty
- total cost
- cost-effectiveness
- minimum performance standard
- public acceptability

Be particularly wary of screening on the basis of public acceptability. Often, this is based on someone's presumption about what stakeholders will want. Remember that stakeholders' views change as they learn about the alternatives and the values at stake.

Developing Strategies or Portfolios

A "strategy" or "portfolio" is a logical combination of actions designed to be implemented as a package. Usually in a management or policy context, there are several categories of possible management actions, and creating a strategy involves selecting one or more actions from each category and combining them to create a comprehensive strategy, normally with some kind of theme.

For example, to develop a plan for reducing emissions, a market-based strategy might define a range of market instruments for different sources; a regulatory strategy might establish updated standards, and a hybrid strategy might include a mix of the two.

Alternatively, the "theme" for strategies might also be oriented to specific standards (one strategy may be designed to achieve a 25% reduction in emissions vs. another that is designed to achieve a 50% reduction). This is particularly relevant when there is a continuum of environmental benefits from increasingly strict standards, rather than a clear threshold below which impacts are acceptable and above which they are not; in this case the decision process involves deciding how much to spend for incremental benefits. This is usefully explored through alternatives as it allows exploration of what would it take (in terms of money and other trade-offs) to get the incremental benefits.

In species at risk recovery planning, it might be useful to explore one recovery strategy that aims to maintain the current population of the species and another that aims to increase it (see Strategy Table example). Or, one strategy that achieves 95% probability of recovery, and another that achieves 75% probability.

For emissions management, themes might reflect increasingly stringent emission reduction targets, or increasing degrees of precaution: "50% reduction" vs. "20% reduction", or it might reflect different approaches such as "50% reduction in all emission types" vs. "focus on priority contaminants". This approach to creating and evaluating distinct and alternative strategies allows decision makers to explore the implications - for all objectives - of these different management choices before making firm policy commitments.

A Strategy Table or Portfolio Builder is a visual structuring tool used to develop strategies (or portfolios). The categories of alternatives are listed as column headings, with the possible actions within each category listed below. It is one of the most useful tools for developing creative alternatives when there are dozens of individual actions to choose from.

To develop portfolios:

Brainstorm a list of possible alternatives.

- From this list, group similar alternatives into categories.
- Start a table on a white board. Put the category names as column headings.
- Enter the individual alternatives in the appropriate categories. At this point, you should start to consider how to frame the individual alternatives in a way that will allow you to create useful portfolio themes. It is usually useful to put "do nothing" or "status quo" as the first item in the column. Below this, enter distinctly different alternatives. The level of detail will depend on the context.
- Define several distinct themes that represent either significantly different approaches to achieving the objectives or significantly different relative emphasis on different objectives.
- Select (circle or otherwise highlight) the alternatives that are included in each portfolio and label the portfolio with its theme.

Common Pitfalls & Refining Alternatives

Some common pitfalls when developing alternatives include:

- Anchoring and Tweaking - Starting from the status quo or the first proposed alternative or what's going on in a neighboring jurisdiction and making only minor incremental changes.
- Recommending - Developing a single recommended alternative and trying to get everyone to buy into it.
- Accepting constraints - when they could be removed or softened.

- Considering sunk costs - Choosing alternatives that justify past decisions.
- Avoiding trade-offs - Not presenting an alternative because it would be controversial and/or glossing over difficult value-based choices or trying to eliminate them too soon -
- Not knowing when to quit - You can introduce new alternatives at any time, but at some point (when the incremental gains are not worth the incremental effort) you need to satisfied.

Refining Alternatives and Criteria

You'll never get it all right the first time. The key to good alternatives is iteration. Eliminate clear losers ""dominated alternatives" and look for win-wins or joint gains. You are developing the best possible alternatives for decision makers to consider. Their job is to make value-based judgments, not technical refinements.

Lay out the alternatives in a consequence table. Characterize their impacts on each evaluation criterion, either quantitatively or qualitatively. In the early stages you may have many criteria and many alternatives. Often they can be reduced in number by testing the alternatives for dominance, and testing the criteria for sensitivity.

One alternative is dominated by another if it performs worse on at least one evaluation criterion and the same or worse on every other criterion. It can be removed from further consideration, since there is no constituency that would prefer it.

A criterion is insensitive to the alternatives when its value does not change across the range of alternatives. When a criterion is insensitive to the alternatives - regardless of how important it is in a general sense, if a criterion is insensitive to the alternatives, then it is not useful in selecting among them and can be eliminated for this decision, and for this set of alternatives.

Step 4: Estimate Consequences

Step 4 is an analytical exercise in which the performance of each alternative is estimated in terms of the evaluation criteria developed in Step 2. Care must be taken to determine the focal areas of uncertainty and to ensure that these are represented properly in the analysis.

This step involves estimating the consequences of the alternatives with respect to the evaluation criteria using available knowledge and predictive tools. The assignment of consequences is an analytical task, conducted by technical experts, with in some cases, input from stakeholders in the form of selecting the experts and defining their terms of reference.

There are, in a social and ecological context, inevitably more uncertainties than budgets and timelines can address. One of the key challenges involves identifying which uncertainties are critical to decision making, prioritizing and scoping studies accordingly, and ensuring an honest exploration of key risk factors.

An important principle for ensuring decision quality and for managing project timelines and budgets is a commitment to decision focused information. Data collection and analysis resources should be allocated across the evaluation criteria in proportion to the extent to which they are expected to contribute useful information for decision making. Expert judgment must be considered as a means of filling data gaps, but must, like modeling and data collection, be performed according to accepted standards, incorporating best practices related to expert selection, elicitation protocols, bias avoidance, and treatment of uncertainty, documentation and peer review.

Proposed studies should be scoped to deliver information directly relevant to the decision process; in most cases this will be by improving the estimates of impacts with respect to stated objectives and evaluation criteria, or in some cases, by identifying which criteria are most relevant. Models must be designed as decision aids not as complex mechanistic models of ecological or economic processes – the latter may have benefits in terms of an overall management and/or research plan, but it should not be assumed that such models will be useful for decision making. From a project management perspective, this focus will help to minimize scope creep. In all, the structured decision framework will create linkages among and a focus for tasks such as scientific data collection and modeling as well as consultation, and overall should serve to improve both the relevance and efficiency of information gathering.

Ultimately, objectives, evaluation criteria and alternatives are linked in a consequence table. A consequence table is a kind of "table of contents" that concisely summarizes estimates of the predicted consequences of the alternatives, relative to the objectives and criteria. It exposes key trade-offs among objectives across the alternatives under consideration.

The Consequence Table

A consequence table is a summary matrix illustrating the performance of each alternative on each objective. It can take a variety of forms depending on the complexity of the problem and the depth of analysis that is possible with the resources available.

Simple Consequence Tables

In its simplest form, a consequence table may just use a simple rating (such as a rough and ready 5-star rating) to describe the performance of each alternative. In the example illustrated below, in each case, one star (*) represents the worst performing alternative one objective (e.g. Alternative 1 is the most expensive), and 5 stars (*****) represents the best performing alternative one objective (e.g. Alternative 1 offers the most incremental protection to a species at risk.

* = Worst performing alternative and ***** = Best performing alternative)

	Alternative 1	Alternative 2	Alternative 3
Cost	*	**	*****
Incremental protection offered to spp at Risk	*****	****	*
Inconvenience to recreational users of a resource	*****	***	***

Simple consequence tables can be very useful at the scoping stages of any decision, or may be all that is required in simple or budget-challenged cases. In most cases, they can be developed on a flipchart in a single group session, and can provide many insights about all the other steps in the decision process (e.g. problems with problem definition, which objectives to use etc). Simple consequence tables may also be useful for describing the broad-brush outline of a decision problem to people unfamiliar with the issues.

There are obvious shortcomings with this level of analysis, however. Among these are:

- It provides no sense of how important the difference is between one star and five stars (e.g. what difference in actual protection is offered by "*****" relative to "*"?).
- Because they are sketched in, no rigor is applied in the assignation of the stars.
- There is little scope to undertake a 'trade-off analysis' of people's values based on these ratings (See step 5).

Because of these and other problems, a more quantitative consequence table is usually appropriate.

More Complex Consequence Tables

Below is an example of a consequence table developed to summarize some alternative power supply options to a remote community:

Because real-world consequence tables can be more difficult to take in and understand, a handy trick is to use colour-coding techniques offered by programs such as Microsoft Excel to highlight the difference in performance across alternatives. In this example, "negatives" (e.g. cost) have been shaded with an appropriately-sized red bar and "positives" (e.g. jobs) have been shaded with an appropriately-sized red bar.

Note that in this example, objectives have not been organized hierarchically, though it is easy to see how they could have been. More complex decisions may have two or even three levels of objective hierarchy.

Recognizing & Incorporating Uncertainty

Uncertainty will be an important factor in many decisions. In most cases, the goal of further analysis of uncertainty is not necessarily to reduce it, but to better understand it and its implications for the decision. There are many analytical methods for treating uncertainty (e.g., sensitivity analysis, scenario analysis, Monte carlo simulation, etc.); the choice depends on the technical details of the problem. However, some general guidelines for dealing with uncertainty in the decision process include:

- Document uncertainties and identify those most likely to have an impact on the decision. There will be many uncertainties – only a few will matter.

- Characterize these uncertainties as explicitly and unambiguously as possible. This could be in the form of assigning probabilities to competing hypotheses, or developing probability distributions for uncertain parameters.
- Estimate the consequences of management alternatives probabilistically or under alternative scenarios. If the results are insensitive, either the uncertainty is unimportant in the context of the decision, or the evaluation criteria need to be re-defined to reflect the impact of the uncertainty on the decision.
- When different management alternatives have different distributions of outcomes, some alternatives being more risky than others, ensure that presentation of consequences captures the risk trade-offs. Use graphic representations such as risk profiles to support the consequence table where necessary.
- Report the level of agreement and disagreement among experts; this is important information for decision makers.
- Provide context for understanding the relevance and significance of uncertainty. For example, are results close to a recognized or legal standard? Are results near a threshold of severe impact or near a steep part of a cost curve? In general, what are the consequences of being wrong, and are there alternatives that are more robust than others?

Where relevant, identify options for reducing uncertainty to aid future decisions (e.g., potential research, monitoring, and management initiatives). Ensure that there is in fact some future decision that this reduction in uncertainty will support.

Step 5: Evaluate Trade-Offs and Select

SDM is not a black box, and group discussion should always play a central role in evaluating preferences for alternatives. However, in many cases, preference assessment techniques (such as swing weighting) may be used to help people understand their preferred alternatives.

Although the SDM process often delivers "win-wins" most decision will still involve trade-offs of some kind and hence the next step involves evaluating these trade-offs and making value-based choices. For example, it may be possible to deliver different levels of environmental protection (environmental flows for example) at different levels of investment, or it may be necessary to set priorities among different development objectives (e.g., irrigation versus rural electrification or drinking water provision). These trade-offs will be exposed and efforts will be made to gain an understanding of how the people most affected view them. Who is consulted and who participates in making choices may vary by the decision – with the involvement of senior government officials and national/international civil society organizations for strategic decisions and with their local counterparts for project-level decisions.

Under SDM, it is not the method (SDM) or some external analysis that does the evaluation, but those seen as legitimate stakeholders, based on their own values and their understanding of the values of those affected. The SDM process requires that decision makers make explicit choices about which alternative is preferred. This can be done holistically by reviewing the trade-offs in the consequence table and assigning ranks or preferences to the alternatives directly. In this approach, participants implicitly think about which impacts are more or less important, and which set of trade-offs is more or less acceptable. Alternatively, structured methods for more explicitly weighting the evaluation criteria, making trade-offs, and scoring and ranking the alternatives may be used.

The SDM process is designed to support, but not require, such structured preference assessment methods. When they are used, they should be designed to provide insight and guidance to decision makers, rather than to prescribe a formulaic answer. They can be used to focus deliberations on productive areas and maintain a performance-based dialogue, rather than a positional one. Structured methods can be demanding, but participants are generally enthusiastic about exploring their own trade-offs, learning about the values and choices of others, and knowing that (in the case of stakeholders) their input has been systematically recorded and taken to decision makers. At minimum, an emphasis on deliberative quality requires that stakeholders and decision makers involved at this stage should be expected to:

- demonstrate an understanding of the decision scope and context, how it is related to other decisions, why the problem matters, and for whom the consequences are most relevant;
- demonstrate an understanding of the evaluation criteria, the alternatives and the key trade-offs among the alternatives;
- demonstrate an understanding of key uncertainties and their impact on the performance of the alternatives;

- Articulate their preferences for the alternatives in terms of the trade-offs that are presented in the consequence table.

While stakeholder consensus is desirable in the SDM process, it is not mandatory. Areas of agreement and disagreement among stakeholders and the reasons for disagreement should be documented and presented to decision makers. To the extent that there is a significant difference between the views of technical specialists and the views of non-technical stakeholders, these differences and the reasons for them should be highlighted.

Step 6: Implement and Monitor

The last step in the decision process then is to identify mechanisms for on-going monitoring to ensure accountability with respect to on-ground results, research to improve the information base for future decisions, and a review mechanism so that new information can be incorporated into future decisions.

Unstructured Decision Making

Unstructured decision making is a dynamic process where an individual must create an alternative because one is not available or provided. In this type of a decision, an individual may not have formed preferences or may not know the path to arrive at a solution. As opposed to selecting from existing alternatives, little research examines when decision makers create an alternative. Electronic commerce websites allow individuals to create a product by customizing it. A web-based simulation called Interactive Choice was developed for the investigation.

It is an interactive naturalistic decision space permitting experimental controls such as random placement of participants into conditions and random display of stimuli. Participants customized three products (pizza, cell phones, and shoes). Building on theoretical foundations of unfolding model and Image Theory, a model asserts the presentation of the information and preparation of the decision maker influences a decision maker. A phased examination explores decision makers' cognitive processes by measuring participants' evaluations of the product created and the process to create it. In the first phase, three experiments find, contrary to previous independent investigations, participants rarely retain a pre-selected default value. Logistic regression reveals that the odds ratio of predicting default retention is dependent on product type.

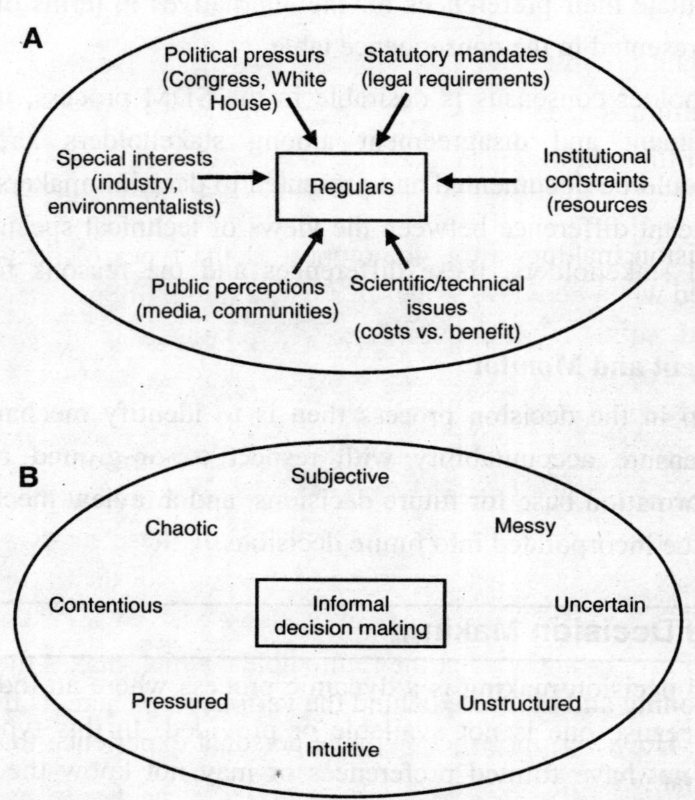

In the second phase, results identify that problem solving instructions influence decision making. Analyses of multidimensional scaling and cluster analysis reveal patterns for default retention and problem solving instructions that define an electronic decision aid called Choice Builder. The dissertation suggests that when an individual creates a product, he or she has more control over the process that subsequently reduces the influence of the default. A new theoretical foundation is proposed identifying that for unstructured decisions individuals construct both decision strategies and preferences while creating an alternative. With an active process of acquiring and evaluating information, an individual forms a decision strategy and updates preferences to achieve an ideal outcome. This dissertation makes four contributions that include 1) a research tool, Interactive Choice, for exploration, 2) the identification of cognitive processes involved, 3) a proposal of a new theoretical approach, and 4) an electronic decision aid, Choice Builder.

There are **many types of decision making** and these can be easily categorized into the following 4 groups:

- Rational

- Intuitive
- Recognition primed decision making
- The ultimate decision making model

Let's consider these in more detail.

Rational

Rational decision making is the commonest of the types of decision making that is taught and learned when people consider that they want to improve their decision making. These are **logical, sequential** models where the emphasis is on listing many potential options and then working out which is the best. Often the pros and cons of each option are also listed and scored in order of importance.

The rational aspect indicates that there is considerable reasoning and thinking done in order to select the optimum choice. Because we put such a heavy emphasis on thinking and getting it right in our society, there are many of these models and they are very popular. People like to know what the steps are and many of these models have steps that are done in order.

People would love to know what the future holds, which makes these models popular. Because the reasoning and rationale behind the various steps here, is that if you do x, then y should happen. However, most people have personal experience that the world usually doesn't operate that way!

Intuitive

The second of the types of decision making are the intuitive models. The idea here is that there may be absolutely no reason or logic to the decision making process. Instead, there is an inner knowing, or intuition, or some kind of sense of what the right thing to do is.

And there are probably as many intuitive types of decision making as there are people. People can feel it in their heart, or in their bones, or in their gut and so on. There are also a variety of ways for people to receive information, either in pictures or words or voices.

People talk about extra sensory perception as well. However, they are still actually picking up the information through their five senses. Clairsentience is where people feel things, clairaudience is hearing things and clairvoyance is seeing things.

And of course we have phrases such as 'I smell a rat', ' it smells fishy' and 'I can taste success ahead'.

Other types of decision making in the intuitive category might include tossing a coin, throwing dice, tarot cards, astrology, and so on.

Decision wheels are usually more humorous than intuitive but they do have a serious application.

Recognition primed...

Gary Klein has spent considerable time studying human decision making and his results are very interesting. He believes that we make **90 to 95% of our decisions** in a pattern recognition way. He suggests that what we actually do is gather information from our environment in relation to the decision we want to make. We then pick an option that we think will work. We **rehearse it mentally** and if we still think it will work, we go ahead.

If it does not work mentally, we choose another option and run that through in our head instead. If that seems to work, we go with that one. We pick scenarios one by one, mentally check them out, and as soon as we find one that works, we choose it.

He also points out that as we get more experience, we can recognize more patterns, and we make better choices more quickly.

Of interest here is that the military in many countries have adapted his methods because they are considerably more effective than either of the types of decision making we've discussed already. In fact, you could say that his model is a combination of the above two types of decision making.

The ultimate...

In terms of making decisions for your own life, this last of the types of decision making is my favored model. It includes the ideas of the recognition primed decision making model and much more.

Firstly, before you even make a decision, you establish how and who you want to be. You obviously want to be in a good state so that you can make good decisions. But you also want to **be true to yourself**, and that means knowing who 'yourself' is.

Once you learn how to be solid and centered, then and only then, do you make decisions. And the decisions are always organized around staying true to yourself and doing things that are good for and aligned who you are. Doing things that are on your own path, and that allow you to become **even more solid and centered...**

The whole model is organized around having the kinds of experiences that you want to be having, and even when the world upsets your plans with its own, you learn how to use this and manipulate it so that **you still get what you want** anyway...

Organizational Decision

The organizational decision making process involves proper and efficient implementation of strategic plans and methods to achieve desired business objective. Let's examine some key areas that affect the overall process.

Often one difficulty facing an organization is that multiple divisions are involved in the overall decision making process. Making a decision can have different implications for each respective division. Gaining agreement from all stakeholders can be a challenge. When a companies overall strategy depends on the support of all business units, organization wide support is crucial.

Key strategic evaluation and planning is crucial. This planning needs to address the overall strategic goals of the organization but also the end effects that impact workers outside of the decision chain. Organizational dysfunction and worker resistance can result if proper thought and attention is not directed towards front line efforts. Organizational change professional deal specifically with these issues. Unifying the company at all levels is very important. A failure to calculate and anticipate the implications of key decisions can derail a company's goals and objectives.

Organizational change management and planning processes seek to address the implications that a change in one input can have on the corresponding output. The evaluation and process evaluation that comprises part of the change management approach seeks to measure and anticipate the effect strategic decisions will have on company resources and labor. This permits the careful monitoring and benchmarking to adjust process as required to more closely align organizational objectives with desired outcomes.

With the businesses of today facing shortened product lifecycles, organizations are facing intense competitive pressures to build market share to stay ahead of rivals. Process changes, the introduction of new and improved disruptive technologies are forcing companies to adapt new business goals and objectives in shortened timeframes. This places corresponding stresses on all levels of the organization. As business units are forced to respond to top level management goals, flexibility has become a modern day requirement.

Organizational change management is a growing discipline to help managers become better positioned to understand how the decision making process can affect individuals at a cognitive level. Performance improvement is intimately linked to this. As companies transition into the future, change management is expected to become increasingly important.

Enterprise Decision Management

Enterprise decision management, commonly abbreviated "EDM", entails all aspects of managing automated decision design and deployment that an organization uses to manage its interactions with customers, employees and suppliers. Computerization has changed the way organizations are approaching their decision-making because it has enabled "information-based decisions" - decisions based on analysis of historical behavioral data, prior decisions, and their outcomes.

Enterprise decision management is described as an "emerging important discipline, due to an increasing need to automate high-volume decisions across the enterprise and to impart precision, consistency, and agility in the decision-making process." EDM is implemented "via the use of rule-based system and analytic models for enabling high-volume, automated decision making."

Organizations seek to improve their decision yield (the value created through each decision) by deploying business processes and software solutions that better manage the tradeoffs between precision, consistency, agility, speed, and cost of decision-making within organizations. The concept of decision yield focuses on five key attributes of decision-making: more targeted decisions (precision); in the same way, over and over again (consistency); while being able to adapt "on-the-fly" (business agility) while reducing cost and improving speed, is an overall metric for how well an organization is making a particular decision.

Organizations are adopting EDM technology and business processes because they need a higher return from previous infrastructure investments, are dealing with increasing business decision complexity, face competitive pressure for more sophisticated decisions and because increasingly short windows of competitive advantage means that the speed of business is outpacing speed of information technology to react.

The topic of EDM has recently been extensively covered in the book "Smart (Enough) System", which argues that applying the approach to operational decisions is an effective way to make information system smart enough to be useful (as distinct from intelligent in the sense of Artificial Intelligence).[3]

Other terms used include "intelligent process automation" (where EDM is combined with business process management) and "decision Management".

Planning for Decision Making

While decision making without planning is fairly common, it is often not pretty. The terms used to describe it--crisis management, putting out fires, seat-of-the-pants governing--all reveal the inelegance and awkwardness of this way of life. Planning allows decisions to be made in a much more comfortable and intelligent way. Planning even makes decisions easier by providing guidelines and goals for the decision. We might even say that planning is a type of decision simplification technique (see the discussion of these techniques below).

Decision makers will find four major benefits to planning:

1. Planning allows the establishment of independent goals. The vision which will shape the decisions is set apart from surrounding events. Decisions are not made only as reactions to external stimuli. "Management by firefighting" is replaced by a conscious and directed series of choices. Managers now steer the organization, individuals now steer their lives, rather than being steered by external forces. Sometimes the difference between planning and not planning is described as "proactive" (taking control of the situation) versus "reactive" (responding to stimuli).

2. Planning provides a standard of measurement. A plan provides something to measure against, so that you can discover whether or not you are achieving or heading toward your goals. As the proverb says, *if you don't know where you're going, it doesn't matter which way you go.*

3. Planning converts values to action. When you are faced with a decision, you can consult your plan and determine which decision will help advance your plan best. Decisions made under the guidance of planning can work together in a coherent way to advance company or individual goals.

Planning is useful in emergency situations, too. When a crisis arises, a little thought about the overall plan will help determine which decision to make that will not only help resolve the crisis but will also help advance the overall plan. Without a plan, crises are dealt with haphazardly and decisions are made which may ultimately be in conflict with each other.

4. Planning allows limited resources to be committed in an orderly way. Budgets, time, effort, manpower--all are limited. Their best use can be made when a plan governs their use.

- A simple example would be planning to buy a house or a car. Rather than having to decide between buying the item right now with all cash or never having it, you can plan to buy it over several years by making payments. Or, you might combine this plan with the plan to buy a smaller house and add rooms later as they could be afforded. By planning you can thus accomplish things that might otherwise look impossible.

Decision Levels

We all recognize that some decisions are more important than others, whether in their immediate impact or long term significance. As a means of understanding the significance of a decision so that we can know how much time and resources to spend on it, three levels of decision have been identified:

1. Strategic. Strategic decisions are the highest level. Here a decision concerns general direction, long term goals, philosophies and values. These decisions are the least structured and most imaginative; they are the most risky and of the most uncertain outcome, partly because they reach so far into the future and partly because they are of such importance.

For example: Decisions about what to do with your life, what to learn, or what methods to use to gain knowledge (travel, work, and school) would be strategic. Whether to produce a low priced product and gain market share or produce a high priced product for a niche market would be a strategic decision.

2. Tactical. Tactical decisions support strategic decisions. They tend to be medium range, medium significance, with moderate consequences.

For example: If your strategic decision were to become a forest ranger, a tactical decision would include where to go to school and what books to read. Or if your company decided to produce a low priced product, a tactical decision might be to build a new factory to produce them at a low manufacturing cost.

3. Operational. These are every day decisions, used to support tactical decisions. They are often made with little thought and are structured. Their impact is immediate, short term, short range, and usually low cost. The consequences of a bad operational decision will be minimal, although a series of bad or sloppy operational decisions can cause harm. Operational decisions can be preprogrammed, pre-made, or set out clearly in policy manuals.

For example: If your tactical decision is to read some books on forestry, your operational decision would involve where to shop for the books. You might have a personal policy of shopping for books at a certain store or two. Thus, the operational decision is highly structured: "Whenever books are needed, look at Joe's Books."

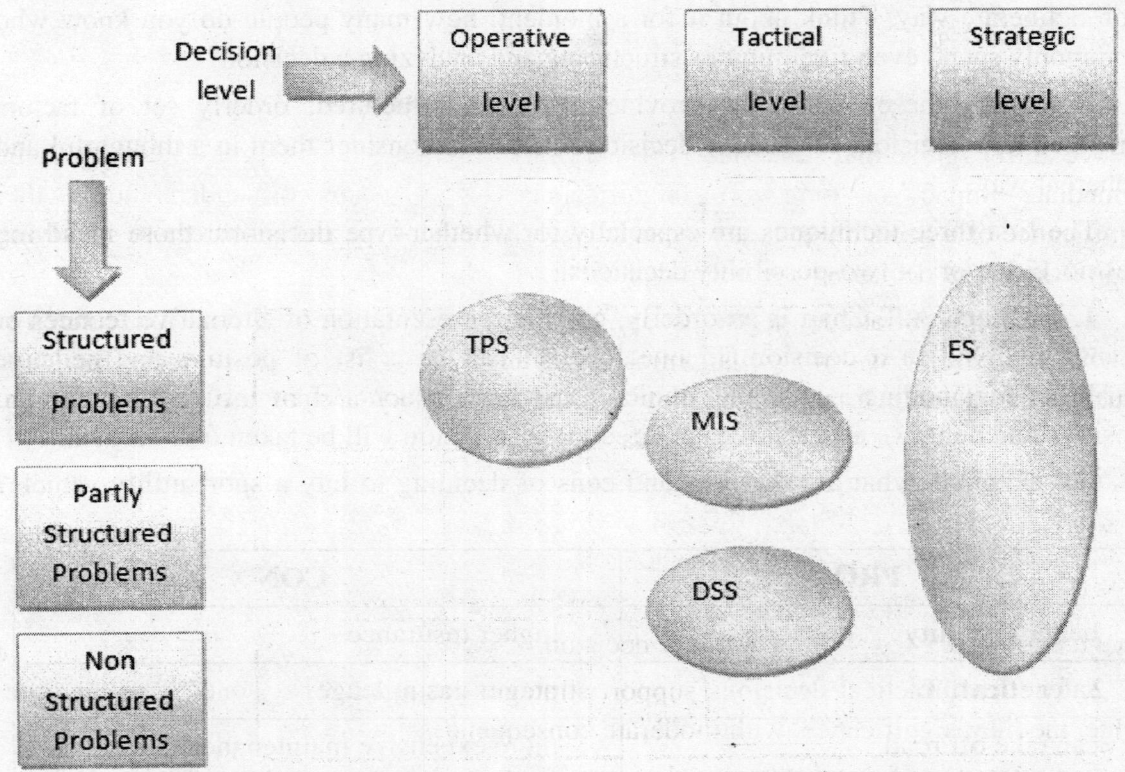

Decision level

An important comment should be made here. Issues should be examined and decisions should be made at all of these levels. If you discover that nearly all of your thinking and decision making is taking place at the operational level, then you are probably not doing enough strategic thinking and planning. As a result you will lead a reactive life, responding only to the forces around you and never getting control of your life, your direction or your goals.

SOME USEFUL TECHNIQUES FOR DECISION MAKING

This is a list of easy, practical techniques that can be applied to simple or complex decisions. They share the assumption that circumspect analysis is the key to making good decisions. Many decisions are made with too little information and too little thought, in a non-deliberate way. Think about it for a moment: how many people do you know who commonly spend even five minutes structuring and analyzing a decision?

Note how these techniques provide a visible, structured, orderly set of factors involved in a decision, so that the decision maker can consider them in a thoughtful and coherent way.

The first three techniques are especially for whether-type decisions, those involving yes/no, either/or, or two-possibility decisions.

1. T-Chart. A T-Chart is an orderly, graphic representation of alternative features or points involved in a decision. In one form, it can be a list of positive and negative attributes surrounding a particular choice. Drawing up such a chart insures that both the positive and negative aspects of each direction or decision will be taken into account.

For example, what are the pros and cons of deciding to buy a sport utility vehicle?

PRO	CON
better visibility	higher insurance
safer structure	poorer gas mileage
can take off road	more expensive maintenance

In another form, two possible choices are listed, with the good points or arguments or effects listed for each. Suppose your company is trying to decide whether to create its own advertising or hire an agency.

Use Outside Agency	Write Ads In-House
professional work	faster product
expertise of ideas	better knowledge of product
media connections	use same ad in flyers

To fill out this latter form, more than two choices can be included, and a list of negatives for each choice can be added as well.

2. PMI. Edward de Bono refines the T-Chart idea into a three part structure, which he calls PMI for plus, minus, and interesting. Here you first list all the plus or good points of the idea, then all the minus or bad points, and finally all the interesting points--consequences, areas of curiosity or uncertainty, or attributes that you simply don't care to view as either good or bad at this point (consequences that some people might view as good and others might view as bad, for example). The "interesting" category also allows exploration of the idea or choice outside the context of judgment--you don't have to evaluate the attribute into a positive or negative category.

As simple as this technique seems to be, and as often as others will tell you, "Well, of course, everyone does that all the time," this is a very powerful but much neglected technique. Most people believe they list the pluses and minuses of a decision before making it, but in actual practice, many people make a decision or form an opinion before they consider the evidence in an orderly way. Only after they make a decision do they hunt around for reasons to support it.

Considering the evidence on both (or all) sides before you commit yourself emotionally and psychologically to a position will have a major impact on the quality of your decision making.

For example, suppose you are on a jury and must decide the guilt or innocence of the accused (or to hold for the plaintiff or defendant in a civil trial, if you prefer). What happens on most juries is that after the members meet in the room and choose a foreman, a preliminary vote is taken. "Let's find our where we all stand now," the foreman might say. Unfortunately, beginning a decision making session this way creates more problems than it solves. Before the jurors have had time to think over the issues or to discuss them to clarify the facts, they are asked to give their opinions. Giving an opinion is, in our society, accompanied by an ego investment, because we do not like to be wrong. As a result, each juror becomes emotionally committed to his first opinion and will very often proceed to look for arguments and facts that support this opinion (and hence defend his ego), rather than listen thoughtfully to the facts and decide the case on its merits.

If, on the other hand, the foreman said, "Instead of a preliminary vote on the case, let's work together to draw up a list, first of all the evidence that would argue for the defendant's guilt, then all the evidence that would argue for his innocence. And as we make the lists, we can also write down facts that are interesting but that don't necessarily argue either for guilt or innocence." Now all the jurors will work together, have the opportunity to ask questions and resolve doubts, consider evidence they might not otherwise have remembered, and can change their minds back and forth as many times as they want, all without a threat to their egos or their need to be correct. Notice that the PMI technique turns the jurors into collaborators, working together, instead of competitive debaters arguing for victory (rather than truth).

As another example, suppose that you are on the board of a missionary and relief organization and your group has decided to improve the roads in a small South American village. You as chairman must present the alternatives, which are that you have enough gravel either to pave half the roads completely or to fix the worst spots and holes in all the roads. If you stand up and say, "Well that's it; what do you think?" you'll get the usual off-the-cuff first impression opinions, backed up later by whatever arguments those who have committed to them can dredge up. But suppose you say, "Let's make two PMI lists, first one of all the good and bad points for paving half the roads completely, and then one for the good and bad of fixing the worst problems on all the roads. Then we will have all the ideas and reasons before us when we make a decision." This way, you will be pooling your ideas and working together without the threat of being wrong or the need to defend your first opinion.

Yes, this simple technique of deliberate pro and con identification is extremely powerful and extremely neglected. Get into the habit of using it and you'll see your decision making quality improve remarkably.

What is Decision Making?

Some Definitions

1. Decision making is the study of identifying and choosing alternatives based on the values and preferences of the decision maker: Making a decision implies that there are alternative choices to be considered, and in such a case we want not only to identify as many of these alternatives as possible but to choose the one that (1) has the highest probability of success or effectiveness.

2. Best fits with our goals, desires, lifestyle, values, and so on: Decision making is the process of sufficiently reducing uncertainty and doubt about alternatives to allow a reasonable choice to be made from among them.

This definition stresses the information-gathering function of decision making. It should be noted here that uncertainty is *reduced* rather than eliminated. Very few decisions are made with absolute certainty because complete knowledge about all the alternatives is seldom possible. Thus, every decision involves a certain amount of risk. If there is no uncertainty, you do not have a decision; you have an algorithm-- a set of steps or a recipe that is followed to bring about a fixed result.

Kinds of Decisions

There are several basic kinds of decisions.

1. Decisions whether: This is the yes/no, either/or decision that must be made before we proceed with the selection of an alternative. Should I buy a new TV? Should I travel this summer? Decisions whether are made by weighing reasons pro and cons. The PMI technique discussed in the next chapter is ideal for this kind of decision.

It is important to be aware of having made a decision whether, since too often we assume that decision making begins with the identification of alternatives, *assuming that the decision to choose one has already been made.*

2. Decisions which: These decisions involve a choice of one or more alternatives from among a set of possibilities, the choice being based on how well each alternative measures up to a set of predefined criteria.

3. Contingent decisions: These are decisions that have been made but put on hold until some condition is met.

For example, I have decided to buy that car **if** I can get it for the right price; I have decided to write that article **if** I can work the necessary time for it into my schedule. OR even, we'll take the route through the valley if we can control the ridge and if we detect no enemy activity to the north.

Most people carry around a set of already made, contingent decisions, just waiting for the right conditions or opportunity to arise. Time, energy, price, availability, opportunity, encouragement--all these factors can figure into the necessary conditions that need to be met before we can act on our decision. Some contingent decisions are unstated or even exist below the awareness of the decision maker. These are the type that occurs when we seize opportunity. We don't walk around thinking, "If I see a new laser printer for $38, I'll buy it," but if we happen upon a deal like that and we have been contemplating getting a new printer, the decision is made quickly. Decisions made in sports and warfare is like this. The best contingent and opportunistic decisions are made by the prepared mind· one that has thought about criteria and alternatives in the past.

Decision Making is a Recursive Process

A critical factor that decision theorists sometimes neglect to emphasize is that in spite of the way the process is presented on paper, **decision making is a nonlinear', recursive process.** That is, most decisions are made by moving back and forth between the choice of criteria (the characteristics we want our choice to meet) and the identification of alternatives (the possibilities we can choose from among). The alternatives available influence the criteria we apply to them, and similarly the criteria we establish influence the alternatives we will consider. Let's look at an example to clarify this.

Suppose someone wants to decide, Should I get married? Notice that this is a decision whether. A linear approach to decision making would be to decide this question by weighing the reasons pro and cons (what are the benefits and drawbacks of getting married) and then to move to the next part of the process, the identification of criteria (supportive, easy going, competent, affectionate, etc.). Next, we would identify alternatives likely to have these criteria (Kathy, Jennifer, Michelle, Julie, etc.). Finally we would evaluate each alternative according to the criteria and choose the one that best meets the criteria. We would thus have a scheme like this:

Decision whether ... select criteria ... identify alternatives ... match criteria to alternatives ... make choice

However, the fact is that our decision whether to get married may really be a contingent decision. "I'll get married **if** I can find the right person." It will thus be influenced by the identification of alternatives, which we usually think of as a later step in the process. Similarly, suppose we have arrived at the "identify alternatives" stage of the process when we discover that Jennifer (one of the girls identified as an alternative) has a wonderful personality characteristic that we had not even thought of before, but that we now really want to have in a wife. We immediately add that characteristic to our criteria. Thus, the decision making process continues to move back and forth, around and around as it progresses in what will eventually be a linear direction but which in its actual workings is highly recursive.

Key point, then, is that the characteristics of the alternatives we discover will often revise the criteria we have previously identified.

The Components of Decision Making

The Decision Environment

Every decision is made within a decision environment, which is defined as the collection of information, alternatives, values, and preferences *available at the time of the decision.* An ideal decision environment would include all possible information, all of it accurate, and every possible alternative. However, both information and alternatives are constrained because the time and effort to gain information or identify alternatives are limited. The time constraint simply means that a decision must be made by a certain time. The effort constraint reflects the limits of manpower, money, and priorities. (You wouldn't want to spend three hours and half a tank of gas trying to find the very best parking place at the mall.) Since decisions must be made within this constrained environment, we can say that *the major challenge of decision making is uncertainty,* and a major goal of decision analysis is to reduce uncertainty. We can almost never have all information needed to make a decision with certainty, so most decisions involve an undeniable amount of risk.

The fact that decisions must be made within a limiting decision environment suggests two things. First, it explains why hindsight is so much more accurate and better at making decisions that foresight. As time passes, the decision environment continues to grow and expand. New information and new alternatives appear--even after the decision must be made. Armed with new information after the fact, the hindsighters can many times look back and make a much better decision than the original maker, *because the decision environment has continued to expand.*

The second thing suggested by the decision-within-an-environment idea follows from the above point. Since the decision environment continues to expand as time passes, it is often advisable to put off making a decision until close to the deadline. Information and alternatives continue to grow as time passes, so to have access to the most information and to the best alternatives, do not make the decision too soon. Now, since we are dealing with real life, it is obvious that some alternatives might no longer be available if too much time passes; that is a tension we have to work with, a tension that helps to shape the cutoff date for the decision.

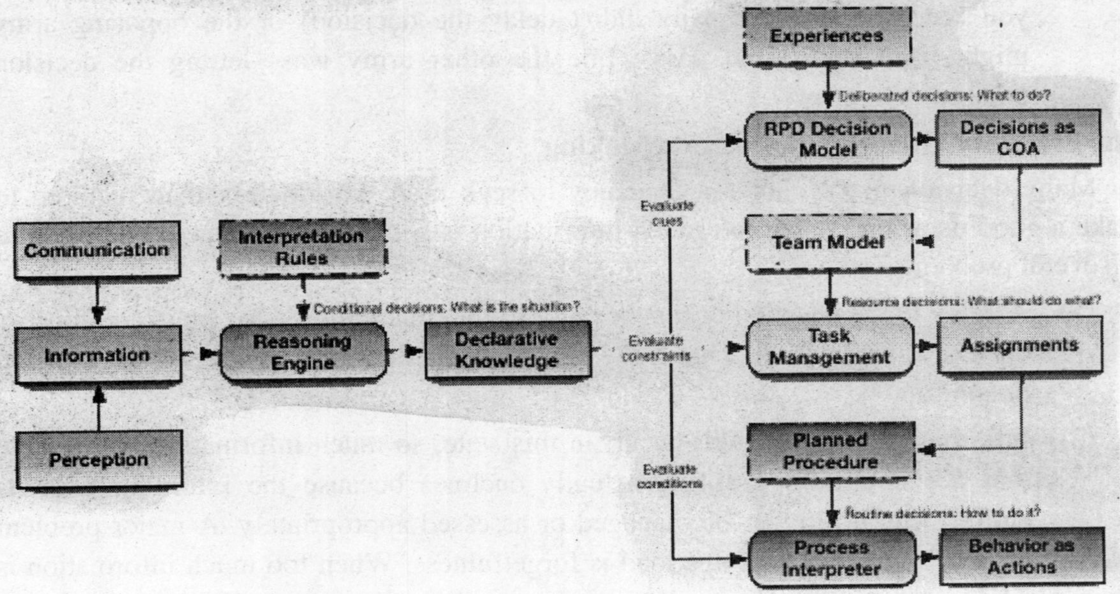

Delaying a decision as long as reasonably possible, then, provides three benefits:

- The decision environment will be larger, providing more information. There is also time for more thoughtful and extended analysis.
- New alternatives might be recognized or created. Version 2.0 might be released.
- The decision maker's preferences might change. With further thought, wisdom, and maturity, you may decide not to buy car X and instead to buy car Y.

And delaying a decision involves several risks:

1. As the decision environment continues to grow, the decision maker might become overwhelmed with too much information and either makes a poorer decision or else face decision paralysis.
2. Some alternatives might become unavailable because of events occurring during the delay. In a few cases, where the decision was between two alternatives (attack the pass or circle around behind the large rock), both alternatives might become unavailable, leaving the decision maker with nothing. And we have all had the experience of seeing some amazing bargain only to hesitate and find that when we go back to buy the item, it is sold out.
3. In a competitive environment, a faster rival might make the decision and gain advantage. Another manufacturer might bring a similar product to market before you (because that company didn't delay the decision) or the opposing army might have seized the pass while the other army was "letting the decision environment grow."

The Effects of Quantity on Decision Making

Many decision makers have a tendency to seek more information than required to make a good decision. When too much information is sought and obtained, one or more of several problems can arise.

(1) A delay in the decision occurs because of the time required to obtain and process the extra information. This delay could impair the effectiveness of the decision or solution.

(2) Information overload will occur. In this state, so much information is available that decision-making ability actually declines because the information in its entirety can no longer be managed or assessed appropriately. A major problem caused by information overload is forgetfulness. When too much information is taken into memory, especially in a short period of time, some of the information (often that received early on) will be pushed out.

The example is sometimes given of the man who spent the day at an information-heavy seminar. At the end of the day, he was not only unable to remember the first half of the seminar but he had also forgotten where he parked his car that morning.

(3) Selective use of the information will occur. That is, the decision maker will choose from among all the information available only those facts which support a preconceived solution or position.

(4) Mental fatigue occurs, which results in slower work or poor quality work.

(5) Decision fatigue occurs where the decision maker tires of making decisions. Often the result is fast, careless decisions or even decision paralysis--no decisions are made at all.

The quantity of information that can be processed by the human mind is limited. Unless information is consciously selected, processing will be biased toward the first part of the information received. After that, the mind tires and begins to ignore subsequent information or forget earlier information. (Have you ever gone shopping for something where you looked at many alternatives--cars, knives, phones, TVs--only to decide that you liked the first one best?)

Decision Streams

A common misconception about decision making is that decisions are made in isolation from each other: you gather information, explore alternatives, and make a choice, without regard to anything that has gone before. The fact is, decisions are made in a context of other decisions. The typical metaphor used to explain this is that of a stream. There is a stream of decisions surrounding a given decision, many decisions made earlier have led up to this decision and made it both possible and limited. Many other decisions will follow from it.

Another way to describe this situation is to say that most decisions involve a choice from a group of preselected alternatives, made available to us from the universe of alternatives by the previous decisions we have made. Previous decisions have "activated" or "made operable" certain alternatives and "deactivated" or "made inoperable" others.

For example, when you decide to go to the park, your decision has been enabled by many previous decisions. You had to decide to live near the park; you had to decide to buy a car or learn about bus routes, and so on. And your previous decisions have constrained your subsequent ones: you can't decide to go to a park this afternoon if it is three states away. By deciding to live where you do, you have both enabled and disabled a whole series of other decisions.

As another example, when you enter a store to buy a DVD player or TV, you are faced with the preselected alternatives stocked by the store. There may be 200 models available in the universe of models, but you will be choosing from, say, only a dozen. In this case, your decision has been constrained by the decisions made by others about which models to carry.

We might say, then, that every decision

(1) follows from previous decisions,

(2) Enables many future decisions, and

(3) Prevents other future decisions.

People who have trouble making decisions are sometimes trapped by the constraining nature of decision making. Every decision you make precludes other decisions, and therefore might be said to cause a loss of freedom. If you decide to marry Terry, you no longer can decide to marry Shawn. However, just as making a decision causes a loss of freedom, it also creates new freedom, new choices and new possibilities. So making a decision is liberating as well as constraining. And a decision left unmade will often result in a decision by default or a decision being made for you.

It is important to realize that every decision you make affects the decision stream and the collections of alternatives available to you both immediately and in the future. In other words, decisions have far reaching consequences.

Concepts and Definitions

1. Information: This is knowledge about the decision, the effects of its alternatives, the probability of each alternative, and so forth. A major point to make here is that while substantial information is desirable, the statement that "the more information, the better" is not true. Too much information can actually reduce the quality of a decision. See the discussion on The Effects of Quantity on Decision Making above.

2. Alternatives: These are the possibilities one has to choose from. Alternatives can be identified (that is, searched for and located) or even developed (created where they did not previously exist). Merely searching for preexisting alternatives will result in less effective decision making.

3. Criteria: These are the characteristics or requirements that each alternative must possess to a greater or lesser extent. Usually the alternatives are rated on how well they possess each criterion. For example, alternative Toyota ranks an 8 on the criterion of economy, while alternative Buick ranks a 6 on the same criterion.

4. Goals: What is it you want to accomplish? Strangely enough, many decision makers collect a bunch of alternatives (say cars to buy or people to marry) and then ask, "Which should I choose?" without thinking first of what their goals are, what overall objective they want to achieve. Next time you find yourself asking, "What should I do? What should I choose?" ask yourself first, "What are my goals?"

A component of goal identification should be included in every instance of decision analysis.

5. Value: Value refers to how desirable a particular outcome is, the value of the alternative, whether in dollars, satisfaction, or other benefit.

6. Preferences: These reflect the philosophy and moral hierarchy of the decision maker. We could say that they are the decision maker's "values," but that might be confusing with the other use of the word, above. If we could use that word here, we would say that personal values dictate preferences. Some people prefer excitement to calmness, certainty to risk, efficiency to esthetics, quality to quantity, and so on. Thus, when one person chooses to ride the wildest roller coaster in the park and another chooses a mild ride, both may be making good decisions, if based on their individual preferences.

7. Decision Quality: This is a rating of whether a decision is good or bad. A good decision is a logical one based on the available information and reflecting the preferences of the decision maker.

The important concept to grasp here is that the quality of a decision is not related to its outcome: a good decision can have either a good or a bad outcome. Similarly, a bad decision (one not based on adequate information or not reflecting the decision maker's preferences) can still have a good outcome.

For example, if you do extensive analysis and carefully decide on a certain investment based on what you know about its risks and your preferences, then your decision is a good one, even though you may lose money on the investment. Similarly, if you throw a dart at a listing of stocks and buy the one the dart hits, your decision is a bad one, even though the stock may go up in value.

Good decisions that result in bad outcomes should thus not be cause for guilt or recrimination. If you decide to take the scenic route based on what you know of the road (reasonably safe, not heavily traveled) and your preferences (minimal risk, prefer scenery over early arrival), then your decision is a good one, even though you might happen to get in an accident, or have a flat tire in the middle of nowhere. It is not justified to say, "Well, this was a bad decision."

In judging the quality of a decision, in addition to the concerns of logic, use of information and alternatives, three other considerations come into play:

A. The decision must meet the stated objectives most thoroughly and completely. How well does the alternative chosen meet the goals identified?

B. The decision must meet the stated objectives most efficiently, with concern over cost, energy, side effects. Are there negative consequences to the alternative that make that choice less desirable? We sometimes overlook this consideration in our search for thrills.

C. The decision must take into account valuable byproducts or indirect advantages. A new employee candidate may also have extra abilities not directly related to the job but valuable to the company nonetheless. These should be taken into account.

8. Acceptance: Those who must implement the decision or who will be affected by it must accept it both intellectually and emotionally.

Acceptance is a critical factor because it occasionally conflicts with one of the quality criteria. In such cases, the best thing to do may be to choose a lesser quality solution that has greater acceptance.

For example, when cake mixes first were put on the market, manufacturers put everything into the mix--the highest quality and most efficient solution. Only water had to be added. However, the mixes didn't sell well--they weren't accepted. After investigation, the makers discovered that women didn't like the mixes because using the mixes made them feel guilty: they weren't good wives because they were taking a shortcut to making a cake. The solution was to take the egg and sometimes the milk out of the mix so that the women would have something to do to "make" the cake other than just adding water. Now they had to add egg and perhaps milk, making them feel more useful. The need to feel useful and a contributor is one of the most basic of human needs. Thus, while the new solution was less efficient in theoretical terms, it was much more acceptable. Cake mixes with the new formula became quite popular.

Thus, the inferior method may produce greater results if the inferior one has greater support. One of the most important considerations in decision making, then, is the people factor. Always consider a decision in light of the people implementation.

A decision that may be technologically brilliant but that is sociologically stupid will not work. Only decisions that are implemented, and implemented with thoroughness (and preferably enthusiasm) will work the way they are intended to.

Approaches to Decision Making

There are two major approaches to decision making in an organization, the authoritarian method in which an executive figure makes a decision for the group and the group method in which the group decides what to do.

1. Authoritarian. The manager makes the decision based on the knowledge he can gather. He then must explain the decision to the group and gain their acceptance of it. In some studies, the time breakdown for a typical operating decision is something like this:

Make decision, 5 min.; explain decision, 30 min.; gain acceptance, 30 min.

2. Group. The group shares ideas and analyses, and agrees upon a decision to implement. Studies show that the group often has values, feelings, and reactions quite different from those the manager supposes they have. No one knows the group and its tastes and preferences as well as the group itself. And, interestingly, the time breakdown is something like this:

Group makes decision, 30 min.; explain decision, 0 min.; gain acceptance, 0 min.

Clearly, just from an efficiency standpoint, group decision making is better. More than this, it has been shown many times that *people prefer to implement the ideas they themselves think of.* They will work harder and more energetically to implement their own idea than they would to implement an idea imposed on them by others. We all have a love for our own ideas and solutions, and we will always work harder on a solution supported by our own vision and our own ego than we will on a solution we have little creative involvement with.

There are two types of group decision making sessions. First is **free discussion** in which the problem is simply put on the table for the group to talk about. For example, Joe has been offered a job change from shift supervisor to maintenance foreman. Should he take the job?

The other kind of group decision making is **developmental discussion** or structured discussion. Here the problem is broken down into steps, smaller parts with specific goals. For example, instead of asking generally whether Joe should take the job, the group word works on sub questions: What are Joe's skills? What skills does the new job require? How does Joe rate on each of the skills required? Notice that these questions seek specific information rather than more general impressionistic opinions.

Developmental discussion (1) insures systematic coverage of a topic and (2) insures that all members of the group are talking about the same aspect of the problem at the same time.

Some Decision Making Strategies

As you know, there are often many solutions to a given problem, and the decision maker's task is to choose one of them. The task of choosing can be as simple or as complex as the importance of the decision warrants, and the number and quality of alternatives can also be adjusted according to importance, time, and resources and so on. There are several strategies used for choosing. Among them are the following:

1. Optimizing. This is the strategy of choosing the best possible solution to the problem, discovering as many alternatives as possible and choosing the very best. How thoroughly optimizing can be done is dependent on

A. importance of the problem

B. time available for solving it

C. cost involved with alternative solutions

D. availability of resources, knowledge

E. personal psychology, values

Note that the collection of complete information and the consideration of all alternatives are seldom possible for most major decisions, so that limitations must be placed on alternatives.

2. Satisfying: In this strategy, the first satisfactory alternative is chosen rather than the best alternative. If you are very hungry, you might choose to stop at the first decent looking restaurant in the next town rather than attempting to choose the best restaurant from among all (the optimizing strategy). The word *satisfying* was coined by combining *satisfactory* and *sufficient.* For many small decisions, such as where to park, what to drink, which pen to use, which tie to wear, and so on, the satisfying strategy is perfect.

3. Maxima: This stands for "maximize the maximums." This strategy focuses on evaluating and then choosing the alternatives based on their maximum possible payoff. This is sometimes described as the strategy of the optimist, because favorable outcomes and high potentials are the areas of concern. It is a good strategy for use when risk taking is most acceptable, when the go-for-broke philosophy is reigning freely.

4. Maxim in: This stands for "maximize the minimums." In this strategy, that of the pessimist, the worst possible outcome of each decision is considered and the decision with the highest minimum is chosen. The Maxim in orientation is good when the consequences of a failed decision are particularly harmful or undesirable. Maxim in concentrates on the salvage value of a decision, or of the guaranteed return of the decision. It's the philosophy behind the saying, "A bird in the hand is worth two in the bush."

Quiz shows exploit the uncertainty many people feel when they are not quite sure whether to go with a maximax strategy or a maxim in one: "Okay, Mrs. Freen, you can now choose to take what you've already won and go home, or risk losing it all and find out what's behind door number three."

Example: I could put my $10,000 in a genetic engineering company, and if it creates and patents new bacteria that help plants resist frost, I could make $50,000. But I could also lose the whole $10,000. But if I invest in a soap company, I might make only $20,000, but if the company goes completely broke and gets liquidated, I'll still get back $7,000 of my investment, based on its book value.

Example: its fourth down and ten yards to go on your twenty yard line. Do you go for a long pass or punt? Maxima would be to pass; Maxim in would be to punt.

Decision Making Procedure

As you read this procedure, remember our discussion earlier about the recursive nature of decision making. In a typical decision making situation, as you move from step to step here, you will probably find yourself moving back and forth also.

1. Identify the decision to be made together with the goals it should achieve: Determine the scope and limitations of the decision. Is the new job to be permanent or temporary or is that not yet known (thus requiring another decision later)? Is the new package for the product to be put into all markets or just into a test market? How might the scope of the decision be changed--that is, what are its possible parameters?

When thinking about the decision, be sure to include a clarification of goals: We must decide whom to hire for our new secretary, *one who will be able to create an efficient and organized office.* Or, we must decide where to go on vacation, *where we can relax and get some rest from the fast pace of society.*

2. Get the facts: But remember that you cannot get all the facts. Get as many facts as possible about a *decision within the limits of time imposed on you and your ability to process them*, but remember that virtually every decision must be made in partial ignorance. Lack of complete information must not be allowed to paralyze your decision. A decision based on partial knowledge is usually better than not making the decision when a decision is really needed. The proverb that "any decision is better than no decision," while perhaps extreme, shows the importance of choosing. When you are racing toward a bridge support, you must decide to turn away to the right or to the left. Which way you turn is less important than the fact that you do indeed turn.

As part of your collection of facts, list your feelings, hunches, and intuitive urges. Many decisions must ultimately rely on or be influenced by intuition because of the remaining degree of uncertainty involved in the situation.

Also as part of your collection of facts, consult those who will be affected by and who will have to implement your decision. Input from these people not only helps supply you with information and help in making the decision but it begins to produce the acceptance necessary in the implementers because they feel that they are part of the decision making process. As Russell Ackoff noted in *The Art of Problem Solving*, not consulting people involved in a decision is often perceived as an act of aggression.

3. Develop alternatives: Make a list of all the possible choices you have, including the choice of doing nothing. Not choosing one of the candidates or one of the building sites is in itself a decision. Often a non decision is harmful as we mentioned above--not choosing to turn either right or left is to choose to drive into the bridge. But sometimes the decision to do nothing is useful or at least better than the alternatives, so it should always be consciously included in the decision making process.

Also be sure to think about not just identifying available alternatives but creating alternatives that don't yet exist. For example, if you want to choose which major to pursue in college, think not only of the available ones in the catalog, but of designing your own course of study.

4. Rate each alternative: This is the evaluation of the value of each alternative. Consider the negative of each alternative (cost, consequences, problems created, time needed, etc.) and the positive of each (money saved, time saved, added creativity or happiness to company or employees, etc.). Remember here that the alternative that you might like best or that would in the best of all possible worlds be an obvious choice will, however, not be functional in the real world because of too much cost, time, or lack of acceptance by others.

Also don't forget to include indirect factors in the rating. If you are deciding between machines X, Y, and Z and you already have an employee who knows how to operate machine Z, that fact should be considered. If you are choosing an investigative team to send to Japan to look at plant sites and you have very qualified candidates A, B, and C, the fact that B is a very fast typist, a superior photographer or has some other side benefit in addition to being a qualified team member, should be considered. In fact, what you put on your hobbies and interests line on your resume can be quite important when you apply for a job just because employers are interested in getting people with a good collection of additional abilities.

5. Rate the risk of each alternative: In problem solving, you hunt around for a solution that best solves a particular problem, and by such a hunt you are pretty sure that the solution will work. In decision making, however, there is always some degree of uncertainty in any choice. Will Bill really work out as the new supervisor? If we decide to expand into Canada, will our sales and profits really increase? If we let Jane date Fred at age fifteen, will the experience be good? If you decide to marry person X or buy car Y or go to school Z, will that be the best or at least a successful choice?

Risks can be rated as percentages, ratios, rankings, grades or in any other form that allows them to be compared. See the section on risk evaluation for more details on risking.

6. Make the decision: If you are making an individual decision, apply your preferences (which may take into account the preferences of others). Choose the path to follow, whether it includes one of the alternatives, more than one of them (a multiple decision) or the decision to choose none.

And of course, don't forget to implement the decision and then evaluate the implementation, just as you would in a problem solving experience.

One important item often overlooked in implementation is that when explaining the decision to those involved in carrying it out or those who will be affected by it, don't just list the projected benefits: frankly explain the risks and the drawbacks involved and tell why you believe the proposed benefits outweigh the negatives. Implementers are much more willing to support decisions when they (1) understand the risks and (2) believe that they are being treated with honesty and like adults.

Remember also that very few decisions are irrevocable. Don't cancel a decision prematurely because many new plans require time to work--it may take years for your new branch office in Paris to get profitable--but don't hesitate to change directions if a particular decision clearly is not working out or is being somehow harmful. You can always make another decision to do something else.

Risking

Because making decisions involves a degree of risk, it would be helpful to examine risk and risk analysis in this chapter in order to gain an understanding of what is involved. Risk and uncertainty create anxiety, yet they are necessary components of an active life.

General Comments on Risk Taking

1. Only the risk takers are truly free. All decisions of consequence involve risk. Without taking risks, you cannot grow or improve or even live.

2. There is really no such thing as permanent security in anything on earth. Not taking risks is really not more secure than taking them, for your present state can always be changed without action on your part. If you don't take the risk of dying by driving to the store, your house could collapse on you and kill you anyway.

3. You are supposed to be afraid when you risk. Admit your fears--of loss, of rejection, of failure.

4. Risking normally involves a degree of separation anxiety--the anxiety you feel whenever you are removed from something that makes you feel secure. Many children feel this when they first leave their parents for school. Some college students feel this when they go off to college. Travelers sometimes feel it when they get homesick. The way to overcome separation anxiety is to build a bridge between the familiar and secure and the new. Find out what the new place--school or country--is like and how its elements compare to familiar and secure things at home. Take familiar things with you--books, teddy bear, popcorn popper, whatever.

The same is true of all risks. Make the opportunity as familiar as possible and learn as much about it as you can before you release the security of the old. Find out about the new job, its location, the lifestyle of those who live there, and so on.

The five classical functions of a manager are:

- **Planning** – the direction a company takes e.g. diversifying, where to operate.
- **Organising** - resources such as people, space, equipment and services.
- **Coordinating** - the activities of various departments.
- **Decision-making** - about the organisation, products or services made or sold, the employees, use of I.T.
- **Controlling** - monitoring and supervising the activities of others.

The role of a **management information system** (MIS) is to provide a manager with sufficient information to make informed decisions to help him to carry out the above functions. The best definition of an MIS is:

The role of a management information system is to convert data from **internal** and **external** sources into information that can be used to aid in making **effective decisions** for planning, directing and controlling.

We need to make the distinction between a data-processing system and an information system:

- **Data processing system** record day to day transactions, e.g. sale of a CD to a customer.
- **Operational Information system** read the collected data and do things like producing lists of items that need to be re-ordered.
- The **MIS** will analyse the sales data to highlight sales trends of different product lines, to enable decisions to be made as to whether the product needs special promotion, or whether it should be discontinued.

The MIS deals with internal and external information. The internal information can be got quite easily from the various system on the company network, e.g. sales figures for each product line. The external information is gathered from:

- Intelligence about competitors' activities. This can come through reading articles in the press, leaks, or even industrial espionage.
- Information about population shifts. As the population gets older, the less likely they are to be interested in pop-music or customising cars, but are more likely to be interested in weight-loss products or holidays for the over 50s.

- Economic and social factors. Sales of cars would go down in an area where a major employer had just closed down a plant.
- Government Legislation. Financial forecasts would change if the minimum wage rose.

The MIS can be used to gather information from both **formal** and **informal flows** of information.

- A **formal flow** of information is one in which a **procedure** is adopted, e.g. the downloading of sales figures from several branches first thing on a Monday morning. External data can be collected using specialised **data collection agencies** such as *Dun and Bradstreet* who produce economic data for academic and commercial organizations. Formal flows can also come from people working on the same document at several locations, or by use of **e-mail**, or by use of **company intranets**.
- **Informal** information flows come from chance meetings, reading magazines or newspapers, or watching the news on TV.

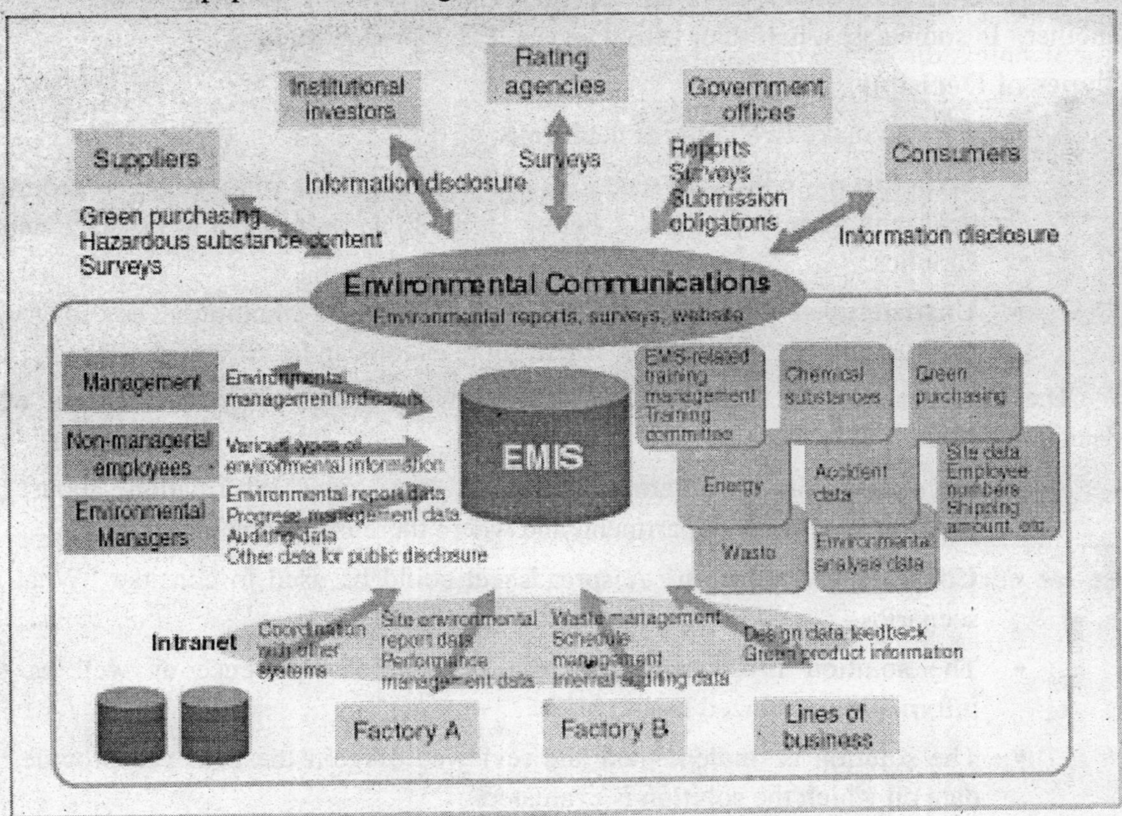

The MIS must produce information for managers on three levels:

- **Operational** – day-to-day decisions such as ordering in more stock;
- **Tactical** – decisions that have a short to medium term effect, e.g. introducing a new product to a particular retail outlet;
- **Strategic** – long term decisions that will affect the future of the organisation, e.g. whether to open a new store, or take over a rival concern.

In 1973 a study showed the following about the time taken by a manager on various different tasks:

- Desk work – 22%
- Travel – 3%
- Unscheduled meetings – 10%
- Scheduled meetings (the practical alternative to work) – 59%
- Telephone calls – 6%.

Some chief executives have to change their attention rapidly form one task to another. In some cases, half their activities last less than nine minutes.

Types of Decision

A manager can make two kinds of decision:

- **Structured –** which are repetitive and need a definite routine and procedure to deal with them, e.g. stock is below 15 %, so an order need to be place with a supplier.
- **Unstructured –** require knowledge, insight, and evaluation. They may well crop up without warning, and the right decision can be critical.

The manager may well go through the following stages when considering what decision to take:

- **Recognise the problem**. The MIS may give information about the performance of the department, and where there is a problem.
- **Consider the solution**. A spreadsheet could be used to consider "What if" scenarios.
- The solution is chosen using the manager's experience as well as the information produced by the MIS.
- The solution is implemented and reviewed. Again the MIS can provide the data on which the solution is evaluated.

Often solutions do not proceed smoothly and there may have to be backtracking from one stage to another.

Exercise

Q. 1. "Decision making is the primary task of the Manager." Explain the various theories of decision making in context of this statement.

Q. 2. What is Decision Making? Discuss aids to Decision Making and theories of Decision Making in brief.

Q. 3. Why people fail in planning? Explain how to create an environment for effective planning.

Q. 4. Explain the concept of Decision Making. Discuss the different aids to Decision Making.

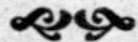

6 Database Management System

A **Database Management System (DBMS)** is a set of computer programs that controls the creation, maintenance, and the use of a database. It allows organizations to place control of database development in the hands of database administrators (DBAs) and other specialists. A DBMS is a system software package that helps the use of integrated collection of data records and files known as databases. It allows different user application programs to easily access the same database.

DBMSs may use any of a variety of database models, such as the network model or relational model. In large system, a DBMS allows users and other software to store and retrieve data in a structured way. Instead of having to write computer programs to extract information, user can ask simple questions in a query language. Thus, many DBMS packages provide Fourth-generation programming language (4GLs) and other application development features. It helps to specify the logical organization for a database and access and use the information within a database. It provides facilities for controlling data access, enforcing data integrity, managing concurrency, and restoring the database from backups. A DBMS also provides the ability to logically present database information to users.

In fact, most of today's database system are referred to as a *Relational Database Management System (RDBMS)*, because of their ability to store related data across multiple tables.

Some of the more popular relational database management system include:

- Microsoft Access
- File maker
- Microsoft SQL Server

- MySQL
- Oracle

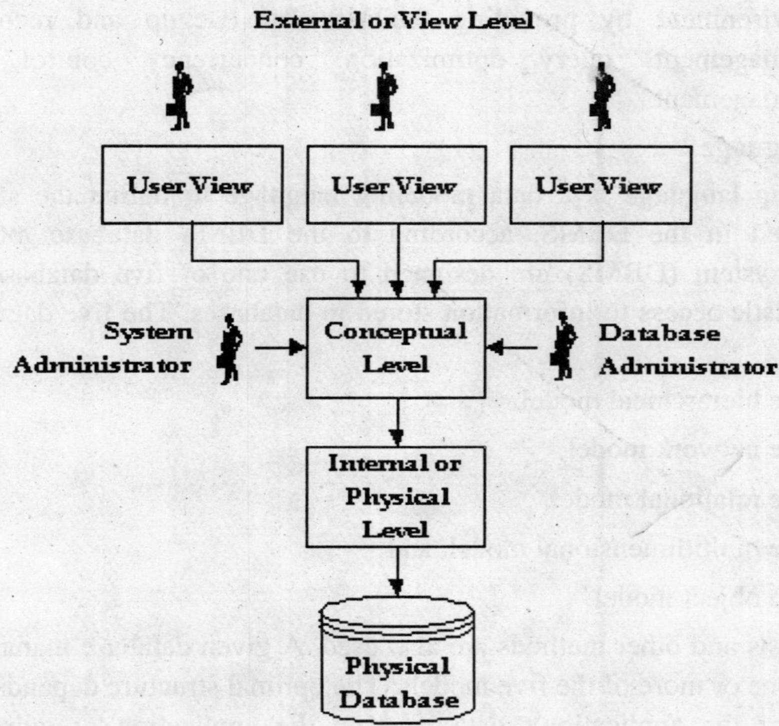

DOMS Components

- **DBMS Engine** accepts logical request from the various other DBMS subsystem, converts them into physical equivalents, and actually accesses the database and data dictionary as they exist on a storage device.
- **Data Definition Subsystem** helps user to create and maintain the data dictionary and define the structure of the files in a database.
- **Data Manipulation Subsystem** helps user to add, change, and delete information in a database and query it for valuable information. Software tools within the data manipulation subsystem are most often the primary interface between user and the information contained in a database. It allows user to specify its logical information requirements.
- **Application Generation Subsystem** contains facilities to help users to develop transaction-intensive applications. It usually requires that user

perform a detailed series of tasks to process a transaction. It facilitates easy-to-use data entry screens, programming languages, and interfaces.

- **Data Administration Subsystem** helps users to manage the overall database environment by providing facilities for backup and recovery, security management, query optimization, concurrency control, and change management.

Modeling language

A modeling language is a data modeling language to define the schema of each database hosted in the DBMS, according to the DBMS database model. Database management system (DBMS) are designed to use one of five database structures to provide simplistic access to information stored in databases. The five database structures are:

- The hierarchical model,
- The network model,
- The relational model,
- The multidimensional model, and
- The object model.

Inverted lists and other methods are also used. A given database management system may provide one or more of the five models. The optimal structure depends on the natural organization of the application's data, and on the application's requirements, which include transaction rate (speed), reliability, maintainability, scalability, and cost.

The **hierarchical structure** was used in early mainframe DBMS. Records' relationships form a treelike model. This structure is simple but nonflexible because the relationship is confined to a one-to-many relationship. IBM's IMS system and the RDM Mobile are examples of a hierarchical database system with multiple hierarchies over the same data. RDM Mobile is a newly designed embedded database for a mobile computer system. The hierarchical structure is used primarily today for storing geographic information and file system.

The **network structure** consists of more complex relationships. Unlike the hierarchical structure, it can relate to many records and accesses them by following one of several paths. In other words, this structure allows for many-to-many relationships.

The **relational structure** is the most commonly used today. It is used by mainframe, midrange and microcomputer system. It uses two-dimensional rows and columns to store data. The tables of records can be connected by common key values. While working for

IBM, E.F. Codd designed this structure in 1970. The model is not easy for the end user to run queries with because it may require a complex combination of many tables.

The **multidimensional structure** is similar to the relational model. The dimensions of the cube-like model have data relating to elements in each cell. This structure gives a spreadsheet-like view of data. This structure is easy to maintain because records are stored as fundamental attributes - in the same way they are viewed - and the structure is easy to understand. Its high performance has made it the most popular database structure when it comes to enabling online analytical processing (OLAP).

The **object oriented structure** has the ability to handle graphics, pictures, voice and text, types of data, without difficultly unlike the other database structures. This structure is popular for multimedia Web-based applications. It was designed to work with object-oriented programming languages such as Java.

The dominant model in use today is the ad hoc one embedded in SQL, despite the objections of purists who believe this model is a corruption of the relational model since it violates several fundamental principles for the sake of practicality and performance. Many DBMSs also support the Open Database Connectivity API that supports a standard way for programmers to access the DBMS.

Data structure

Data structures (fields, records, files and objects) optimized to deal with very large amounts of data stored on a permanent data storage device (which implies relatively slow access compared to volatile main memory).

Database query language

A database query language and report writer allows users to interactively interrogate the database, analyze its data and update it according to the user's privileges on data. It also controls the security of the database. Data security prevents unauthorized users from viewing or updating the database. Using passwords, users are allowed access to the entire database or subsets of it called subschemas. For example, an employee database can contain all the data about an individual employee, but one group of users may be authorized to view only payroll data, while others are allowed access to only work history and medical data.

If the DBMS provides a way to interactively enter and update the database, as well as interrogate it, this capability allows for managing personal databases. However, it may not leave an audit trail of actions or provide the kinds of controls necessary in a multi-user organization. These controls are only available when a set of application programs are customized for each data entry and updating function.

Transaction mechanism

A database transaction mechanism ideally guarantees ACID properties in order to ensure data integrity despite concurrent user accesses (concurrency control), and faults (fault tolerance). It also maintains the integrity of the data in the database. The DBMS can maintain the integrity of the database by not allowing more than one user to update the same record at the same time. The DBMS can help prevent duplicate records via unique index constraints; for example, no two customers with the same customer numbers (key fields) can be entered into the database. See ACID properties for more information (Redundancy avoidance).

DBMS topics

External, Logical and Internal view

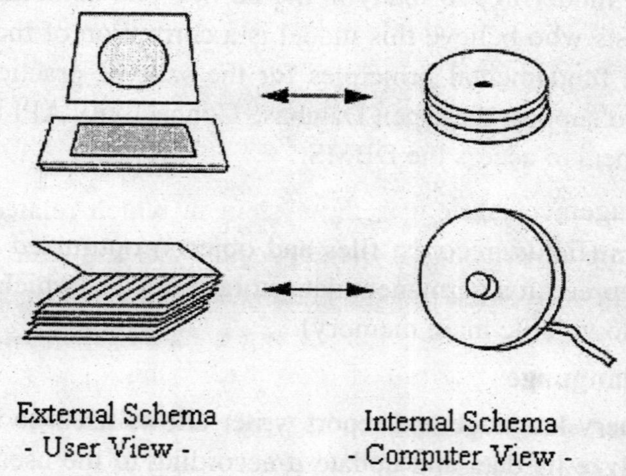

Traditional View of Data

A database management system provides the ability for many different users to share data and process resources. But as there can be many different users, there are many different database needs. The question now is: How can a single, unified database meet the differing requirement of so many users?

A DBMS minimizes these problems by providing two views of the database data: an external view (or User view), logical view (or conceptual view) and physical (or internal) view. The user's view, of a database program represents data in a format that is meaningful to a user and to the software programs that process those data.

One strength of a DBMS is that while there is typically only one conceptual (or logical) and physical (or internal) view of the data, there can be an endless number of different External views. This feature allows users to see database information in a more business-related way rather than from a technical, processing viewpoint. Thus the logical view refers to the way user views data, and the physical view to the way the data are physically stored and processed.

DBMS Features and Capabilities

Alternatively, and especially in connection with the relational model of database management, the relation between attributes drawn from a specified set of domains can be seen as being primary. For instance, the database might indicate that a car that was originally "red" might fade to "pink" in time, provided it was of some particular "make" with an inferior paint job. Such higher arity relationships provide information on all of the underlying domains at the same time, with none of them being privileged above the others.

DBMS Simple Definition

Data base management system is the system in which related data is stored in an "efficient" and "compact" manner. Efficient means that the data which is stored in the DBMS is accessed in very quick time and compact means that the data which is stored in DBMS covers very little space in the computer's memory. In the above definition the phrase "related data" is used which means that the data which is stored in the DBMS is about some particular topic.

Throughout recent history specialized databases have existed for scientific, geospatial, imaging, and document storage and like uses. Functionality drawn from such applications has lately begun appearing in mainstream DBMSs as well. However, the main focus, at least when aimed at the commercial data processing market, is still on descriptive attributes on repetitive record structures.

Thus, the DBMSs of today roll together frequently needed services or features of attribute management. By externalizing such functionality to the DBMS, applications effectively share code with each other and are relieved of much internal complexity. Features commonly offered by database management system include:

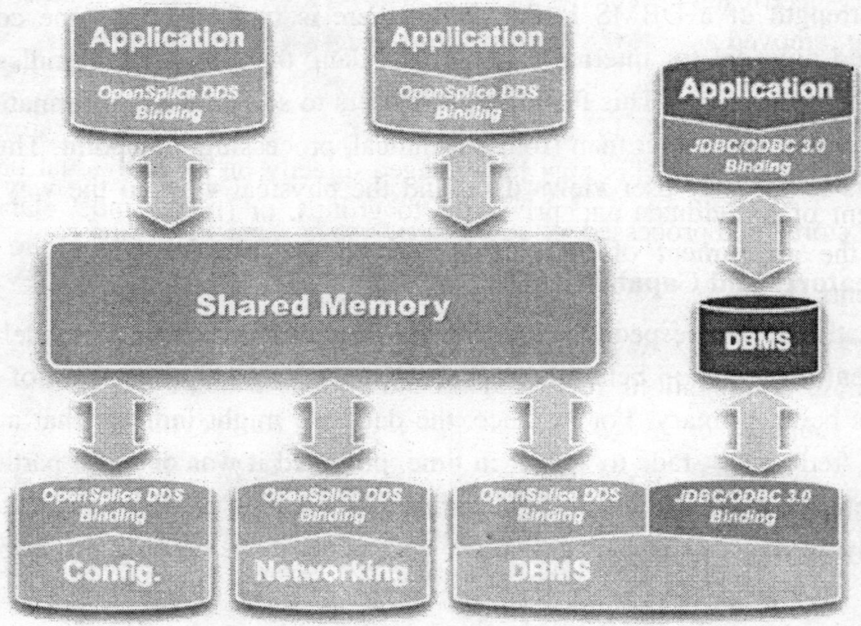

Query ability

Querying is the process of requesting attribute information from various perspectives and combinations of factors. Example: "How many 2-door cars in Texas are green?" A database query language and report writer allow users to interactively interrogate the database, analyze its data and update it according to the users privileges on data.

Backup and replication

Copies of attributes need to be made regularly in case primary disks or other equipment fails. A periodic copy of attributes may also be created for a distant organization that cannot readily access the original. DBMS usually provide utilities to facilitate the process of extracting and disseminating attribute sets. When data is replicated between database servers, so that the information remains consistent throughout the database system and users cannot tell or even know which server in the DBMS they are using, the system is said to exhibit replication transparency.

Rule enforcement

Often one wants to apply rules to attributes so that the attributes are clean and reliable. For example, we may have a rule that says each car can have only one engine associated with it (identified by Engine Number). If somebody tries to associate a second engine with a given car, we want the DBMS to deny such a request and display an error message. However, with changes in the model specification such as, in this example, hybrid gas-electric cars, rules may need to change. Ideally such rules should be able to be added and removed as needed without significant data layout redesign.

Security

For security reasons, it is desirable to limit who can see or change specific attributes or groups of attributes. This may be managed directly on an individual basis, or by the assignment of individuals and privileges to groups, or (in the most elaborate models) through the assignment of individuals and groups to roles which are then granted entitlements.

Computation

Common computations requested on attributes are counting, summing, averaging, sorting, grouping, cross-referencing, and so on. Rather than have each computer application implement these from scratch, they can rely on the DBMS to supply such calculations.

Change and access logging

This describes who accessed which attributes, what was changed, and when it was changed. Logging services allow this by keeping a record of access occurrences and changes.

Automated optimization

For frequently occurring usage patterns or requests, some DBMS can adjust themselves to improve the speed of those interactions. In some cases the DBMS will merely provide tools to monitor performance, allowing a human expert to make the necessary adjustments after reviewing the statistics collected.

Meta-data repository

Metadata is data describing data. For example, a listing that describes what attributes are allowed to be in data sets is called "meta-information".

Advanced DBMS

An example of an advanced DMBS is Distributed Data Base Management System (DDBMS), a collection of data which logically belong to the same system but are spread out over the sites of the computer network. The two aspects of a distributed database are distribution and logical correlation:

- **Distribution:** The fact that the data are not resident at the same site, so that we can distinguish a distributed database from a single, centralized database.

- **Logical Correlation:** The fact that the data have some properties which tie them together, so that we can distinguish a distributed database from a set of local databases or files which are resident at different sites of a, computer network.

Distributed Database

A **distributed database** is a database that is under the control of a central database management system (DBMS) in which storage devices are not all attached to a common CPU. It may be stored in multiple computers located in the same physical location, or may be dispersed over a network of interconnected computers.

Collections of data (e.g. in a database) can be distributed across multiple physical locations. A distributed database can reside on network servers on the Internet, on corporate intranets or extranets, or on other company networks. Replication and distribution of databases improve database performance at end-user worksites. To ensure that the distributive databases are up to date and current, there are two processes: replication and duplication. Replication involves using specialized software that looks for changes in the distributive database. Once the changes have been identified, the replication process makes all the databases look the same. The replication process can be very complex and time consuming depending on the size and number of the distributive databases. This process can also require a lot of time and computer resources. Duplication on the other hand is not as complicated. It basically identifies one database as a master and then duplicates that database. The duplication process is normally done at a set time after hours. This is to ensure that each distributed location has the same data. In the duplication process, changes to the master database only are allowed. This is to ensure that local data will not be overwritten. Both of the processes can keep the data current in all distributive locations.

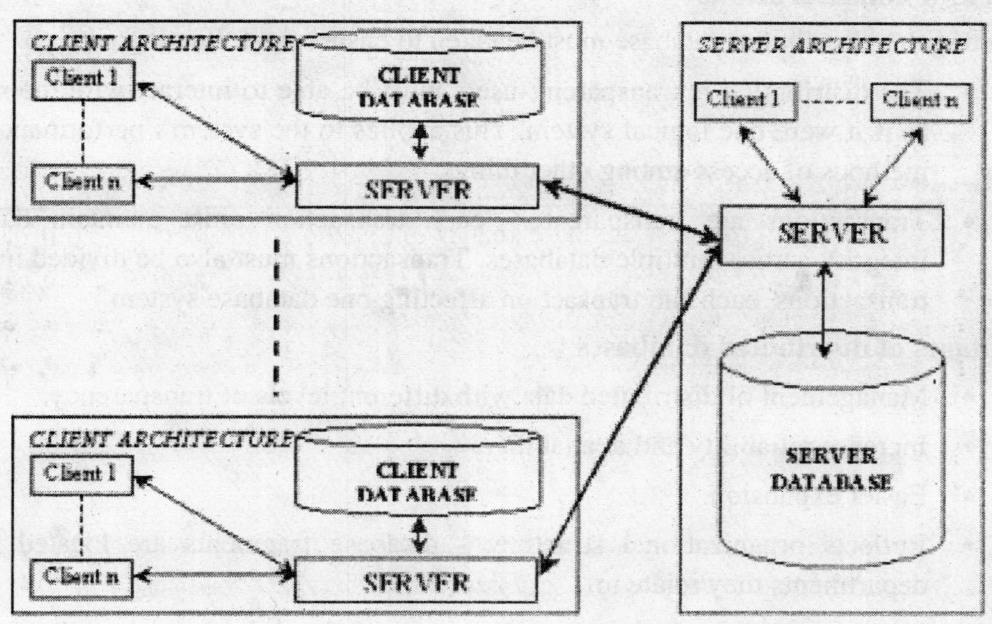

Besides distributed database replication and fragmentation, there are many other distributed database design technologies. For example, local autonomy, synchronous and asynchronous distributed database technologies. These technologies' implementation can and does depend on the needs of the business and the sensitivity/confidentiality of the data to be stored in the database, and hence the price the business is willing to spend on ensuring data security, consistency and integrity.

Basic Architecture

A database User accesses the distributed database through:

Local applications

Applications which do not require data from other sites.

Global applications

Applications which do require data from other sites.

A distributed database does not share main memory or disks.

Important considerations

Care with a distributed database must be taken to ensure the following:

- The distribution is transparent:-users must be able to interact with the system as if it were one logical system. This applies to the system's performance, and methods of access among other things.
- Transactions are transparent: - each transaction must maintain database integrity across multiple databases. Transactions must also be divided into sub transactions, each sub transaction affecting one database system.

Advantages of distributed databases

- Management of distributed data with different levels of transparency.
- Increase reliability and availability.
- Easier expansion.
- Reflects organizational structure: - database fragments are located in the departments they relate to.
- Local autonomy: - a department can control the data about them (as they are the ones familiar with it.)
- Protection of valuable data:-if there were ever a catastrophic event such as a fire, all of the data would not be in one place, but distributed in multiple locations.
- Improved performance:-data is located near the site of greatest demand, and the database system themselves are parallelized, allowing load on the databases to be balanced among servers. (A high load on one module of the database won't affect other modules of the database in a distributed database.)
- Economics: - it costs less to create a network of smaller computers with the power of a single large computer.
- Modularity: - system can be modified, added and removed from the distributed database without affecting other modules (system).
- Reliable transactions - Due to replication of database.
- Hardware, Operating System, Network, Fragmentation, DBMS, Replication and Location Independence.
- Continuous operation.
- No reliance on central site.

- Distributed Query processing.
- Distributed Transaction management.

Single site failure does not affect performance of system. All transactions follow A.C.I.D. property: a-atomicity, the transaction takes place as whole or not at all; c-consistency, maps one consistent DB state to another; i-isolation, each transaction sees a consistent DB; d-durability, the results of a transaction must survive system failures. The Merge Replication Method used to consolidate the data between databases.

Disadvantages of Distributed Databases

- **Complexity:** extra work must be done by the DBAs to ensure that the distributed nature of the system is transparent. Extra work must also be done to maintain multiple disparate system, instead of one big one. Extra database design work must also be done to account for the disconnected nature of the database—for example, joins become prohibitively expensive when performed across multiple system.
- **Economics:** increased complexity and a more extensive infrastructure means extra labour costs.
- **Security:** remote database fragments must be secured, and they are not centralized so the remote sites must be secured as well. The infrastructure must also be secured (e.g., by encrypting the network links between remote sites).
- **Difficult to maintain integrity:** in a distributed database, enforcing integrity over a network may require too much of the network's resources to be feasible.
- **Inexperience:** distributed databases are difficult to work with, and as a young field there is not much readily available experience on proper practice.
- **Lack of standards:** there are no tools or methodologies yet to help users convert a centralized DBMS into a distributed DBMS.
- **Database design more complex:** besides of the normal difficulties, the design of a distributed database has to consider fragmentation of data, allocation of fragments to specific sites and data replication.
- Additional software is required.
- Operating System should support distributed environment.
- **Concurrency control:** it is a major issue. It is solved by locking and time stamping.

Centralized System

Centralized System: A modern, general-purpose computer system consists of one to a few CPUs & a number of device controllers that are connected through a common bus that provides access to shared memory. The CPUs have local cache memories that store local copies of parts of the memory, to speed up access to data. Each device controller is in charge of a specific type of device (for example, a disk drive, an audio device, or a video display). The CPUs & the device controllers can execute concurrently, competing for memory access. Cache memory reduces the contention for memory access, since it reduces the number of times that the CPU needs to access shared memory.

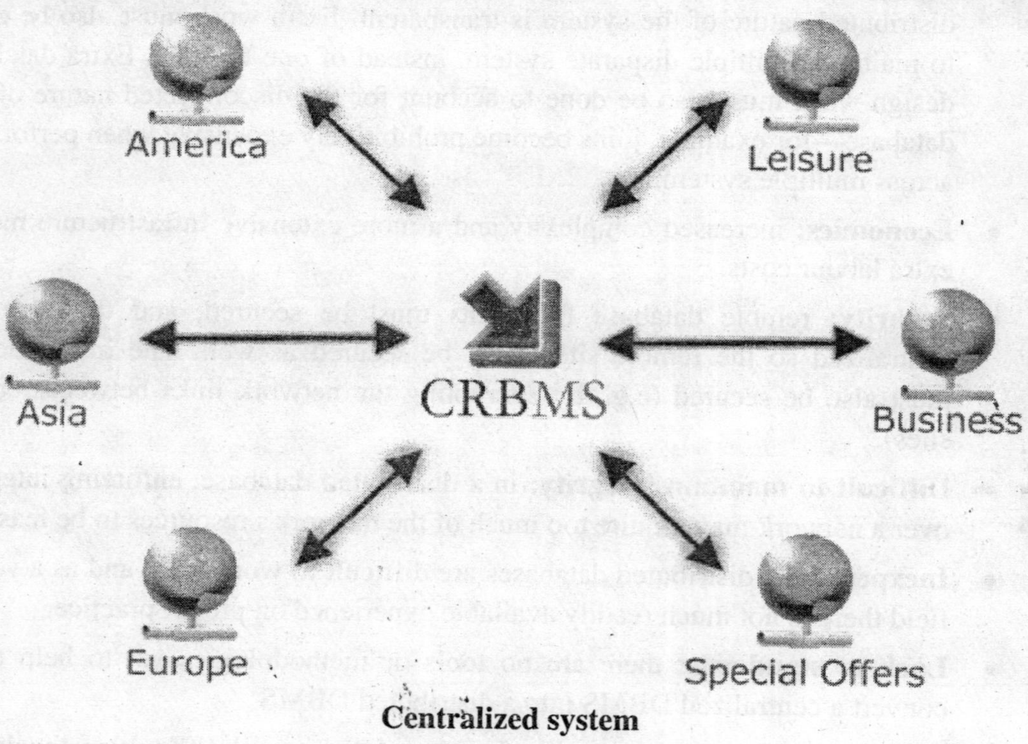

Centralized system

In a distributed database system, the database is stored on several computers. The computers in a distributed system communicate with one another through various communication media, such as high-speed networks or telephone lines. They do not share main memory or disks. The computers in a distributed system may vary in size & function, ranging from workstations up to mainframe system.

The main difference between centralized & distributed databases is that the distributed databases are typically geographically separated, are separately administered, & have slower interconnection. Also in distributed databases we differentiate between local & global transactions. A local transaction is one that accesses data only from sites where the transaction originated. A global transaction, on the other hand, is one that either accesses data in a site different from the one at which the transaction was initiated, or accessed data in several different sites.

Summary

A DBMS is a set of software programs that controls the organization, storage, management, and retrieval of data in a database. DBMSs are categorized according to their data structures or types. The DBMS accepts requests for data from an application program and instructs the operating system to transfer the appropriate data. The queries and responses must be submitted and received according to a format that conforms to one or more applicable protocols. When a DBMS is used, information system can be changed much more easily as the organization's information requirements change. New categories of data can be added to the database without disruption to the existing system.

Database servers are computers that hold the actual databases and run only the DBMS and related software. Database servers are usually multiprocessor computers, with generous memory and RAID disk arrays used for stable storage. Hardware database accelerators, connected to one or more servers via a high-speed channel, are also used in large volume transaction processing environments. DBMSs are found at the heart of most database applications. DBMSs may be built around a custom multitasking kernel with built-in networking support, but modern DBMSs typically rely on a standard operating system to provide these functions.

Exercise

Q. 1. What is database?

Ans. A database is a logically coherent collection of data with some inherent meaning, representing some aspect of real world and which is designed, built and populated with data for a specific purpose.

Q. 2. What is DBMS?

Ans.

(*a*) Redundancy is controlled.

(*b*) Unauthorized access is restricted.

(*c*) Providing multiple user interfaces.

(*d*) Enforcing integrity constraints.

(*e*) Providing backup and recovery.

Q. 3. What is a Database system?

Ans. The database and DBMS software together is called as Database system.

Q. 4. Disadvantage in File Processing System?

Ans.

(*a*) Data redundancy & inconsistency.

(*b*) Difficult in accessing data.

(*c*) Data isolation.

(*d*) Data integrity.

(*e*) Concurrent access is not possible.

(*f*) Security Problems.

Q. 5. Describe the three levels of data abstraction?

Ans. There are three levels of abstraction:

(*a*) **Physical level:** The lowest level of abstraction describes how data are stored.

(*b*) **Logical level:** The next higher level of abstraction, describes what data are stored in database and what relationship among those data.

(*c*) **View level:** The highest level of abstraction describes only part of entire database.

Q. 6. Define the "integrity rules"

Ans. There are two Integrity rules.

(*a*) Entity Integrity: States that? Primary key cannot have NULL value?

(*b*) Referential Integrity: States that? Foreign Key can be either a NULL value or should be Primary Key value of other relation.

Q. 7. What is extension and intension?

Ans. Extension -It is the number of tuples present in a table at any instance. This is time dependent.

Intension – It is a constant value that gives the name, structure of table and the constraints laid on it.

Q. 8. What is System R? What are its two major subsystem?

Ans. System R was designed and developed over a period of 1974-79 at IBM San Jose Research Center . It is a prototype and its purpose was to demonstrate that it is possible to build a Relational System that can be used in a real life environment to solve real life problems, with performance at least comparable to that of existing system.

Its two subsystem are:

(*a*) Research Storage

(*b*) System Relational Data System.

Q. 9. How is the data structure of System R different from the relational structure?

Ans. Unlike Relational system in System R

(*a*) Domains are not supported.

(*b*) Enforcement of candidate key uniqueness is optional.

(*c*) Enforcement of entity integrity is optional.

(*d*) Referential integrity is not enforced.

Q. 10. What is Data Independence?

Ans. Data independence means that the application is independent of the storage structure and access strategy of data. In other words, The ability to modify the schema definition in one level should not affect the schema definition in the next higher level.

Two types of Data Independence:

(*a*) Physical Data Independence : Modification in physical level should not affect the logical level.

(*b*) Logical Data Independence : Modification in logical level should affect the view level.

Note: Logical Data Independence is more difficult to achieve.

Q. 11. What is a view? How it is related to data independence?

Ans. A view may be thought of as a virtual table, that is, a table that does not really exist in its own right but is instead derived from one or more underlying base table. In other words, there is no stored file that direct represents the view instead a definition of view is stored in data dictionary. Growth and restructuring of base tables is not reflected in views. Thus, the view can insulate users from the effects of restructuring and growth in the database. Hence, accounts for logical data independence.

Q. 12. What is Data Model?

Ans. A collection of conceptual tools for describing data, data relationships data semantics and constraints.

Q. 13. What is E-R model?

Ans. This data model is based on real world that consists of basic objects called entities and of relationship among these objects. Entities are described in a database by a set of attributes.

Q. 14. What is Object Oriented model?

Ans. This model is based on collection of objects. An object contains values stored in instance variables within the object. An object also contains bodies of code that operate on the object. These bodies of code are called methods. Objects that contain same types of values and the same methods are grouped together into classes.

Q. 15. What is an Entity?

Ans. It is a 'thing' in the real world with an independent existence.

Q. 16. What is an Entity type?

Ans. It is a collection (set) of entities that have same attributes.

Q. 17. What is an Entity set?

Ans. It is a collection of all entities of particular entity type in the database.

Q. 18. What is an Extension of entity type?

Ans. The collections of entities of a particular entity type are grouped together into an entity set.

Q. 19. What is Weak Entity set?

Ans. An entity set may not have sufficient attributes to form a primary key, and its primary key compromises of its partial key and primary key of its parent entity, then it is said to be Weak Entity set.

Q. 20. What is an attribute?

Ans. It is a particular property, which describes the entity.

Q. 21. What is a Relation Schema and a Relation?

Ans. A relation Schema denoted by $R(A_1, A_2, ?, A_n)$ is made up of the relation name R and the list of attributes Ai that it contains. A relation is defined as a set of tuples. Let r be the relation which contains set tuples $(t_1, t_2, t_3, \ldots, t_n)$. Each tuple is an ordered list of n-values $t = (v_1, v_2, \ldots, v_n)$.

Q. 22. What is degree of a Relation?

Ans. It is the number of attribute of its relation schema.

Q. 23. What is Relationship?

Ans. It is an association among two or more entities.

Q. 24. What is Relationship set?

Ans. The collection (or set) of similar relationships.

Q. 25. What is Relationship type?

Ans. Relationship type defines a set of associations or a relationship set among a given set of entity types.

Q. 26. What is degree of Relationship type?

Ans. It is the number of entity type participating.

Q. 27. What is Data Storage – Definition Language?

Ans. The storage structures and access methods used by database system are specified by a set of definition in a special type of DDL called data storage-definition language.

Q. 28. What is DML (Data Manipulation Language)?

Ans. This language that enable user to access or manipulate data as organised by appropriate data model.

(*a*) Procedural DML or Low level: DML requires a user to specify what data are needed and how to get those data.

(*b*) Non-Procedural DML or High level: DML requires a user to specify what data are needed without specifying how to get those data.

Q. 29. What is VDL (View Definition Language)?

Ans. It specifies user views and their mappings to the conceptual schema.

Q. 30. What is DML Compiler?

Ans. It translates DML statements in a query language into low-level instruction that the query evaluation engine can understand.

Q. 31. What is Query evaluation engine?

Ans. It executes low-level instruction generated by compiler.

Q. 32. What is DDL Interpreter?

Ans. It interprets DDL statements and record them in tables containing metadata.

Q. 33. What is Record-at-a-time?

Ans. The Low level or Procedural DML can specify and retrieve each record from a set of records. This retrieve of a record is said to be Record-at-a-time.

Q. 34. What is Set-at-a-time or Set-oriented?

Ans. The High level or Non-procedural DML can specify and retrieve many records in a single DML statement. This retrieve of a record is said to be Set-at-a-time or Set-oriented.

Q. 35. What is Relational Algebra?

Ans. It is procedural query language. It consists of a set of operations that take one or two relations as input and produce a new relation.

Q. 36. What is Relational Calculus?

Ans. It is an applied predicate calculus specifically tailored for relational databases proposed by E.F. Codd. E.g. of languages based on it are DSL ALPHA, QUEL.

Q. 37. How does Tuple-oriented relational calculus differ from domain-oriented relational calculus.

Ans. The tuple-oriented calculus uses a tuple variables i.e., variable whose only permitted values are tuples of that relation. E.g. QUEL

The domain-oriented calculus has domain variables i.e., variables that range over the underlying domains instead of over relation. E.g. ILL, DEDUCE.

Q. 38. What is normalization?

Ans. It is a process of analysing the given relation schemas based on their Functional Dependencies (FDs) and primary key to achieve the properties.

(*a*) Minimizing redundancy

(*b*) Minimizing insertion, deletion and update anomalies.

Q. 39. What is Functional Dependency?

Ans. A Functional dependency is denoted by X Y between two sets of attributes X and Y that are subsets of R specifies a constraint on the possible tuple that can form a relation state r of R. The constraint is for any two tuples t_1 and t_2 in r if $t_1[X] = t_2[X]$ then they have $t_1[Y] = t_2[Y]$. This means the value of X component of a tuple uniquely determines the value of component Y.

Q. 40. When is a functional dependency F said to be minimal?

Ans.

(*a*) Every dependency in F has a single attribute for its right hand side.

(*b*) We cannot replace any dependency X A in F with a dependency Y A where Y is a proper subset of X and still have a set of dependency that is equivalent to F.

(*c*) We cannot remove any dependency from F and still have set of dependency that is equivalent to F.

Q. 41. What is Multivalued dependency?

Ans. Multivalued dependency denoted by X Y specified on relation schema R, where X and Y are both subsets of R, specifies the following constraint on any relation r of R: if two tuples t_1 and t_2 exist in r such that $t_1[X] = t_2[X]$ then t_3 and t_4 should also exist in r with the following properties.

(*a*) $t_3[x] = t_4[X] = t_1[X] = t_2[X]$

(*b*) $t_3[Y] = t_1[Y]$ and $t_4[Y] = t_2[Y]$

(*c*) $t_3[Z] = t_2[Z]$ and $t_4[Z] = t_1[Z]$

where $[Z = (R-(X \cup Y))]$

Q. 42. What is Lossless join property?

Ans. It guarantees that the spurious tuple generation does not occur with respect to relation schemas after decomposition.

Q. 43. What is 1 NF (Normal Form)?

Ans. The domain of attribute must include only atomic (simple, indivisible) values.

Q. 44. What is Fully Functional dependency?

Ans. It is based on concept of full functional dependency. A functional dependency X Y is fully functional dependency if removal of any attribute A from X means that the dependency does not hold any more.

Q. 45. What is 2NF?

Ans. A relation schema R is in 2NF if it is in 1NF and every non-prime attribute A in R is fully functionally dependent on primary key.

Q. 46. What is 3NF?

Ans. A relation schema R is in 3NF if it is in 2NF and for every FD X A either of the following is true

(*a*) X is a Super-key of R.

(*b*) A is a prime attribute of R.

In other words, if every non prime attribute is non-transitively dependent on primary key.

Q. 47. What is BCNF (Boyce-Codd Normal Form)?

Ans. A relation schema R is in BCNF if it is in 3NF and satisfies an additional constraint that for every FD X A, X must be a candidate key.

Q. 48. What is 4NF?

Ans. A relation schema R is said to be in 4NF if for every Multivalued dependency X Y that holds over R, one of following is true.

(*a*) X is subset or equal to (or) XY = R.

(*b*) X is a super key.

Q. 49. What is 5NF?

Ans. A Relation schema R is said to be 5NF if for every join dependency {R_1, R_2, ..., R_n} that holds R, one the following is true

(*a*) Ri = R for some i.

(*b*) The join dependency is implied by the set of FD, over R in which the left side is key of R.

I will hope by going through this all questions your DBMS concepts will get strong.

7 Business Application of Information Technology

Information Technology Basic

Management Information System (M.I.S.) is basically concerned with processing data into information. Which is then communicated to the various Departments in an organization for appropriate decision-making?

- Data
- Information
- Communication
- Decisions

Data collection involves the use of Information Technology (IT) comprising: computers and telecommunications networks (E-Mail, Voice Mail, Internet, telephone, etc.) Computers are important for more quantitative, than qualitative, data collection, storage and retrieval; Special features are speed and accuracy, and storage of large amount of data. Telecommunications provide the means for one way or two-way communication and for the transmission of messages. A combination of IT is used:

Telephone, computer, processor, printer, etc. A lot of time and money are saved and the security of data and messages is ensured. MIS provides several benefits to the business organization: the means of effective and efficient coordination between Departments; quick and reliable referencing; access to relevant data and documents; use of less labour; improvement in organizational and departmental techniques; management of day-to-day activities (as accounts, stock control, payroll, etc.); day-to-day assistance in a Department and closer contact with the rest of the world. It is important to note that whatever IT is installed must be appropriate to the organization, and to each department (Ref. to 'Functional Areas').

1. Accessing Information Using Computer System

Introduction

With the introduction of the Internet and the World Wide Web, students are able to access information faster and more efficiently using modern Computer System. In the past, one had to visit national and school libraries and spend large amounts of time accessing information. Presently any individual can quickly access, save and print information from any location. One can access the internet from Cyber Cafes, schools, mobile phones, at home and even at modern libraries through internet service providers and telecommunication links. Apart from the internet, information e.g. encyclopedias, tutorials and documentaries can be accessed from Compact Discs which are read from computer system.

Components of a Computer System

Modern computer system consist of a central processing unit, primary storage, secondary storage, input, and output and communication devices.

- The ***central processing unit*** (CPU) manipulates data and controls the other parts of the computer system.
- *Primary storage* (RAM) temporarily stores data and program instructions during processing.
- ***Secondary storage*** (hard disk drives) stores data and instructions when they are not used in processing.
- ***Input devices*** (keyboard, mouse) convert data and instructions for processing in the computer.
- ***Output devices*** (monitor, printer) present data in a form that people can understand, and
- ***Communications devices*** (modems) control the passing of information to and from communications networks Computers are differently classified. We can use size and processing speed to categorize contemporary computers as mainframes, midrange computers, personal Computers, workstations, and supercomputers. Accessing information using the Internet or compact discs require a minimum of a desktop or laptop personal computer. These system

once equipped with a modem, browser software and CD-ROM are, sufficient enough for individuals to access and track information.

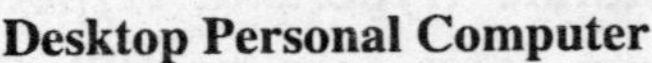

Desktop Personal Computer **Laptop Personal Computer**

What is the Internet?

The Internet is a network of networks, linking computers to computers sharing the TCP/IP protocols. Each runs software to provide or "serve" information and/or to access and view information. The Internet is the transport vehicle for the information stored in files or documents on another computer. It can be compared to an international communications utility servicing computers. The Internet itself does not contain information. It is a slight misstatement to say a "document was found on the Internet." It would be more correct to say it was found through or using the Internet. What it was found in (or on) is one of the computers linked to the Internet. Computers on the Internet may use one or all of the following Internet services:

- ***Electronic mail (e-mail)***. Permits you to send and receive mail. Provides access to discussion groups often called Listservs® after the software they operate under.
- ***Telnet or remote login***. Permits your computer to log onto another computer and use it as if you were there.
- ***FTP or File Transfer Protocol***. Allows your computer to rapidly retrieve complex files intact from a remote computer and view or save them on your computer.

- ***Gopher***. An early, text-only method for accessing internet documents. Gopher has been almost entirely subsumed in the World Wide Web, but you may still find gopher documents linked to in web pages.
- The ***World Wide Web (WWW or "the Web")***.

The largest, fastest growing activity on the Internet.

What is the World Wide Web and what makes it work?

The WWW incorporates all of the Internet services above and much more. You can retrieve documents, view images, animation, and video, listen to sound files, speak and hear voice, and view programs that run on practically any software in the world, providing your computer has the hardware and software to do these things. When you log onto the Internet using Netscape or Microsoft's Internet Explorer or some other browser, you are viewing documents on the World Wide Web. The current foundation on which the WWW functions is the programming language called HTML. It is HTML and other programming imbedded within HTML that make possible Hypertext. Hypertext is the ability to have web pages containing links, which are areas in a page or buttons or graphics on which you can click your mouse button to retrieve another document into your computer. This "click ability" using Hypertext links is the feature which is unique and revolutionary about the Web.

What is a Browser? What are Netscape and Internet Explorer?

A browser is a computer program that resides on your computer enabling you to use the computer to view WWW documents and access the Internet taking advantage of text formatting, hypertext links, images, sounds, motion, and other features. Netscape and Internet Explorer are currently the leading "graphical browsers" in the world (meaning they facilitate the viewing of graphics such as images and video and more). There are other browsers (e.g., Mozilla Firefox, Opera). Most offer many of the same features and can be successfully used to retrieve documents and activate many kinds of programs.

Search engines use software programs that use the browsers and enable the user to locate specific information on the internet. Most operate by searching for specific key words among the millions of sites on the web. Some of the major search websites are Google, Yahoo, and Excite. There are many different search websites, and each is organized according to slightly different principles. The best way to use these websites is to locate one that works for you and then continue to use it; as you learn more about a specific search engine your searches will become more efficient and successful.

The search engine has a textbox where one can type in a word or phrase. Pressing enter on the keyboard will display a list of related topics corresponding to the word or phrase typed. To view the information, one has to click on a link with the mouse and a new page will open with that topic. Each browser has navigation buttons for users to go back, forward, stop, refresh or go to the home page.

2. Using the Internet to Access Information

Requirements for the Internet

Logging onto the internet and getting information is a process which is very similar to that of searching a large public library for information. But the process is a lot faster using the internet services which are currently available on computers. In a large library, our first objective is to obtain a catalog number then proceed to the bookshelf, get the required book [according to the author's name or subject title] and search for the relevant chapters depending upon the topic.

In the case of using the internet, the user must have access to a:

- Personal Computer equipped with a modem [modulator/demodulator] – this part is used to
- Convert digital signals to analog signals and vice versa
- Username and Password – obtainable only after signing up is completed with the Internet Service Provider [example Tstt or Interserv or Carib Link]
- Telephone line connections which is attached directly to the modem of the computer
- Browser software such as ***Netscape Navigator*** or ***Internet Explorer*** – normally obtained from the supplier of the software for computers

Connecting to the Internet

After entering the User name and Password, the user establishes contact with the internet and searching for information can now begin by:

- Selecting a search engine such as ***Yahoo*** or ***Excite*** or ***Google***. There are many others available depending upon the nature of the search
- Entering the website using the keyboard, in the box provided by the search engine

The search is now carried out after pressing the **ENTER** key or using the mouse and clicking on **search** to determine the amount of information available.

The user is now invited to traverse the subtopics [using the scroll knob] which are presented on the screen and choose one subtopic using the mouse. The contents can be viewed, printed out, or saved on the ***Hard Drive*** or ***Floppy diskette*** for later use.

Using the Browser and Search Engine

In the following Example, the ***Internet Explorer*** is chosen as the ***Browser software*** and ***Excite*** is selected as the ***search engine***. Suppose we are searching for information on the topic "SOLE BUSINESS OWNERSHIP" The steps are as follows:

[1] Start up the computer and establish connection with the internet by entering your username and password.

[2] Double Click on the ***Internet Explorer*** Icon using the mouse or Click Once using the mouse then press ENTER on the keyboard.

[3] Now Type in the name of the topic in the search box provided-in this case ***Sole Business Ownership*** then press ENTER or click on **search** using the mouse.

The following pages display the results of the search

1. SBA - Legal Aspects | Forms of ***Business Ownership***

   a ***Sole*** Proprietorship: Easiest and least expensive form of ***ownership*** to organize … ***Sole***

   Proprietors receive all income generated by the ***business*** to keep …

2. Doing ***Business*** as a ***Sole*** Proprietor

   The ***sole*** proprietorship is perhaps the most common form of ***business ownership***. … If you are

   the ***sole*** owner, your ***business*** will still is a ***sole*** proprietorship.

Internet

The Internet is a global system of interconnected computer networks that use the standardized Internet Protocol Suite (TCP/IP) to serve billions of users worldwide. It is a network of networks that consists of millions of private and public, academic, business, and government networks of local to global scope that are linked by copper wires, fiber-optic cables, wireless connections, and other technologies.

The Internet carries a vast array of information resources and services, most notably the inter-linked hypertext documents of the World Wide Web (WWW) and the infrastructure to support electronic mail. In addition, it supports popular services such as online chat, file transfer and file sharing, gaming, commerce, social networking, publishing, video on demand, and teleconferencing and telecommunications. Voice (VoIP) applications allow person-to-person communication via voice and video.

The origins of the Internet reach back to the 1960s when the United States funded research projects of its military agencies to build robust, fault-tolerant and distributed computer networks. This research and a period of civilian funding of a new U.S.

backbone by the National Science Foundation spawned worldwide participation in the development of new networking technologies and led to the commercialization of an international network in the mid 1990s, and resulted in the following popularization of countless applications in virtually every aspect of modern human life. As of 2009, an estimated quarter of Earth's population uses the services of the Internet.

Terminology

The terms *Internet* and *World Wide Web* are often used in everyday speech without much distinction. However, the Internet and the World Wide Web are not one and the same. The Internet is a global data communications system. It is a hardware and software infrastructure that provides connectivity between computers. In contrast, the Web is one of the services communicated via the Internet. It is a collection of interconnected documents and other resources, linked by hyperlinks and URLs. The term *the Internet*, when referring to *the* Internet has traditionally been treated as a proper noun and written with an initial capital letter. There is a trend to regard it as a generic term or common noun and thus write it as "the internet", without the capital.

History

The USSR's launch of Sputnik spurred the United States to create the Advanced Research Projects Agency, known as ARPA, in February 1958 to regain a technological lead.

ARPA created the Information Processing Technology Office (IPTO) to further the research of the Semi Automatic Ground Environment (SAGE) program, which had networked country-wide radar system together for the first time. J. C. R. Licklider was selected to head the IPTO. Licklider moved from the Psycho-Acoustic Laboratory at Harvard University to MIT in 1950, after becoming interested in information technology. At MIT, he served on a committee that established Lincoln Laboratory and worked on the SAGE project. In 1957, he became a Vice President at BBN, where he bought the first production PDP-1 computer and conducted the first public demonstration of time-sharing.

Professor Leonard Kleinrock with one of the first ARPANET Interface Message Processors at UCLA

At the IPTO, Licklider got Lawrence Roberts to start a project to make a network, and Roberts based the technology on the work of Paul Baran, who had written an exhaustive study for the United States Air Force that recommended packet switching (opposed to circuit switching) to achieve better network robustness and disaster survivability. UCLA professor Leonard Kleinrock had provided the theoretical foundations for packet networks in 1962, and later, in the 1970s, for hierarchical routing, concepts which have been the underpinning of the development towards today's Internet.

After much work, the first two nodes of what would become the ARPANET were interconnected between UCLA's School of Engineering and Applied Science and SRI International (SRI) in Menlo Park, California, on October 29, 1969. The ARPANET was one of the "eve" networks of today's Internet. Following on from the demonstration that packet switching worked on the ARPANET, the British Post Office, Telnet, DATAPAC and TRANSPAC collaborated to create the first international packet-switched network service. In the UK, this was referred to as the International Packet Switched Service (IPSS), in 1978. The collection of X.25-based networks grew from Europe and the US to cover Canada, Hong Kong and Australia by 1981. The X.25 packet switching standard was developed in the CCITT (now called ITU-T) around 1976.

A plaque commemorating the birth of the Internet at Stanford University X.25 was independent of the TCP/IP protocols that arose from the experimental work of DARPA on the ARPANET, Packet Radio Net and Packet Satellite Net during the same time period. Vinton Cerf and Robert Kahn developed the first description of the TCP protocols during 1973 and published a paper on the subject in May 1974. Use of the term "Internet" to describe a single global TCP/IP network originated in December 1974 with the publication of RFC 675, the first full specification of TCP that was written by Vinton Cerf, Yogen Dalal and Carl Sunshine, then at Stanford University.

During the next nine years, work proceeded to refine the protocols and to implement them on a wide range of operating system. The first TCP/IP-based wide-area network was operational by January 1, 1983 when all hosts on the ARPANET were switched over from the older NCP protocols. In 1985, the United States' National Science Foundation (NSF) commissioned the construction of the NSFNET, a university 56 kilobit/second network backbone using computers called "fuzzballs" by their inventor, David L. Mills. The following year, NSF sponsored the conversion to a higher-speed 1.5 megabit/second network. A key decision to use the DARPA TCP/IP protocols was made by Dennis Jennings, then in charge of the Supercomputer program at NSF.

The opening of the network to commercial interests began in 1988. The US Federal Networking Council approved the interconnection of the NSFNET to the commercial MCI Mail system in that year and the link was made in the summer of 1989. Other commercial electronic e-mail services were soon connected, including OnTyme, Telemail and Compuserve. In that same year, three commercial Internet service providers (ISPs) were created: UUNET, PSINet and CERFNET. Important, separate networks that offered gateways into, then later merged with, the Internet include Usenet and BITNET. Various other commercial and educational networks, such as Telnet, Tymnet, CompuServe and JANET were interconnected with the growing Internet.

Telnet (later called Sprint net) was a large privately funded national computer network with free dial-up access in cities throughout the U.S. that had been in operation since the 1970s. This network was eventually interconnected with the others in the 1980s as the TCP/IP protocol became increasingly popular. The ability of TCP/IP to work over virtually any pre-existing communication networks allowed for a great ease of growth, although the rapid growth of the Internet was due primarily to the availability of an array of standardized commercial routers from many companies, the availability of commercial Ethernet equipment for local-area networking, and the widespread implementation and rigorous standardization of TCP/IP on UNIX and virtually every other common operating system.

This NeXT Computer was used by Berners-Lee at CERN and became the world's first Web server.

Although, the basic applications and guidelines that make the Internet possible had existed for almost two decades, the network did not gain a public face until the 1990s. On 6 August 1991, CERN, a pan European organization for particle research, publicized the new World Wide Web project. The Web was invented by English scientist Tim Berners-Lee in 1989. An early popular web browser was ViolaWWW, patterned after HyperCard and built using the X Window System.

It was eventually replaced in popularity by the Mosaic web browser. In 1993, the National Center for Supercomputing Applications at the University of Illinois released version 1.0 of Mosaic, and by late 1994 there was growing public interest in the previously academic, technical Internet. By 1996 usage of the word *Internet* had become commonplace, and consequently, so had its use as a synecdoche in reference to the World Wide Web.

Meanwhile, over the course of the decade, the Internet successfully accommodated the majority of previously existing public computer networks (although some networks, such as FidoNet, have remained separate). During the 1990s, it was estimated that the Internet grew by 100 percent per year, with a brief period of explosive growth in 1996 and 1997. This growth is often attributed to the lack of central administration, which allows organic growth of the network, as well as the non-proprietary open nature of the Internet protocols, which encourages vendor interoperability and prevents any one company from exerting too much control over the network. Using various statistics, Advanced Micro Devices estimated the population of Internet users to be 1.5 billion as of January 2009.

Technology

Protocols

The complex communications infrastructure of the Internet consists of its hardware components and a system of software layers that control various aspects of the architecture. While the hardware can often be used to support other software system, it is the design and the rigorous standardization process of the software architecture that characterizes the Internet and provides the foundation for its scalability and success. The responsibility for the architectural design of the Internet software system has been delegated to the Internet Engineering Task Force (IETF).

The IETF conducts standard-setting work groups; open to any individual, about the various aspects of Internet architecture. Resulting discussions and final standards are published in a series of publications, called Request for Comments (RFCs), freely available on the IETF web site. The principal methods of networking that enable the Internet are contained in specially designated RFCs that constitute the Internet Standards.

These standards describe a framework known as the Internet Protocol Suite. This is a model architecture that divides methods into a layered system of protocols (RFC 1122, RFC 1123). The layers correspond to the environment or scope in which their services operate. At the top is the Application Layer, the space for the application-specific networking methods used in software applications, e.g., a web browser program. Below this top layer, the Transport Layer connects applications on *different hosts* via the network (e.g., client-server model) with appropriate data exchange methods. Underlying these layers are the core networking technologies, consisting of two layers.

The Internet Layer enables computers to identify and locate each other via Internet Protocol (IP) addresses, and allows them to connect to one-another via intermediate (transit) networks. Lastly, at the bottom of the architecture, is a software layer, the Link Layer, that provides connectivity between hosts on the same local network link, such as a local area network (LAN) or a dial-up connection. The model, also known as TCP/IP, is designed to be independent of the underlying hardware which the model therefore does not concern itself with in any detail. Other models have been developed, such as the Open System Interconnection (OSI) model, but they are not compatible in the details of description, nor implementation, but many similarities exist and the TCP/IP protocols are usually included in the discussion of OSI networking.

The most prominent component of the Internet model is the Internet Protocol (IP) which provides addressing system (IP addresses) for computers on the Internet. IP enables internetworking and essentially establishes the Internet itself. IP Version 4 (IPv4) is the initial version used on the first generation of the today's Internet and is still in dominant use. It was designed to address up to ~4.3 billion (10^9) Internet hosts. However, the explosive growth of the Internet has led to IPv4 address exhaustion which is estimated to enter its final stage in approximately 2011. A new protocol version, IPv6, was developed in the mid 1990s which provides vastly larger addressing capabilities and more efficient routing of Internet traffic. IPv6 is currently in commercial deployment phase around the world and Internet address registries (RIRs) have begun to urge all resource managers to plan rapid adoption and conversion.

IPv6 is not interoperable with IPv4. It essentially establishes a "parallel" version of the Internet not directly accessible with IPv4 software. This means software upgrades or translator facilities are necessary for every networking device that needs to communicate on the IPv6 Internet. Most modern computer operating system are already converted to operate with both versions of the Internet Protocol. Network infrastructures, however, are still lagging in this development.

Aside from the complex physical connections that make up its infrastructure, the Internet is facilitated by bi- or multi-lateral commercial contracts (e.g., peering agreements), and by technical specifications or protocols that describe how to exchange data over the network. Indeed, the Internet is defined by its interconnections and routing policies.

Modern Uses

The Internet is allowing greater flexibility in working hours and location, especially with the spread of unmetered high-speed connections and web applications.

The Internet can now be accessed almost anywhere by numerous means, especially through mobile Internet devices. Mobile phones, data cards, handheld game consoles and cellular routers allow users to connect to the Internet from anywhere there is a wireless network supporting that device's technology. Within the limitations imposed by small screens and other limited facilities of such pocket-sized devices, services of the Internet, including email and the web, may be available. Service providers may restrict the services offered and wireless data transmission charges may be significantly higher than other access methods.

The Internet has also become a large market for companies; some of the biggest companies today have grown by taking advantage of the efficient nature of low-cost advertising and commerce through the Internet, also known as e-commerce. It is the fastest way to spread information to a vast number of people simultaneously. The Internet has also subsequently revolutionized shopping—for example; a person can order a CD online and receive it in the mail within a couple of days, or download it directly in some cases.

The Internet has also greatly facilitated personalized marketing which allows a company to market a product to a specific person or a specific group of people more so than any other advertising medium. Examples of personalized marketing include online communities such as MySpace, Friendster, Orkut, Face book and others which thousands of Internet users join to advertise themselves and make friends online. Many of these users are young teens and adolescents ranging from 13 to 25 years old. In turn, when they advertise themselves they advertise interests and hobbies, which online marketing companies can use as information as to what those users will purchase online, and advertise their own companies' products to those users.

The low cost and nearly instantaneous sharing of ideas, knowledge, and skills has made collaborative work dramatically easier, with the help of collaborative software. Not only can a group cheaply communicate and share ideas, but the wide reach of the Internet allows such groups to easily form in the first place. An example of this is the free software movement, which has produced, among other programs, Linux, Mozilla Firefox, and OpenOffice.org. Internet "chat", whether in the form of IRC chat rooms or channels, or via instant messaging system, allow colleagues to stay in touch in a very convenient way when working at their computers during the day. Messages can be exchanged even more quickly and conveniently than via e-mail. Extensions to these system may allow files to be exchanged, "whiteboard" drawings to be shared or voice and video contact between team members.

The Internet allows computer users to remotely access other computers and information stores easily, wherever they may be across the world. They may do this with or without the use of security, authentication and encryption technologies, depending on the requirements. This is encouraging new ways of working from home, collaboration and information sharing in many industries.

An accountant sitting at home can audit the books of a company based in another country, on a server situated in a third country that is remotely maintained by IT specialists in a fourth. These accounts could have been created by home-working bookkeepers, in other remote locations, based on information e-mailed to them from offices all over the world. Some of these things were possible before the widespread use of the Internet, but the cost of private leased lines would have made many of them infeasible in practice. An office worker away from their desk, perhaps on the other side of the world on a business trip or a holiday, can open a remote desktop session into his normal office PC using a secure Virtual Private Network (VPN) connection via the Internet. This gives the worker complete access to all of his or her normal files and data, including e-mail and other applications, while away from the office. This concept is also referred to by some network security people as the Virtual Private Nightmare, because it extends the secure perimeter of a corporate network into its employees' homes.

Services

Information

Many people use the terms *Internet* and *World Wide Web* (or just the *Web*) interchangeably, but, as discussed earlier, the two terms are not synonymous. The World Wide Web is a global set of documents, images and other resources, referenced and interconnected by Uniform Resource Locators (URLs) and hyperlinks. These URLs allow users to address the web servers and other devices that store these resources and access them as required using the Hypertext Transfer Protocol (HTTP). HTTP is only one of the communication protocols used on the Internet. Web services may also use HTTP to allow software system to communicate in order to share and exchange business logic and data.

Software products that can access the resources of the Web are often called *user agents*. In normal use, web browsers, such as Internet Explorer, Firefox, Opera, Apple Safari, and Google Chrome, let users navigate from one web page to another via hyperlinks. Documents on the web may contain any combination of computer data, including graphics, sounds, text, video, multimedia and interactive content including games, office applications and scientific demonstrations. Through keyword-driven Internet research using search engines like Yahoo! and Google, users worldwide have easy, instant access to a vast and diverse amount of online information. Compared to printed encyclopedias and traditional libraries, the World Wide Web has enabled a sudden and extreme decentralization of information and data.

Using the Web, it is also easier than ever before for individuals and organizations to publish ideas and information to a potentially large audience. Publishing a web page, a blog, or building a website involves little initial cost and many cost-free services are available. Publishing and maintaining large, professional web sites with attractive, diverse and up-to-date information is still a difficult and expensive proposition, however. Many individuals and some companies and groups use *web logs* or blogs, which are largely used as easily updatable online diaries. Some commercial organizations encourage staff to communicate advice in their areas of specialization in the hope that visitors will be impressed by the expert knowledge and free information, and be attracted to the corporation as a result. One example of this practice is Microsoft, whose product developers publish their personal blogs in order to pique the public's interest in their work. Collections of personal web pages published by large service providers remain popular, and have become increasingly sophisticated. Whereas operations such as Angel fire and GeoCities have existed since the early days of the Web, newer offerings from, for example, Facebook and MySpace currently have large followings. These operations often brand themselves as social network services rather than simply as web page hosts.

Advertising on popular web pages can be lucrative, and e-commerce or the sale of products and services directly via the Web continues to grow. In the early days, web pages were usually created as sets of complete and isolated HTML text files stored on a web server. More recently, websites are more often created using content management or wiki software with, initially, very little content. Contributors to these system, who may be paid staff, members of a club or other organization or members of the public, fill underlying databases with content using editing pages designed for that purpose, while casual visitors view and read this content in its final HTML form. There may or may not be editorial, approval and security system built into the process of taking newly entered content and making it available to the target visitors.

Communication

E-mail is an important communications service available on the Internet. The concept of sending electronic text messages between parties in a way analogous to mailing letters or memos predates the creation of the Internet. Today it can be important to distinguish between internet and internal e-mail system. Internet e-mail may travel and be stored unencrypted on many other networks and machines out of both the sender's and the recipient's control. During this time it is quite possible for the content to be read and even tampered with by third parties, if anyone considers it important enough. Purely internal or intranet mail system, where the information never leaves the corporate or organization's network, are much more secure, although in any organization there will be IT and other personnel whose job may involve monitoring, and occasionally accessing, the e-mail of other employees not addressed to them. Pictures, documents and other files can be sent as e-mail attachments. E-mails can be sent to multiple e-mail addresses.

Internet telephony is another common communications service made possible by the creation of the Internet. VoIP stands for Voice-over-Internet Protocol, referring to the protocol that underlies all Internet communication. The idea began in the early 1990s with walkie-talkie-like voice applications for personal computers. In recent years many VoIP system have become as easy to use and as convenient as a normal telephone. The benefit is that, as the Internet carries the voice traffic, VoIP can be free or cost much less than a traditional telephone call, especially over long distances and especially for those with always-on Internet connections such as cable or ADSL. VoIP is maturing into a competitive alternative to traditional telephone service. Interoperability between different providers has improved and the ability to call or receive a call from a traditional telephone is available. Simple, inexpensive VoIP network adapters are available that eliminate the need for a personal computer.

Voice quality can still vary from call to call but is often equal to and can even exceed that of traditional calls. Remaining problems for VoIP include emergency telephone number dialing and reliability. Currently, a few VoIP providers provide an emergency service, but it is not universally available. Traditional phones are line-powered and operate during a power failure; VoIP does not do so without a backup power source for the phone equipment and the Internet access devices. VoIP has also become increasingly popular for gaming applications, as a form of communication between players. Popular VoIP clients for gaming include Ventrilo and Team speak. Wii, PlayStation 3, and Xbox 360 also offer VoIP chat features.

Data transfer

File sharing is an example of transferring large amounts of data across the Internet. A computer file can be e-mailed to customers, colleagues and friends as an attachment. It can be uploaded to a website or FTP server for easy download by others. It can be put into a "shared location" or onto a file server for instant use by colleagues. The load of bulk downloads to many users can be eased by the use of "mirror" servers or peer-to-peer networks. In any of these cases, access to the file may be controlled by user authentication, the transit of the file over the Internet may be obscured by encryption, and money may change hands for access to the file.

The price can be paid by the remote charging of funds from, for example, a credit card whose details are also passed—usually fully encrypted—across the Internet. The origin and authenticity of the file received may be checked by digital signatures or by MD5 or other message digests. These simple features of the Internet, over a worldwide basis, are changing the production, sale, and distribution of anything that can be reduced to a computer file for transmission. This includes all manner of print publications.

software products, news, music, film, video, photography, graphics and the other arts. This in turn has caused seismic shifts in each of the existing industries that previously controlled the production and distribution of these products.

Streaming media refers to the act that many existing radio and television broadcasters promote Internet "feeds" of their live audio and video streams (for example, the BBC). They may also allow time-shift viewing or listening such as Preview, Classic Clips and Listen Again features.

These providers have been joined by a range of pure Internet "broadcasters" who never had on-air licenses. This means that an Internet-connected device, such as a computer or something more specific, can be used to access on-line media in much the same way as was previously possible only with a television or radio receiver. The range of material is much wider, from pornography to highly specialized, technical webcasts. Podcasting is a variation on this theme, where—usually audio—material is downloaded and played back on a computer or shifted to a portable media player to be listened to on the move. These techniques using simple equipment allow anybody, with little censorship or licensing control, to broadcast audio-visual material worldwide.

Webcams can be seen as an even lower-budget extension of this phenomenon. While some webcams can give full-frame-rate video, the picture is usually either small or updates slowly. Internet users can watch animals around an African waterhole, ships in the Panama Canal, traffic at a local roundabout or monitor their own premises, live and in real time. Video chat rooms and video conferencing are also popular with many uses being found for personal webcams, with and without two-way sound.

YouTube was founded on 15 February 2005 and is now the leading website for free streaming video with a vast number of users. It uses a flash-based web player to stream and show video files. Registered users may upload an unlimited amount of video and build their own personal profile. YouTube claims that its users watch hundreds of millions, and upload hundreds of thousands, of videos daily.

Accessibility

Common methods of Internet access in homes include dial-up, landline broadband (over coaxial cable, fiber optic or copper wires), Wi-Fi, satellite and 3G technology cell phones. Public places to use the Internet include libraries and Internet cafes, where computers with Internet connections are available. There are also Internet access points in many public places such as airport halls and coffee shops, in some cases just for brief use while standing. Various terms are used, such as "public Internet kiosk", "public access terminal", and "Web payphone". Many hotels now also have public terminals, though these are usually fee-based.

These terminals are widely accessed for various usages like ticket booking, bank deposit, online payment etc. Wi-Fi provides wireless access to computer networks, and therefore can do so to the Internet itself. Hotspots providing such access include Wi-Fi cafes, where would-be users need to bring their own wireless-enabled devices such as a laptop or PDA. These services may be free to all, free to customers only, or fee-based. A hotspot need not be limited to a confined location. A whole campus or park, or even an entire city can be enabled. Grassroots efforts have led to wireless community networks. Commercial Wi-Fi services covering large city areas are in place in London, Vienna, Toronto, San Francisco, Philadelphia, Chicago and Pittsburgh.

The Internet can then be accessed from such places as a park bench. Apart from Wi-Fi, there have been experiments with proprietary mobile wireless networks like Ricochet, various high-speed data services over cellular phone networks, and fixed wireless services. High-end mobile phones such as smart phones generally come with Internet access through the phone network. Web browsers such as Opera are available on these advanced handsets, which can also run a wide variety of other Internet software. More mobile phones have Internet access than PCs, though this is not as widely used. An Internet access provider and protocol matrix differentiates the methods used to get online.

Social impact

The Internet has made possible entirely new forms of social interaction, activities and organizing, thanks to its basic features such as widespread usability and access. Social networking websites such as Face book and MySpace have created a new form of socialization and interaction. Users of these sites are able to add a wide variety of items to their personal pages, to indicate common interests, and to connect with others. It is also possible to find a large circle of existing acquaintances, especially if a site allows users to utilize their real names, and to allow communication among large existing groups of people. Sites like meetup.com exist to allow wider announcement of groups which may exist mainly for face-to-face meetings, but which may have a variety of minor interactions over their group's site at meetup.org, or other similar sites.

The first generation is now being raised with widespread availability of Internet connectivity, with consequences for privacy, identity, and copyright concerns. These "Digital natives" face a variety of concerns that were not present for prior generations.

In democratic societies, the Internet has achieved new relevance as a political tool, leading to Internet censorship by some states. The presidential campaign of Howard Dean in 2004 in the United States became famous for its ability to generate donations via the Internet. Many political groups use the Internet to achieve a whole new method of organizing, in order to carry out Internet activism. Some governments, such as those of

Iran, North Korea, Myanmar, the People's Republic of China, and Saudi Arabia, restrict what people in their countries can access on the Internet, especially political and religious content. This is accomplished through software that filters domains and content so that they may not be easily accessed or obtained without elaborate circumvention.

In Norway, Denmark, Finland and Sweden, major Internet service providers have voluntarily (possibly to avoid such an arrangement being turned into law) agreed to restrict access to sites listed by police. While this list of forbidden URLs is only supposed to contain addresses of known child pornography sites, the content of the list is secret. Many countries, including the United States, have enacted laws making the possession or distribution of certain material, such as child pornography, illegal, but do not use filtering software. There are many free and commercially available software programs, called content-control software, with which a user can choose to block offensive websites on individual computers or networks, such as to limit a child's access to pornography or violence.

The Internet has been a major source of leisure since before the World Wide Web, with entertaining social experiments such as MUDs and MOOs being conducted on university servers, and humor-related Usenet groups receiving much of the main traffic. Today, many Internet forums have sections devoted to games and funny videos; short cartoons in the form of Flash movies are also popular. Over 6 million people use blogs or message boards as a means of communication and for the sharing of ideas. The pornography and gambling industries have both taken full advantage of the World Wide Web, and often provide a significant source of advertising revenue for other websites. Although many governments have attempted to put restrictions on both industries' use of the Internet, this has generally failed to stop their widespread popularity.

One main area of leisure on the Internet is multiplayer gaming. This form of leisure creates communities, bringing people of all ages and origins to enjoy the fast-paced world of multiplayer games. These range from MMORPG to first-person shooters, from role-playing games to online gambling.

This has revolutionized the way many people interact and spend their free time on the Internet. While online gaming has been around since the 1970s, modern modes of online gaming began with services such as Game Spy and Player, to which players of games would typically subscribe. Non-subscribers were limited to certain types of game play or certain games. Many use the Internet to access and download music, movies and other works for their enjoyment and relaxation. As discussed above, there are paid and unpaid sources for all of these, using centralized servers and distributed peer-to-peer technologies. Some of these sources take more care over the original artists' rights and over copyright laws than others.

Many use the World Wide Web to access news, weather and sports reports, to plan and book holidays and to find out more about their random ideas and casual interests. People use chat, messaging and e-mail to make and stay in touch with friends worldwide, sometimes in the same way as some previously had pen pals. Social networking websites like MySpace, Face book and many others like them also put and keep people in contact for their enjoyment. The Internet has seen a growing number of Web desktops, where users can access their files, folders, and settings via the Internet. Cyber slacking can become a serious drain on corporate resources; the average UK employee spent 57 minutes a day surfing the Web while at work, according to a 2003 study by Peninsula Business Services.

Electronic Commerce

Electronic Commerce, commonly known as (electronic marketing) **e-commerce** or **ecommerce**, consists of the buying and selling of products or services over electronic system such as the Internet and other computer networks. The amount of trade conducted electronically has grown extraordinarily with widespread Internet usage. The use of commerce is conducted in this way, spurring and drawing on innovations in electronic funds transfer, supply chain management, Internet marketing, online transaction processing, electronic data interchange (EDI), inventory management system, and automated data collection system. Modern electronic commerce typically uses the World Wide Web at least at some point in the transaction's lifecycle, although it can encompass a wider range of technologies such as e-mail as well.

A large percentage of electronic commerce is conducted entirely electronically for virtual items such as access to premium content on a website, but most electronic commerce involves the transportation of physical items in some way. Online retailers are sometimes known as e-tailors and online retail is sometimes known as e-tail. Almost all big retailers have electronic commerce presence on the World Wide Web.

Electronic commerce that is conducted between businesses is referred to as business-to-business or B_2B. B_2B can be open to all interested parties (e.g. commodity exchange) or limited to specific, pre-qualified participants (private electronic market). Electronic commerce that is conducted between businesses and consumers, on the other hand, is referred to as business-to-consumer or B_2C. This is the type of electronic commerce conducted by companies such as Amazon.com.

Electronic commerce is generally considered to be the sales aspect of e-business. It also consists of the exchange of data to facilitate the financing and payment aspects of the business transactions.

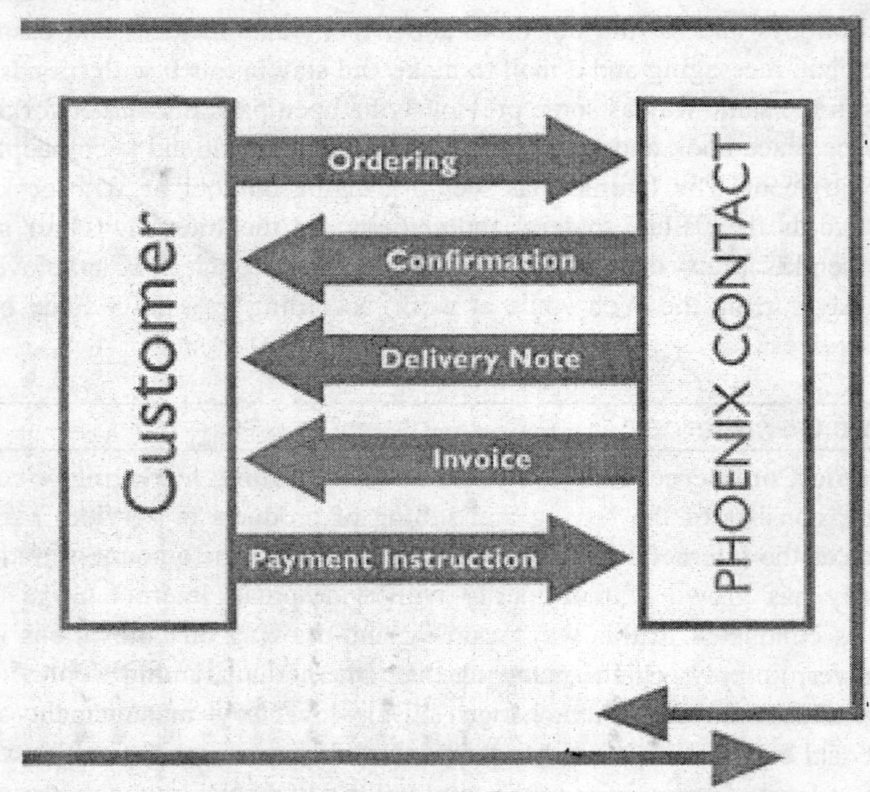

History

Early development

The meaning of electronic commerce has changed over the last 30 years. Originally, electronic commerce meant the facilitation of commercial transactions electronically, using technology such as Electronic Data Interchange (EDI) and Electronic Funds Transfer (EFT). These were both introduced in the late 1970s, allowing businesses to send commercial documents like purchase orders or invoices electronically. The growth and acceptance of credit cards, automated teller machines (ATM) and telephone banking in the 1980s were also forms of electronic commerce. Another form of e-commerce was the airline reservation system typified by Saber in the USA and Travicom in the UK.

Online shopping, an important component of electronic commerce was invented by Michael Aldrich in the UK in 1979. The world's first recorded B2B was Thomson Holidays in 1981 The first recorded B2C was Gateshead SIS/Tesco in 1984 The world's first recorded online shopper was Mrs. Jane Snowball of Gates head, England During the 1980s, online shopping was also used extensively in the UK by auto manufacturers such as Ford, Peugeot-Talbot, General Motors and Nissan. All these organizations and others used the Aldrich system. The system used the switched public telephone network in dial-up and leased line modes. There was no broadband capability.

From the 1990s onwards, electronic commerce would additionally include enterprise resource planning system (ERP), data mining and data warehousing.

An early example of many-to-many electronic commerce in physical goods was the Boston Computer Exchange, a marketplace for used computers launched in 1982. An early online information marketplace, including online consulting, was the American Information Exchange, another pre Internet online system introduced in 1991.

In 1990 Tim Berners-Lee invented the World Wide Web and transformed an academic telecommunication network into a worldwide everyman everyday communication system called internet/www. Commercial enterprise on the Internet was strictly prohibited until 1991. Although, the Internet became popular worldwide around 1994 when the first internet online shopping started, it took about five years to introduce security protocols and DSL allowing continual connection to the Internet. By the end of 2000, many European and American business companies offered their services through the World Wide Web. Since then people began to associate a word "ecommerce" with the ability of purchasing various goods through the Internet using secure protocols and electronic payment services.

Timeline

- 1979: Online shopping was invented in the UK by Michael Aldrich.
- 1982: Minitel was introduced nationwide in France by France Telecom and used for online ordering.
- 1987: Swreg begins to provide software and shareware authors means to sell their products online through an electronic Merchant account.
- 1990: Tim Berners-Lee writes the first web browser, Worldwide Web, using a NeXT computer.
- 1992: J.H. Snider and Terra Zippering publish Future Shop: How New Technologies Will Change the Way We Shop and What We Buy. St. Martin's Press. ISBN 0312063598.

- 1994: Netscape releases the Navigator browser in October under the code name Mozilla. Pizza Hut offers pizza ordering on its Web page. The first online bank opens. Attempts to offer flower delivery and magazine subscriptions online. Adult materials also becomes commercially available, as do cars and bikes. Netscape 1.0 is introduced in late 1994 SSL encryption that made transactions secure.
- 1995: Jeff Bezos launches Amazon.com and the first commercial-free 24 hour, internet-only radio stations, Radio HK and NetRadio start broadcasting. Dell and Cisco begin to aggressively use Internet for commercial transactions. eBay is founded by computer programmer Pierre Omidyar as AuctionWeb.
- 1998: Electronic postal stamps can be purchased and downloaded for printing from the Web.
- 1999: Business.com sold for US $7.5 million to eCompanies, which was purchased in 1997 for US $149,000. The peer-to-peer file sharing software Napster launches. ATG Stores launches to sell decorative items for the home online.
- 2000: The dot-com bust.
- 2002: eBay acquires PayPal for $1.5 billion. Niche retail companies CSN Stores and Net Shops are founded with the concept of selling products through several targeted domains, rather than a central portal.
- 2003: Amazon.com posts first yearly profit.
- 2007: Business.com acquired by R.H. Donnelley for $345 million.
- 2008: US ecommerce and Online Retail sales projected to reach $204 billion, an increase of 17 percent over 2007.

Business Application

Some common applications related to electronic commerce are the following:

- Email
- Enterprise content management
- Instant messaging
- Newsgroups
- Online shopping and order tracking
- Online banking
- Online office suites
- Domestic and international payment system
- Shopping cart software
- Teleconferencing
- Electronic tickets

Government regulations

In the United States, some electronic commerce activities are regulated by the Federal Trade Commission (FTC). These activities include the use of commercial e-mails, online advertising and consumer privacy. The CAN-SPAM Act of 2003 establishes national standards for direct marketing over e-mail. The Federal Trade Commission Act regulates all forms of advertising, including online advertising, and states that advertising must be truthful and non-deceptive. Using its authority under Section 5 of the FTC Act, which prohibits unfair or deceptive practices, the FTC has brought a number of cases to enforce the promises in corporate privacy statements, including promises about the security of consumers' personal information. As result, any corporate privacy policy related to e-commerce activity may be subject to enforcement by the FTC.

The Ryan Height Online Pharmacy Consumer Protection Act of 2008, which came into law in 2008, amends the Controlled Substances Act to address online pharmacies.

Forms

Contemporary electronic commerce involves everything from ordering "digital" content for immediate online consumption, to ordering conventional goods and services, to "meta" services to facilitate other types of electronic commerce.

On the consumer level, electronic commerce is mostly conducted on the World Wide Web. An individual can go online to purchase anything from books or groceries, to expensive items like real estate. Another example would be online banking, i.e. online bill payments, buying stocks, transferring funds from one account to another, and initiating wire payment to another country. All of these activities can be done with a few strokes of the keyboard.

On the institutional level, big corporations and financial institutions use the internet to exchange financial data to facilitate domestic and international business. Data integrity and security are very hot and pressing issues for electronic commerce today.

Intranet

An **intranet** is a private network that uses Internet protocols to securely share any part of an organization's information or operational system within that organization. The term is used in contrast to *internet* - a network between organizations - and instead refers to a network *within* an organization. Sometimes the term refers only to the organization's internal website, but may be a more extensive part of the organization's information technology infrastructure.

Characteristics

An intranet is built from the same concepts and technologies used for the Internet, such as client-server computing and the Internet Protocol Suite (TCP/IP). Any of the well known Internet protocols may be found in an intranet, such as HTTP (web services), SMTP (e-mail), and FTP (file transfer). Internet technologies are often deployed to provide modern interfaces to legacy information system hosting corporate data.

An intranet can be understood as a private version of the Internet, or as a private extension of the Internet confined to an organization by a firewall. The first intranet websites and home pages began to appear in organizations in 1990 - 1991. Although, not officially noted, the term intranet first became common-place with early adopters, such as universities and technology corporations, in 1992.

Intranets are also contrasted with *extranets*; the former are generally restricted to employees of the organization, while the latter may also be accessed by customers, suppliers, or other approved parties. Extranets extend a private network onto the Internet with special provisions for access, authorization, and authentication.

An organization's intranet does not necessarily have to provide access to the Internet. When such access is provided it is usually through a network gateway with a firewall, shielding the intranet from unauthorized external access. The gateway often also implements user authentication, encryption of messages, and often virtual private network (VPN) connectivity for off-site employees to access company information, computing resources and internal communications.

Uses

Increasingly, intranets are being used to deliver tools and applications, e.g., collaboration (to facilitate working in groups and teleconferencing) or sophisticated corporate directories, sales and customer relationship management tools, project management etc., to advance productivity.

Intranets are also being used as corporate culture-change platforms. For example, large numbers of employees discussing key issues in an intranet forum application could lead to new ideas in management, productivity, quality, and other corporate issues.

In large intranets, website traffic is often similar to public website traffic and can be better understood by using web metrics software to track overall activity. User surveys also improve intranet website effectiveness. Larger businesses allow users within their intranet to access public internet through firewall servers. They have the ability to screen messages coming and going keeping security intact.

When part of an intranet is made accessible to customers and others outside the business, that part becomes part of an extranet. Businesses can send private messages through the public network, using special encryption/decryption and other security safeguards to connect one part of their intranet to another.

Intranet user-experience, editorial, and technology teams work together to produce in-house sites. Most commonly, intranets are managed by the communications, HR or CIO departments of large organizations, or some combination of these.

Because of the scope and variety of content and the number of system interfaces, intranets of many organizations are much more complex than their respective public websites. Intranets and their use are growing rapidly. According to the Intranet design annual 2007 from Nielsen Norman Group, the number of pages on participants' intranets averaged 200,000 over the years 2001 to 2003 and has grown to an average of 6 million pages over 2005–2007.

Benefits of Intranets

- **Workforce productivity:** Intranets can also help users to locate and view information faster and use applications relevant to their roles and responsibilities. With the help of a web browser interface, users can access data held in any database the organization wants to make available, anytime and - subject to security provisions - from anywhere within the company workstations, increasing employees' ability to perform their jobs faster, more accurately, and with confidence that they have the right information. It also helps to improve the services provided to the users.
- **Time:** With intranets, organizations can make more information available to employees on a "pull" basis (i.e., employees can link to relevant information at a time which suits them) rather than being deluged indiscriminately by emails.
- **Communication:** Intranets can serve as powerful tools for communication within an organization, vertically and horizontally. From a communications standpoint, intranets are useful to communicate strategic initiatives that have a global reach throughout the organization. The type of information that can easily be conveyed is the purpose of the initiative and what the initiative is aiming to achieve, who is driving the initiative, results achieved to date, and who to speak to for more information. By providing this information on the intranet, staff has the opportunity to keep up-to-date with the strategic focus of the organization. Some examples of communication would be chat, email, and or blogs. A great real world example of where an intranet helped a company communicate is when

Nestle had a number of food processing plants in Scandinavia. Their central support system had to deal with a number of queries every day (McGovern, Gerry). When Nestle decided to invest in an intranet, they quickly realized the savings. McGovern says the savings from the reduction in query calls was substantially greater than the investment in the intranet.

- **Web publishing allows '*cumbersome*'** corporate knowledge to be maintained and easily accessed throughout the company using hypermedia and Web technologies. Examples include: employee manuals, benefits documents, company policies, business standards, newsfeeds, and even training, can be accessed using common Internet standards (Acrobat files, Flash files, CGI applications). Because each business unit can update the online copy of a document, the most recent version is always available to employees using the intranet.
- **Business operations and management:** Intranets are also being used as a platform for developing and deploying applications to support business operations and decisions across the internetworked enterprise.
- **Cost-effective:** Users can view information and data via web-browser rather than maintaining physical documents such as procedure manuals, internal phone list and requisition forms. This can potentially save the business money on printing, duplicating documents, and the environment as well as document maintenance overhead. "PeopleSoft, a large software company, has derived significant cost savings by shifting HR processes to the intranet".
- **Gerry McGovern** goes on to say the manual cost of enrolling in benefits was found to be USD109.48 per enrollment. "Shifting this process to the intranet reduced the cost per enrollment to $21.79; a saving of 80 percent". PeopleSoft also saved some money when they received requests for mailing address change. "For an individual to request a change to their mailing address, the manual cost was USD17.77. The intranet reduced this cost to USD4.87, a saving of 73 percent". PeopleSoft was just one of the many companies that saved money by using an intranet. Another company that saved a lot of money on expense reports was Cisco. "In 1996, Cisco processed 54,000 reports and the amount of dollars processed was USD19 million".
- **Promote common corporate culture:** Every user is viewing the same information within the Intranet.
- **Enhance Collaboration:** With information easily accessible by all authorized users, teamwork is enabled.

- **Cross-platform Capability:** Standards-compliant web browsers are available for Windows, Mac, and UNIX.
- **Built for One Audience:** Many companies dictate computer specifications. Which, in turn, may allow Intranet developers to write applications that only have to work on one browser (no cross-browser compatibility issues)?
- **Knowledge of your Audience:** Being able to specifically address your "viewer" is a great advantage. Since Intranets are user specific (requiring database/network authentication prior to access), you know exactly who you are interfacing with. So, you can personalize your Intranet based on role (job title, department) or individual ("Congratulations Jane, on your 3rd year with our company!").
- **Immediate Updates:** When dealing with the public in any capacity, laws/specifications/parameters can change. With an Intranet and providing your audience with "live" changes, they are never out of date, which can limit a company's liability.
- **Supports a distributed computing architecture:** The intranet can also be linked to a company's management information system, for example a time keeping system.

Planning and Creating an Intranet

Most organizations devote considerable resources into the planning and implementation of their intranet as it is of strategic importance to the organization's success. Some of the planning would include topics such as:

- The purpose and goals of the intranet
- Persons or departments responsible for implementation and management
- Functional plans, information architecture, page layouts, design.
- Implementation schedules and phase-out of existing system
- Defining and implementing security of the intranet
- How to ensure it is within legal boundaries and other constraints
- Level of interactivity (eg wikis, on-line forms) desired.
- Is the input of new data and updating of existing data to be centrally controlled or devolved.

These are in addition to the hardware and software decisions (like content management system), participation issues (like good taste, harassment, confidentiality), and features to be supported.

The actual implementation would include steps such as:

- Securing senior management support and funding.
- Business requirements analysis.
- Setting up web server access using a TCP/IP network.
- Installing required user applications on computers.
- Creation of document framework for the content to be hosted.
- User involvement in testing and promoting use of intranet.
- Ongoing measurement and evaluation, including through benchmarking against other intranets.

Content is King: A successful Intranet project engages its viewers and provides them with immense corporate value by:

- **Feeding the Intranet:** Key personnel must be assigned and committed to feeding Intranet consumers. The alternative for your project to become the "yellow-pages" (a tool that is used as a last resort).
- **Keep it current:** Information that is current, relevant, informative, and useful to the end-user is the only way to keep them coming back for more.
- **Interact or "Listen":** Allow your users to create content. Social networking must be an integral part of any Intranet project, if a company is serious about providing information to and receiving information from their employees.
- **Feedback:** Allow a specific forum for users to tell you what they want and what they do not like.

Act on Feedback: Your users of the Intranet are typically the employees of the company with their finger on the pulse of your industry. Those that are in the trenches on a daily basis will be able to tell "corporate" what trends are happening in the marketplace before any news source. This two-way communication is critical for any successful Intranet. Company executives must read the input and create responses based on the company's direction. Otherwise, what is the point of any employee taking the time to respond? If an employee submits their opinion or their observation, they need to feel that they have been heard. This is accomplished by:

- **Require management** to review intranet posts on a daily basis and respond to the poster. Let them know that their post has already been addressed, is being reviewed, or is being referred to a department head. This ensures the poster that their post has been read and is being acted upon accordingly. If they do not receive feedback, they will discontinue posting.

- **Broadcast feedback:** The ideas that make it into the "this is a great idea" bucket should become "news-worthy". This makes the poster feel useful and encourages others to follow.
- **Log feedback by users:** This information can be useful when considering an applicant for promotion/transfer, etc. It will also let you know who is focused on the company's benefit and not just "filling a position".
- **Require executives to provide daily/weekly content:** Everyone wants to hear from the person(s) they are working for. The Executive Team needs to lead the way in communicating the company's vision to their associates on a frequent (daily, if possible. If not, no less than weekly) basis.

Extranet

An **extranet** is a private network that uses Internet protocols, network connectivity, and possibly the public telecommunication system to securely share part of an organization's information or operations with suppliers, vendors, partners, customers or other businesses. An extranet can be viewed as part of a company's intranet that is extended to users outside the company, usually via the Internet. It has also been described as a "state of mind" in which the Internet is perceived as a way to do business with a selected set of other companies (business-to-business, B_2B), in isolation from all other Internet users. In contrast, business-to-consumer (B_2C) models involve known servers of one or more companies, communicating with previously unknown consumer users.

An extranet can be understood as an intranet mapped onto the public Internet or some other transmission system not accessible to the general public, but managed by more than one company's administrator(s). For example, military networks of different security levels may map onto a common military radio transmission system that never connects to the Internet. Any private network mapped onto a public one is a virtual private network (VPN), often using special security protocols.

For decades, institutions have been interconnecting to each other to create private networks for sharing information. One of the differences that characterize an extranet, however, is that its interconnections are over a shared network rather than through dedicated physical lines. With respect to Internet Protocol networks, RFC 4364 states "If all the sites in a VPN are owned by the same enterprise, the VPN is a corporate *intranet*.

If the various sites in a VPN are owned by different enterprises, the VPN is an *extranet*. A site can be in more than one VPN; e.g., in an intranet and several extranets. We regard both intranets and extranets as VPNs. In general, when we use the term VPN we will not be distinguishing between intranets and extranets. Even if this argument is valid, the term "extranet" is still applied and can be used to eliminate the use of the above description."

In the quote above from RFC 4364, the term "site" refers to a distinct networked environment. Two *sites* connected to each other across the public Internet backbone comprise a VPN. The term "site" does not mean "website." Thus, a small company in a single building can have an "intranet," but to have a VPN, they would need to provide tunneled access to that network for geographically distributed employees.

Similarly, for smaller, geographically united organizations, "extranet" is a useful term to describe selective access to intranet system granted to suppliers, customers, or other companies. Such access does not involve tunneling, but rather simply an authentication mechanism to a web server. In this sense, an "extranet" designates the "private part" of a website, where "registered users" can navigate, enabled by authentication mechanisms on a "login page".

An extranet requires network security. These can include firewalls, server management, the issuance and use of digital certificates or similar means of user authentication, encryption of messages, and the use of virtual private networks (VPNs) that tunnel through the public network.

Many technical specifications describe methods of implementing extranets, but often never explicitly define an extranet. RFC 3547 presents requirements for remote access to extranets. RFC 2709 discusses extranet implementation using IPSec and advanced network address translation (NAT).

Industry Uses

During the late 1990s and early 2000s, several industries started to use the term "extranet" to describe central repositories of shared data made accessible via the web only to authorized members of particular work groups. Scandinavia, Germany and Belgium, among others. Some applications are offered on a Software as a Service (SaaS) basis by vendors functioning as Application service providers (ASPs).

Specially secured extranets are used to provide virtual data room services to companies in several sectors (including law and accountancy).

For example, in the construction industry, project teams could login to and access a 'project extranet' to share drawings and documents make comments, issue requests for information, etc. In 2003 in the United Kingdom, several of the leading vendors formed the Network of Construction Collaboration Technology Providers, or NCCTP, to promote the technologies and to establish data exchange standards between the different system. The same type of construction-focused technologies has also been developed in the United States and Australia.

Advantages

- Exchange large volumes of data using Electronic Data Interchange (EDI).
- Share product catalogs exclusively with trade partners.
- Collaborate with other companies on joint development efforts.
- Jointly develop and use training programs with other companies.
- Provide or access services provided by one company to a group of other companies, such as an online banking application managed by one company on behalf of affiliated banks.
- Share news of common interest exclusively.

Disadvantages

- Extranets can be expensive to implement and maintain within an organization (e.g., hardware, software, employee training costs)—if hosted internally instead of via an application service provider.
- Security of extranets can be a concern when hosting valuable or proprietary information. System access must be carefully controlled to secure sensitive data.

Introduction of Enterprise Solutions

What is an enterprise?

An **enterprise** is a term for a very large business network. Therefore, the phrase "enterprise solutions" refers to business solutions for large corporations which have large networks. I would, however, consider these solutions for various sized organizations due to the enhanced scalability and efficiency of the system. This term "enterprise" is a very broad term and encompasses all aspects of computer technology business solutions including hardware, software and the employees required to implement the requirements of specific organizations. I have had a very difficult time finding a specific definition to the phrase "enterprise solutions". Therefore, I am led to conclude that it is a term coined by marketing personnel to enhance interest in business solutions provided by specialists. This does not make it insignificant. Quite the contrary, as with all corporate operations, the corporation who is most efficient will have the greatest competitive edge.

This section talks about enterprise solutions with regard to software and servers (operating system platforms and related servers) to be used in the enterprise (corporation).

Enterprise Solutions

Enterprise Solutions provide for a scalable, easy to manage programming solution to providing business management and information accessibility for internal and external clients. Enterprise solutions deal with the problem of providing information to clients both externally and internally. It deals with programming and databases. The main problem being how to most efficiently get our data accessible to those we want to access it. The solution has the following characteristics and more:

- **Security -** Should be able to be sure information is not being stolen by those we don't want to have access to it.
- **Scalability -** Should be able to accommodate an increase in clients.
- **Cost -** Should be easy to program.
- **Management -** Should provide ability to manage the implementation including version control software and software that helps manage team effort with regard to providing the solution.
- **Portable -** Should be able to accommodate changes in technology.

Therefore, in order for a business to properly choose enterprise solutions, a proper requirements definition must be completed. All desired features along with priorities for each feature must be assigned in order to make a suitable decision.

Application Server

Enterprise solutions for implementing distributed system generally revolve around an application server which provides several but not necessarily all of the following services:

- Directory and naming services
- Security
- Distributed transactions
- Fault tolerance management
- Load balancing and clustering
- Database services
- State Tracking

These services are generally called technical infrastructure services. There are many types of application servers that may supply some or all of these functions.

The applications that run on these application servers will receive requests from clients such as web browsers and using API program hooks will request or send information to/from other applications or through the interfaces to the specific service such as a database service. When a reply is received, the client request is responded to by the application.

There are also other areas of functionality that are offered by application servers that make their use easier such as:

- Managing and writing applications
- Integration with other system.

To justify an application server the distributed system should require transaction processing across multiple databases.

For more information on application servers read the section about application servers in the independent platform area of this website.

Software Solutions

The two main current business solutions are:

- J2EE - These are a suite of Java technologies including:
  - EJB - Enterprise Java Beans standardizes the program calls to the application server and standardizes the return calls.
  - JDBC - Java Database Connectivity
  - JNDI - Java Naming and Directory Interface
  - JMS - Java Message Service is a remote asynchronous communication to send messages to other objects. It is different from RMI (Remote Method Invocation) since the message is sent and forgotten.
  - RMI - Remote Method Invocation
  - JTA - Java Transaction API.
  - Java Mail
  - Servlets - Provides interfaces or (API calls) to the CGI (Common Gateway Interface) which interfaces between the web client browser and the web server.

- Microsoft's .NET (Previously known as Microsoft's Web Solution Platform and Distributed internet applications Architecture (DNA)). Based on these technologies:
    - o COM - Component Object Modules
    - o DCOM - Distributed Component Object Modules
    - o MTS - Microsoft Transaction Server
    - o MS-DTC - Microsoft Distributed Transaction Coordinator
    - o MSMQ - Microsoft Message Queue server
    - o MSCS - Microsoft Clustering Technology

According to Microsoft, current Microsoft .NET Servers include (These are Microsoft trademarks):

- o Microsoft Application Center 2000
- o Microsoft BizTalk Server 2000
- o Microsoft Commerce Server 2000
- o Microsoft Exchange Server 2000
- o Microsoft Internet Security and Acceleration Server 2000
- o Microsoft Host Integration Server 2000
- o Microsoft Mobile Information Server 2001
- o Microsoft SQL Server 2000

Summary

Internet-The **Internet** is a global system of interconnected computer networks that use the standardized Internet Protocol Suite (TCP/IP) to serve billions of users worldwide. It is a *network of networks* that consists of millions of private and public, academic, business, and government networks of local to global scope that are linked by copper wires, fiber-optic cables, wireless connections, and other technologies.

Electronic Commerce-Electronic Commerce, commonly known as (electronic marketing) e-commerce or ecommerce, consists of the buying and selling of products or services over electronic system such as the Internet and other computer networks. The amount of trade conducted electronically has grown extraordinarily with widespread Internet usage.

Intranet-An **intranet** is a private network that uses Internet protocols to securely share any part of an organization's information or operational system within that organization. The term is used in contrast to *internet* - a network between organizations -

and instead refers to a network *within* an organization. Sometimes the term refers only to the organization's internal website, but may be a more extensive part of the organization's information technology infrastructure.

Extranet-An **extranet** is a private network that uses Internet protocols, network connectivity, and possibly the public telecommunication system to securely share part of an organization's information or operations with suppliers, vendors, partners, customers or other businesses. An extranet can be viewed as part of a company's intranet that is extended to users outside the company, usually via the Internet. It has also been described as a "state of mind" in which the Internet is perceived as a way to do business with a selected set of other companies (business-to-business, B_2B), in isolation from all other Internet users. In contrast, business-to-consumer (B_2C) models involve known servers of one or more companies, communicating with previously unknown consumer users.

Enterprise Solutions-Enterprise Solutions provide for a scalable, easy to manage programming solution to providing business management and information accessibility for internal and external clients. Enterprise solutions deal with the problem of providing information to clients both externally and internally?

Exercise

Q. 1. Define the terms: information system, data processing system?

Q. 2. Why is it important to have framework for analyzing system? What six elements can be used for summarizing any work system?

Q. 3. Discuss how IT enables system are useful for solving real world business problems.

Q. 4. What is a virtual company? What are the six basic characteristics of a successful virtual company?

Q. 5. Explain the advantages of using expert system in solving business application.

Q. 6. List four major reporting alternatives provided by management information system.

Q. 7. With diagram show how data mining extracts knowledge from data warehouse.

Q. 8. Describe traditional system life cycle approach for building information system.

Q. 9. What are the different ways to control access to data, computer and networks?

Q. 10. Discuss the purpose and importance of communication in business administration. What are Barriers and Break-downs in communication?

